The Best
AMERICAN
ESSAYS
1988

GUEST EDITORS OF
The Best American Essays

1986 Elizabeth Hardwick
1987 Gay Talese
1988 Annie Dillard

The Best AMERICAN ESSAYS 1988

Edited and with an Introduction
by ANNIE DILLARD

ROBERT ATWAN,
Series Editor

TICKNOR & FIELDS   NEW YORK   1988

ISSN 0888-3742
ISBN 0-89919-729-9
ISBN 0-89919-730-2 (pbk.)

Printed in the United States of America

Q 10 9 8 7 6 5 4 3 2 1

"Kinds of Water" by Anne Carson. First published in *Grand Street*. Copyright © 1987 by Anne Carson. Reprinted by permission of the author.

"Beacons Burning Down" by Bernard Cooper. First published in *The Georgia Review*. Copyright © 1987 by Bernard Cooper. Reprinted by permission of the author.

"Gettysburg" by Arthur C. Danto. First published in *Grand Street*. Copyright © 1987 by Arthur C. Danto. Reprinted by permission of the author. The accompanying map of Gettysburg is reprinted by permission of Barbara Westman.

"Wadi-Bashing in Arabia Deserta" by Russell Fraser. First published in *The Virginia Quarterly Review*. Copyright © 1987 by *The Virginia Quarterly Review*. Reprinted by permission of the publisher.

"My Two One-Eyed Coaches" by George Garrett. First published in *The Virginia Quarterly Review*. Copyright © 1987 by *The Virginia Quarterly Review*. Reprinted by permission of the publisher.

"After Yitzl" by Albert Goldbarth. First published in *The Georgia Review*. Copyright © 1987 by Albert Goldbarth. Reprinted by permission of the author.

"The Heart of the Seasons" by Elizabeth Hardwick. First published in *House & Garden*. Copyright © 1987 by Elizabeth Hardwick. Reprinted by permission of the author and the publisher.

"L'Après-midi de Mary Garden" by Paul Horgan. First published in *The Yale Review*. Copyright © 1987 by Yale University. Reprinted by permission of the publisher.

"The Feeling of Flying" by Samuel Hynes. First published in *The Sewanee*

Contents

Foreword

ESSAYS ARE MAKING a remarkable literary comeback. For years they received a bad press. A big part of their problem had to do with the family name: essay. It sounded stiff, stuffy, textbookish. When readers heard the word they cringed a little, thinking of things teachers forced them to read and write in school. When I first proposed the idea of an annual essay collection to a publisher, he replied: "It's a lovely idea. But shouldn't we call it something else?" We ran through a few variations — "Best American Articles," "Best American Nonfiction," "Best American Pieces" — and came to a stop. Essay, we realized, was not just the only word; it was truly the *best* word.

One reason "essay" sounds old-fashioned is that — unlike other literary forms — it was slow in coming to terms with the twentieth century. While Joyce, Eliot, and, later, Beckett were radically transforming fiction, poetry, and drama, the essay pretty much retained its relaxed, genteel nineteenth-century manner. It broke no new ground; it resisted no rules; it violated no conventions. Instead of trying to become modern works of literature in themselves, essays seemed content with simply trying to explain those works — and the works needed a lot of explaining. In the academic community, the essay became synonymous with literary criticism (it still is). Essays were written *about* literature; they weren't written *as* literature.

But the literary status of the essay is beginning to change. As Annie Dillard aptly puts it in her introduction to this volume, the essay "has joined the modern world." Essays are being written out of the same imaginative spirit as fiction and poetry. And essays can rival the best fiction and poetry in artistic accomplishment. Why not? The essayist, too, can master imagery, character, symbol, metaphor, and the ins and outs of narration. Just how splendidly today's essayists achieve these literary effects is the central point of Annie Dillard's edition.

This volume reflects the new spirit of the American essay. The personal essay is once again assuming its place in both quarterlies and general magazines as a significant genre. Never before — except perhaps in the days of Emerson and Thoreau — have so many fine young writers begun to explore its literary possibilities. They come to the essay with enthusiasm for its wonderful malleability — it can be made to incorporate enormous chunks of life and literature.

As they stretch the limits of the form, today's essayists are developing a prose that lives along the borders of fiction and poetry. Taking a cue from Borges, they have even begun to blur the boundaries of criticism, biography, and exposition. Some of the essays in this volume do not sound or behave like the "textbook" essays readers have grown accustomed to. They play tricks with narration, shake up expectations of literary form, undermine our confidence that we can know the writer through the writing.

Still, essayists want to be known. The autobiographical impulse is in their bones. With few exceptions, that impulse dominates this volume. The book opens with Mary Lee Settle's evocative reminiscence of London during the first wave of Hitler's buzz bombs. It closes with Charles Simic's intertwined memories of wartime Yugoslavia and the solitary pleasures of reading. And in between we have probably as many varieties of personal reminiscence and self-disclosure as could be gathered in a single book. Among the subjects: bloody battles, exotic places, old-fashioned summers, athletic coaches, the pleasures of property, the pains of property, a headless rooster, prison sex.

"I didn't think an essay could be like this." I was teaching a nonfiction writing workshop and we were reading Annie Dillard's "Total Eclipse." "Like what?" I asked. The student struggled for a moment, trying to explain his surprise. Then he got it. "It reads just like a short story," he said. "It's got drama and"

— he groped for the words — "and emotional intensity." He looked at me suspiciously, and added: "I didn't think essays had those things. Are you sure it's really an *essay?*"

"It's *really* an essay," I answered, almost as satisfied as if I had written it myself.

The Best American Essays features a selection of the year's outstanding essays, essays of literary achievement that show an awareness of craft and a forcefulness of thought. Essays are gathered and screened from a wide variety of big, little, national, and regional magazines. For this edition, Annie Dillard made her final selections after reading some three hundred essays.

To qualify for selection, the essays must be works of respectable literary quality intended as fully developed, independent essays (not excerpts or reviews) on subjects of general interest (not specialized scholarship), originally written in English (or translated by the author) for first appearance in an American publication during the calendar year. Periodicals that want to make sure their contributions will be considered each year should include the series on their subscription list (Robert Atwan, *The Best American Essays*, P.O. Box 1074, Maplewood, New Jersey 07040).

For this volume, I'd like to thank Charles O'Neill for his invaluable suggestions and assistance. Many editors made Annie Dillard's and my life easier — though our rooms certainly more crowded — by generously sending us magazines and recommendations. I'd like to thank, too, the editors of many state and regional magazines for their enthusiastic support of the series. *The Best American Essays* is fortunate this year to have as guest editor Annie Dillard, whose commitment to the art of the essay is evident throughout the collection.

R.A.

Introduction

PROSE GENRES have been blurred all along.

Lying through his teeth, Daniel Defoe published his *Journal of the Plague Year* as an eyewitness account — fifty-seven years after the plague year, when in fact he had been five years old. Defoe always did that. He fooled readers with "The Apparition of Mrs. Veal," a mystery story packaged as journalism; he roped them in again with *Memoirs of a Cavalier,* and again, most successfully, with *Robinson Crusoe.* He even faked the date at the end of *Moll Flanders* ("Written in the year 1683"). On the other hand, Jonathan Swift used the form of a travel narrative for *Gulliver's Travels,* but he didn't expect anybody to believe it. (An outraged Irish bishop fumed that he could scarcely believe a word of it.)

In the eighteenth and nineteenth centuries, some literary folk considered fiction *ipso facto* trash. Serious writers tried to weasel out of the genre. Fielding originally titled *Tom Jones* "The History of a Foundling," to lend it the artistic dignity that nonfiction alone was then thought to possess. Melville's *Typee,* a work of pretty outrageous fiction, masqueraded as fact in its day; so did *Omoo.* Poe published *The Narrative of A. Gordon Pym* as nonfiction. Twain's first title for his novel was "Huck Finn's Autobiography" — to distinguish it from a mere romance, and thereby to plead for a serious reading.

A bizarre switch has occurred in this century. Fiction is newly intellectually respectable. Some writers want to call their work fiction, no matter what it is — as if the word "fiction" were not descriptive but honorific, as if fiction didn't mean fabrication but artfulness. Truman Capote called *In Cold Blood* fiction, and Norman Mailer called *The Executioner's Song* fiction. Few readers or critics care much about genre, actually, and each of these writers may have had motives wholly unrelated to genre. But the issue interests me. Both narratives are meticulously factual. Dramatic and vivid narration, and character, dialogue, and so forth, are not exclusive to fiction, nor forbidden to nonfiction, as both writers presumably knew. It might be, then, that they judged, or their editors judged, that calling these nonfictions "fiction" would earn them a serious reading. Maybe calling them fiction would alert readers and critics to the possibility that there was meaning afoot here, or skill — as indeed there was. But why fudge genre?

Some other writers call their closely autobiographical narratives fiction: Norman MacLean, who wrote beautiful Montana reminiscences in *A River Runs Through It;* Stratis Haviaras, who remembered his Greek childhood in *When the Tree Sings;* Colette, whose *Break of Day* apparently records her daily life; J. G. Ballard, who described his boyhood in Japanese-occupied Shanghai in *Empire of the Sun;* James Agee, whose *A Death in the Family* and *The Morning Watch* re-create his personal facts; and Henry Roth, who wrote the classic Brownsville memoir, *Call It Sleep.* In the eighteenth and nineteenth centuries, these writers would, I think, have been happy to call their work nonfiction.

Similarly, a great many narrative essays appear in the guise of short stories — at least, many among the hundreds of narratives I read for this volume. My guess is that the writers (quite reasonably) want to be understood as artists, and they aren't sure that the essay form invites the sort of critical analysis the works deserve. One purpose of this volume, then, is to encourage essay writers out of the closet.

The essay is gaining ground. Writers like William Gass, Cynthia Ozick, Francine du Plessix Gray, Elizabeth Hardwick, Edward Hoagland, the late James Baldwin, Richard Selzer, Joan Didion, and Edward Abbey may well be more widely read as essayists than as fiction writers.

II

In this century, it was Loren Eiseley — a scientist — who restored the essay's place in imaginative literature and who extended its symbolic capacity. The symbolic essay isn't the only sort of essay, of course; it is one among many other kinds — like the philosophical essays of Emerson, the personal essays of Montaigne, the occasional essays of Hazlitt, the satirical essays of Swift, and the familiar essays of Lamb. It's an interesting kind, though.

Eiseley lays in narrative symbols with a trowel, splashing mortar right and left — but the symbols hold. In his 1969 essay "The Star Thrower," Eiseley makes meaningful symbols of both private and universal facts: of his trip to a Florida beach, of his wearing sunglasses, of the tornadoes that tear through the plains where he grew up, the eye of a dying octopus he sees washed up on the beach, the unpitying eye of science like the eye of a lighthouse, the violent and unforgiving landscape of Darwinian evolution, and, among many other facts, a torn photograph of his mother.

On the beach, Eiseley encounters a beachcomber who throws dying starfish back into the surf. At the essay's beginning, Eiseley thinks this star thrower a fool — what place has pity in the world of natural selection? Individuals die in their billions, and wash up on the shore. At the essay's end, having mined his private life and his scientific knowledge for pertinent events and images — and having lived through them in the space of the essay, as it were, to an altered and compassionate vision — Eiseley returns to the beach to seek the star thrower. He joins the star thrower under a convenient rainbow; the language grows biblical; the two men sow life back into the sea. By the essay's end, every vivid word in every sentence is heaped with layers of meaning. In metaphorical pattern, this essay is at least as rich as Faulkner's fiction, at least as rich as Wallace Stevens's poems. The beachcomber who throws starfish embodies any hope or mercy that flies in the face of unyielding natural law. He stands finally for the extravagant spirit behind creation as a whole; he is a god hurling solar systems into the void.

Among living writers, essayist James McConkey is working

the same vein, but more subtly. Each of the chapters in his 1981 *Court of Memory* — an apparently straightforward memoir of a rather calm, professorial life — is an artful essay. A landlord's severed arm, preserved in a jar of formaldehyde, functions as both fact and symbol. Some of the essays in Barry Lopez's early *Desert Notes* are allegorical, even: in his essay "The Raven," Lopez elucidates the difference between ravens and crows with intense, hieratic, suggestive imagery. The language, and the language alone, carries the meaning, as it does in a complex lyric poem like, say, "Sailing to Byzantium." Sometimes people call a heightened, language-based essay like "The Raven" a prose poem. In fact, "prose poem" is an ignorant, mongrel term that dishonors the essay with its implication that poets alone, in poems alone, may fashion small literary art objects from imagery.

Other literary genres are shrinking a bit. Poetry seems to have priced itself out of a job; sadly, it often handles few materials of significance and addresses a tiny audience. Literary fiction is scarcely being published; it's getting to be like conceptual art — all the unknown writer can do is tell people about his work, and all they can say is, "good idea." The short story is to some extent going the way of poetry, willfully limiting its subject matter to such narrow surfaces that it cannot address the things that most engage our hearts and minds. So the narrative essay may become the genre of choice for writers devoted to significant literature.

In some ways the essay can deal in both events and ideas better than the short story can, because the essayist — unlike the poet — may introduce the plain, unadorned thought without the contrived entrances of long-winded characters who mouth discourses. This sort of awful device killed "the novel of idea." (But eschewing it served to limit fiction's materials a little further, and likely contributed to our being left with the short story of scant idea.) The essayist may reason; he may treat of historical, cultural, or natural events, as well as personal events, for their interest and meaning alone, without resort to fabricated dramatic occasions. So the essay's materials are larger than the story's.

The essay may deal in metaphor better than the poem can, in some ways, because prose may expand what the lyric poem must compress. Instead of confining a metaphor to half a line, the essayist can devote to it a narrative, descriptive, or reflective couple of pages, and bring forth vividly its meanings. Prose welcomes all sorts of figurative language, of course, as well as alliteration, and even rhyme. The range of rhythms in prose is larger and grander than that of poetry. And it can handle discursive idea, and plain fact, as well as character and story.

The essay can do everything a poem can do, and everything a short story can do — everything but fake it. The elements in any nonfiction should be true not only artistically — the connections must hold at base and must be veracious, for that is the convention and the covenant between the nonfiction writer and his reader. Veracity isn't much of a drawback to the writer; there's a lot of truth out there to work with. And veracity isn't much of a drawback to the reader. The real world arguably exerts a greater fascination on people than any fictional one; many people, at least, spend their whole lives there, apparently by choice. The essayist does what we do with our lives; the essayist thinks about actual things. He can make sense of them analytically or artistically. In either case he renders the real world coherent and meaningful, even if only bits of it, and even if that coherence and meaning reside only inside small texts.

III

You could reason that American literature derives from the essay and hinges on the essay, if only because American literature springs from Emerson and Emerson was an essayist. Emerson wrote essays and poetry. Thoreau wrote essays, nonfiction narratives, and poetry. Some of Mark Twain's best writing is in nonfiction — in both the essay ("Corn-Pone Opinions," "Fenimore Cooper's Literary Offenses") and the book-length narrative like *Life on the Mississippi, Roughing It,* and *Innocents Abroad.* Edgar Allan Poe's essays are an important part of his work; so are, lesserly, the essays of William Dean Howells and Washington Irving.

Hawthorne wrote essays and fiction; he weighted his story books with essays, as if to ground the works in the world. Hawthorne's *Twice-Told Tales*, always referred to as a book of short stories, in fact contains eight essays. His *Mosses from an Old Manse* contains five essays. (Melville's review of *Mosses* singles out for praise only one orthodox short story; critic Nina Baym has shown how deeply Melville distrusted fiction.) The bulk of Melville's book of "stories," *Piazza Tales*, is in fact "The Encantadas" — ten wholly factual sketches, without any pretense of fiction, which Melville cobbled together from his own vanishingly brief experience of the Galápagos Islands and — especially — from published histories.

There is no reason why anyone should read, touch, or publish this brilliant stuff ("The Encantadas") as fiction — except that the world is curiously blind to the essay, and to the essay's imaginative and narrative possibility, as if it didn't exist, or as if a work by its very excellence should have mysteriously tiptoed out of its proper (but dull-sounding) genre and crept into a more fashionable (but incorrect) one.

We can think of the essay as the short form of nonfiction, having its own special intensity and requirements, as the short story is the short form of fiction. Not all fiction is literary fiction, and not all nonfiction is literary, either. But some is.

Autobiographical narratives like *The Education of Henry Adams*, *Walden*, *Life on the Mississippi*, *Up from Slavery*, and Gorki's autobiographical trilogy, Nabokov's *Speak, Memory*, Sartre's magnificent *The Words*, and recently Alfred Kazin's *A Walker in the City*, Frank Conroy's *Stop-Time*, Frederick Buechner's *The Sacred Journey*, Garrison Keillor's *Lake Wobegon Days*, Kate Simon's *Bronx Primitive* — these are autobiography. Conroy calls a spade a spade by publishing his book as nonfiction; he wrote *Stop-Time* in fully dramatized scenes, filled with live dialogue and with driving, rather emotional narrative, like Henry Roth's autobiographical novel *Call It Sleep*.

The narrative, first-person essay, narrowing its sights, nevertheless matches these literary autobiographies in range: George Orwell's pointed "Shooting an Elephant," E. B. White's nostalgic "Once More to the Lake," Loren Eiseley's symbolic "The Star

Thrower." (In this volume, see Albert Goldbarth's "After Yitzl," Charles Simic's "Reading Philosophy at Night," William Kittredge's "Home.")

Some autobiographical narrative stresses a small stretch of an old time at a far place: Orwell's *Down and Out in Paris and London,* Mehta's *Vedi,* Thomas's *The Youngest Science,* Joan Colebrook's beautiful *A House of Trees.* The memoir essay repeats the virtues of the book-length form. Maxine Hong Kingston's *The Woman Warrior* is a collection of vivid narrative essays. So are, at least arguably, *Walden,* Edward Abbey's *Desert Solitaire,* Gretel Ehrlich's *The Solace of Open Spaces,* Saint-Exupéry's *Wind, Sand and Stars,* and Henry Beston's *The Outermost House.* So is *Out of Africa:* linked essays on Kenya subjects, plus journal scraps. No one could say that this makes for bad books. (In this volume, Mary Lee Settle's essay, "London — 1944," evokes that time and place hauntingly. William Manchester's short account of the Battle of Okinawa is an essay, and so is Samuel Hynes's memoir of flying planes in the forties.)

Melville's "The Encantadas" is travel literature; so is much of Washington Irving, Mark Twain, Henry Thoreau, and Henry James. Travel writing need not be purely literal, in this century any more than in the last. Bruce Chatwin's *In Patagonia* is a bookish literary text, not a diary of a journey. (In this volume, Anne Carson recounts a journey across Spain. Her "Kinds of Water" is a modern, disjointed narrative broken by quotations and vatic utterances that enrich the essay's powerful impressionistic surface. It's a toss-up whether the writer of such a piece of prose wants to call it an essay or a short story. I call it an essay because I believe it to be nonfiction; it would be silly to call it a short story just because it's good.)

Some nonfiction books, of course, describe people without being scholarly biographies. Boswell's *Life of Johnson* is literature, and so are Geoffrey Wolff's *The Duke of Deception* (about his father) and Michael Ondaatje's memoir of his family in Sri Lanka, *Running in the Family.* Essays may evoke people as well, and as narratively. (See E. J. Kahn, Jr.'s portrait of South African Member of Parliament Helen Suzman, "The Honorable Member for Houghton," and Paul Horgan's "L'Après-midi de Mary Garden.")

IV

The year 1987 was a good one for the essay — as I think the past twenty years have all been. In this collection I wanted to show how vivid the essay can be. I emphasized a kind of subgenre, the narrative essay. I'm especially interested in narrative essays that mix plain facts and symbolic facts, or that transform plain facts into symbolic facts. See, among many examples, James McConkey, "Heroes Among the Barbarians"; Bernard Cooper, "Beacons Burning Down"; Susan Mitchell, "Dreaming in Public"; and the aforementioned essays by Albert Goldbarth, Charles Simic, Anne Carson, and William Kittredge. These are bold contrivances. Many of these writers narrate in fragments linked by idea. The essay has apparently — long since and without discussion — joined the modern world.

This volume contains a number of straightforward, nonsymbolic narrative essays about people and events, too. There are some descriptive essays, like Elizabeth Hardwick's impressionistic summer still life ("The Heart of the Seasons") and Eleanor Munro's Brueghel-like canvas of Lourdes ("On the Pilgrim's Path to Lourdes"). There is only one analytical essay (Arthur C. Danto's "Gettysburg").

Listed in the "Notable Essays" at the volume's end are many fine essays published in 1987 that weren't narrative (like Justin Kaplan's "In Pursuit of the Ultimate Fiction," and essays by Alfred Kazin, Edward Hoagland, Robert Finch, James Laughlin, and so on). Also listed in "Notable Essays of 1987" are those by essayists like Geoffrey C. Ward, William Gass, Joyce Carol Oates, Donald Hall, Barry Lopez, and Cynthia Ozick, whose work has appeared in earlier editions of this *Best Essays* series.

This collection — incidentally — demonstrates the modern writers' self-conscious interest in writing. George Garrett tells what he learned about the craft and professionalism of writing from a football coach and a boxing coach; he recalls "what the body learns and is taught." Whatever else they're doing, these writers tend to write about artfulness itself. Russell Fraser, writing about a journey in Arabia, reflects on literary possibility. He notes, "This is what all writing comes down to, not imagination but the estimating eye." Arthur C. Danto describes Gettysburg: "A battlefield is already halfway to a work of art."

These writers analyze their own methods and processes; they criticize as they go. "But this keeps becoming fiction," William Kittredge complains. Within his essay, he defends its method: "Proceeding through some incidents in this free-associative manner is in fact a technique, a way of discovery." Albert Goldbarth, in a footnote, calls "After Yitzl" an "essay/poem/story." It is about reinventing history from the present: "If necessary . . . we'll make it up."

Understanding history is a recurrent theme in these essays, as it is in most literary nonfiction. Writers serve as the memory of a people. They chew over our public past. William Manchester remembers the Battle of Okinawa; Arthur C. Danto looks at the Gettysburg battlefield; Mary Lee Settle evokes London in 1944. They pore over their private pasts. Samuel Hynes recalls learning to fly an airplane; Susan Mitchell in her memoir of Provincetown shows, by a richly patterned surface of imagery, how a life's boundaries dissolve and its membranes leak.

Essayists deal with present issues, too. E. J. Kahn, Jr., takes on South Africa in his profile of Helen Suzman. Kimberly Wozencraft writes about prison as an inmate; Kenneth A. McClane writes about prison as a visitor. Richard Selzer, who is a physician, describes the AIDS epidemic in Haiti. Russell Fraser touches, at least, on the issues in the Mideast.

The problem of knowing recurs as a theme. James McConkey's "Heroes Among the Barbarians" — about the Indians who lived on his land — concerns the relationship between owning, loving, and knowing. Listed in the "Notable Essays" are Richard Ford's memoir of his mother and Robert Penn Warren's memoir of his father; both stress unknowing, the unknowingness that is the nub of any intimacy. ("I don't know," Ford writes; "I'll never know. . . . I really have no idea.") Charles Simic's "Reading Philosophy at Night" is a series of narratives about being "greedy for the absolute," the unknowable. We try to see in the dark; we toss up our questions and they catch in the trees.

V

The essay is, and has been, all over the map. There's nothing you cannot do with it; no subject matter is forbidden, no structure is proscribed. You get to make up your own structure every time, a structure that arises from the materials and best contains them. The material is the world itself, which, so far, keeps on keeping on. The thinking mind will analyze, and the creative imagination will link instances, and time itself will churn out scenes — scenes unnoticed and lost, or scenes remembered, written, and saved.

In his essay "Home," William Kittredge remembers Jack Ray, his boyhood hero, whom he later hired as a hand on his Oregon ranch. After a bout in jail, Jack Ray would show up in the bunkhouse grinning. "Well, hell, Jack," Kittredge would say. "It's a new day."

"Kid," he would say, "she's a new world every morning."

ANNIE DILLARD

The Best
AMERICAN
ESSAYS
1988

MARY LEE SETTLE

London — 1944

FROM THE VIRGINIA QUARTERLY REVIEW

How DO I capture a city and a time? It began in the back of a
camouflaged RAF lorry that smelled of oil. I clung to the side
as the driver swung the lorry fast around the curved Cotswold
road from Bourton-on-the-Water to the railway station. All I
had left of the uniform I had worn for ten months as an aircraft
woman second class in the Women's Auxiliary Air Force of the
RAF was the pair of issue shoes, heavy black masculine clodhop-
pers. I carried the suitcase I had kept hidden full of civilian
clothes to wear on leave, a civilian ration book, some clothing
coupons, and my discharge papers (my ticket). I was dressed in
the suit I had worn to go into the WAAF at the recruiting station
in Kingsway. That was the beginning of the time in London,
and it ended, eighteen months later, not in London, but at a
dinner party in New York the evening after I came home from
the war.

Why, after all this time, do I need to recall this? There is an
old man, dreaming of Piccadilly in 1944 when he was young
and drunk and a bomber pilot. A friend who brought back a
hidden wound of one forever relived day has shot himself
nearly forty years later. I know that they, in their way, and I in
mine, have no hope of ever being civilians completely.

Others, now in their seventies, sat on the floor, loose limbed
against a wall, like the Cambridge undergraduates they were
before the war, while one of their number read an elegy to a
dead leader and aesthetic guide when they were brave and
young, and in a naïve intrigue against the worst of the world

that bred them. What they were remembering was being young, in love with dedication and one another, and flirting with the dull edges of legality.

The ones who were children in the years of war are still as fascinated as they were when they played at identifying planes, followed battles, in the illusion that they could be followed. They have missed ever since finding in themselves the answer to the most atavistic question in a man's soul. It is the question that makes *The Red Badge of Courage* a great war book whose author never fought in a battle: "Would I fight or would I turn tail?"

They envy the silence of those of us who find it hard to speak; it is our fault. We have left them to the shallow, to a war told by correspondents or seen in old movies. The witnessed events, the quick impassioned romances they imagine, the over-simple pictures of courage and love — all the iron nostalgia, gleaned from romance and from their own demands that the war be as they imagine it, is the hardest of all to wipe clean with recall.

What we found in London then was controlled by where we came from. Did we come on leave, away from the cold and boredom and waiting of being in the forces to the luxury of London, of baths, and pink gin, and some worn remains of graceful living? Or from America to the first glimpse of the danger and deprivation of a city at war? I had done both of these, so that in October 1943 the city I came to was not a surprise.

I had learned its streets on leave when I had wandered there in the anonymity of my air force blue uniform. It was then that I had found the noontime concerts at the National Gallery, the cheap food at the NAAFI, and what was left of the London of Dickens, of Shakespeare, so familiar to me that I hardly had to ask a direction, even though I had never seen it before. I had walked through miles of London streets, all the day and into the blacked-out night.

Osbert Sitwell wrote that the blackout made a medieval city of London. It didn't. There were no pine torches, no wax tapers shining through windows to defeat the darkness. Instead, it was the opposite. London was plunged into the terrible present century and lay exposed under an open, dangerous sky. The pitch darkness was inside of rooms, as if they were caves deep underground before the blackout curtains were drawn and the lamps were lit.

Outside, in the street, London became country again under a changing sky. The buildings were dark monoliths; the streets canyons between cliffs. There were snaggled bombed-out gaps in the townhouse rows that let the moonlight in through high windows that had once been such private rooms, here a fragment of wallpaper with faded rain-streaked animals of a nursery, there a drunken toilet, still clinging to the wall. Many of the ancient churches were only ruins that looked like stone lace that etched the night sky. During the blitz they had been low on the priorities of the fire fighters.

To new arrivals in London, it seemed pitch black out of doors, too, but not, by 1943, to Londoners. People had become conscious again of the phases of the moon, the light from stars. They had regained their country eyes. The darkness was full of noises, the echo of footsteps, of people talking, the cries for taxis. Sound itself seemed amplified and dependable in the half-blindness of the street. The smell was of dust, of damp plaster in the air, and of the formaldehyde scent of the smoke from dirty coal that lodged in the yellow fog. The stained sandbags, the rust, the dull, peeling paint, damp that made great dark lines down the walls, made London seem like a long-neglected, leaky attic.

It was fear that was medieval, and largely unadmitted to this day, fear of the full moon, the bomber's moon, as our ancestors had shrunk from its insane light and the cry of the wolf.

II

I had been sent to London several weeks before to find a job, on orders from the medical officer of my station who had given me sick leave. I was suffering from signals shock, a common aural breakdown after too many hours of enemy jamming on the transmitter/receiver in flying control. Those of us who suffered from it had begun to hear ghost signals from nonexistent aircraft through the electronic repetitive noise of the German jamming that I can rehear, more than forty years later, as I recall the time. Both the M.O. and I knew that I was not quite sick enough to be invalided out, even though I was of no more use as an R/T operator.

"I wish I had a way to work my ticket, too. I'm bloody cheesed off," he said sadly, sitting on the end of my cot in sick bay, his feet tucked up, his arms around his knees. I see now that he was very young. "Why waste your time issuing repaired shoes when you could do a proper job? You are lucky."

I guess I was. I knew people, unlike the others I had left. So between Herbert Agar and a friend in Parliament I was on my way to the train for London in the back of the RAF lorry two weeks after I came back off sick leave. I left the WAAF an aircraft woman second class, pay fourteen shillings a week, on Saturday, and on Monday I reported to the American Office of War Information in Carlos Place, conveniently across from the Connaught Hotel as a "simulated" major in the American Army, a civilian rank for those of us serving in war zones.

London to me that week, at least, was comfort, good food, clean American people after the months of loneliness, a PX card, and a glamour that I had not expected. I was exhausted, my weight thirty pounds below normal, my nerves jangled from signals shock, and still so enmeshed in the discipline, the deprivation, and the language of the forces, that on the first morning I stood to attention beside a colleague's desk and asked to be excused. "Honey," he said, "you're out of the Army. You can pee whenever you want to."

Almost everybody was old at the Office of War Information. I had come from a world where nobody was over twenty-two, except some high ranking officers, who seemed, in their thirties and the fact that they were regular Air Force, as far away as tin gods, who could not be forgiven their mistakes, their preoccupations, or their power over us.

The people in the OWI were famous, too, or so they seemed to me, and I, who only now realize that I was exotic to them, found them glittering with reputation. The courage of some of them was to be honored more than those I had left in one way. They brought to the war more intelligence and less physical resilience than being there required. Some of them were too old, too tired, too sedentary for what they had volunteered to

do, be in London through the attrition of the days, the "little
blitz," the buzz bombs, the V-2s, and the debilitating atmosphere of neglect, dirt, and exhaustion that had built up.

There they were, those who had wangled their way into war,
at the wrong place, doing, in excesses of patriotism or curiosity
or self-proof, work that was the wrong work, at the wrong time.
They were valuable in some terms I had not run into as an
aircraft woman. There were fine editors, good writers, movie
actors, poets, in the halls of the OWI at Carlos Place, and I
realize now that I was as glamorous to them as they were to me.
Somehow I had touched the war they had come to. I knew
things I couldn't tell. Gaunt, and nervous, aesthetically pleasing
in the fashion that pleases at a given time, an object of interest,
I had had the experience they had come to share. What I had
learned to take for granted, service in the forces was, to them, a
fascination. It made them seem somehow younger than I was.
I had a sense of knowing things — oh, not events — civilians
seem always to expect those — but gray expanses and hours,
days, months, of damp indifference.

They didn't quite know what to do with me. They were
professionals, some of the best of American editors, from prewar publishing when it was an art, from the *Paris Herald Tribune,*
the *Saturday Evening Post,* the Viking Press, the *Louisville Courier
Journal, Harper's Bazaar,* to name only the ones I remember best.
I, who had been hired as a "writer," had no experience at all
beyond a few poems, a few short stories, all unpublished, all
long since lost. I was, to them, an oddity, a rescued fragment.
One of my bosses told me that I would never have passed a
security check in the States, because I was a "premature antifas-
cist," having started trying to join up before we went to war. So
I was used at first as a courier to take VIPs to the BBC for
interviews. Accidentally I was plunged straight from lorry to
limousine, from the barracks to tea at the Savoy with Robert
Sherwood, Alfred Lunt, and Lynn Fontanne.

I took Irving Berlin to the BBC, and he, with a capacity for
friendship I have seen in few other people, made friends. He
was tiny in uniform, too old already to be there; he moved like
a cricket, doing everything anyone asked him to do. He treated
others with a sense of rare peerage, as if it were the norm for

people, and he was the kindest and also the funniest person I met in all the time I was escorting VIPs. He had brought over *This Is the Army* to play for the troops.

One evening we were to meet for a drink at Claridge's, and he was late. He came rushing in, apologizing as he ran, and sat down at the table. He said, "I have just had one of the most embarrassing days of my life. You know, we take 'The Army' around to the hospitals. We have a small show, just the leads, designed so that we don't need a stage. Then I go with two or three of the singers around the wards to entertain the men who can't make it to the performance. There are some wards where they are too badly wounded even for that. The commanding officer was taking me around to them, where I always said a few words, hoping to cheer them up a little. I noticed that we kept passing one ward, not going in. I asked why, and he said that the men were too badly off. I bounced in anyway. I told him that if they were conscious I was sure a few words from home would help a little. It was too late to stop me. There they lay, and I started my little speech about how proud we were of them, what brave men, all that. Usually, even from the very sick I got some reaction. From these — none. So I laid it on a bit thicker. I told them how proud their country was of them, how I represented their parents and their sweethearts to tell them we honored them as great Americans. I got no reaction at all. In the hall I said, 'What is the matter with those men? They don't react at all.' The commanding officer said, 'I tried to tell you, Mr. Berlin. That was the VD ward.' "

III

The entertainers, the people in the OWI, the film divisions, some of the foreign correspondents existed, I'm sure, without knowing it, within a caul of privilege they took for granted. It was not safety; they had come to a city where they could be killed, and most of them had come, as I had, in convoy. But their London, to me, was unreal, a stage on which a play called "the war" was running. Even the uniforms some of them wore were like costumes — well cut, no grease marks, not butt-sprung, no inground dirt, no fading, scratching, no ill-fitting crotch crease — in short, not the issue I was still used to.

Most of them had no experience of the strictures we lived by, of being caught by raids late at night so that we had to sleep where we could, away from the cars they seemed to be able to call at any time. They did not step over the outflung arms of families who had slept in the tube stations for nearly four years. Where once, in uniform, I had been caught in Piccadilly tube station by a raid, in this new time, I trailed my evening skirts along the narrow track between the sleeping bodies and the trains.

Those who ate in restaurants had no inkling of what it was like to live on rationing, on scrounging unrationed food, fish or carbohydrates that means standing in queues hour after hour, gray-faced with fatigue. One time I was in a taxi with a woman, made innocent by money rather than fame, and she saw a queue at the horsemeat shop in Paddington. She said, "Isn't it amazing that those people still keep pets?"

Three days after I arrived I was taken to dinner at a black market restaurant by Burgess Meredith and Paul Douglas, who were in the film division, and who had decided I needed feeding. Where we went I still don't know. We were driven through dark unfamiliar streets by one of those London cabbies who seemed to find his way like a night animal, with only the tiny slits of blue light showing from the masked headlights that gave no light to drive by, but only warned pedestrians.

We walked into an overpowering smell of food, a luxury of clean white tablecloths and damask napkins from "before the war," which had already become a magic time, dimmed and changed by nostalgia. I remember that the room was dark, with that cavelike atmosphere of London restaurants that used to imitate old libraries or men's clubs, with their dark woodwork and their leather banquettes along the walls. In the corner Mac Kriendler from "21" in New York sat with a foreign correspondent I have forgotten. It was the only black market restaurant I ever saw in London.

People who knew each other had turned it into a home away from home where they had the comfort of being with their own in that network of fame I had hardly known existed. There they sat, correspondents, actors, Hollywood writers who had been trained to write too quickly from first impressions, and would write about the war in the same way, imagining the rest. Many a hungry GI slogged through minds in such meeting places, or the Ritz Bar, while the professionals and the shallow gambled with war, having no idea that they were missing everything about it but the events.

They ordered for me with great care. They treated me gently, but unwisely. I had been living on wartime rations, only two thirds of that issued to men in the forces, on the theory that women were smaller and needed less food. I can still see the plate of food, and smell it. A lamb chop, two inches thick, a baked potato with two weeks' ration of butter melting on it, and green beans. The smell of melting fat, of rich meat, made my gorge rise; I prayed to get to the ladies' room in time. I was violently sick. The rest of the evening was spent with them taking turns holding my head over the loo while I had the dry heaves. After that I learned to face carefully both the new food and a certain aura of fame.

By the winter of 1943–44, in the first preparations for the invasion, troops from all over the world gathered on leave in the West End of London. Cries for taxis and women in all their languages were plaintive in the blackout. Small, dim, blue lights, the only color allowed, read *Bar, Pub, Restaurant.* When the blackout curtains, which were hung like labyrinths at the doors, were pushed aside, you were met by a wall of light and noise, and the uniforms, by that year, of all the Allies.

Sometimes there were mistakes. The Tivoli Bar at the Ritz had all the elegance and aloofness of a London club. It was another home for a mixture of the kind of Americans who knew about the Ritz, Guards officers, and assorted English ladies with what Hilaire Belloc called "loud and strident voices." Outside, in Piccadilly, it had a faint blue sign like all the rest.

Two American officers, new to the darkness of the streets, had picked up two girls of the hundreds who haunted the West End. They had seen only the faint blue word "bar," and they pushed aside the blackout curtains and escorted the girls into one of the most exclusive rooms in London.

The two girls had been a long time in the streets. One's teeth were snaggled, the other had dirt scratched down her bare legs. Their clothes were filthy. It was obvious, but only for a second, that the two young men were actually seeing them for the first time. There was hardly a pause. They showed them to the table, pulled back their chairs, and followed the perfect Chesterfieldian advice, "Treat the duchess like a whore and the whore like a duchess." There was not a word said by the waiter, who entered into the scene with all the arrogant politeness he would have shown any other customer. I was never prouder of my countrymen than I was then, when they, far more insouciant than the British around them, soothed the feelings of a pair of embarrassed Piccadilly whores.

We spent the days in make-work and met in bars, in restaurants, and turned them into havens. There was no place else to go. The Petit Club Française had more movie actors, ballet girls, and American writers than the Free French it had been opened for. The long front room of the Connaught, which looks comfortably like a large drawing room, gathered the OWI and the foreign correspondents. There were scores of places, all over London, where people found their own.

It took time for me. I seemed flung from group to group at first. I remember Claude Cockburn, who was Frank Pitcairn of the *Daily Worker,* to whom I lent ten pounds when he had run out of money one night in the back bar of the Café Royal. He paid me back with ten shares of *The Week,* a Communist broadsheet he published every week with all the lowlife "capitalist" intrigues he could find in either the British or the American government. It earned me a black dossier as a part owner of a Communist magazine. I was fascinated with all of this, with the paradox of a mixture of secrecy as a flirtation and of naïve hope among most of the intelligent people I met then.

I had lunch, through Cockburn, in one of London's fashionable restaurants with the editor of the *Daily Worker* and a Communist deputy from Belgium who looked like the bust of Beethoven. I asked him when he became a Communist. He smiled and said, "When I was fifty. It was not, with me, a youthful error."

Maybe I was being recruited, I don't know. I must have disappointed them if I was; I was too curious, too questioning, and, by then, far too experienced at being a pawn to blind authority to be attracted to dictatorship, proletarian or otherwise. Only a few months before I had had to run along behind a proletarian sergeant who was as mean as a snake, as she rode her bicycle through an RAF station.

I sat on the stairs in a gold satin dress at a ball in one of the grand houses in Grosvenor Street with a pink Guards officer, nineteen years old. He looked with some disdain at the people dancing. He said, "I'm frightfully sorry you see us like this. Before the war [that already magic time] half these people would not have been asked here."

I said, "Before the war I would probably not have been asked here." He was killed in the invasion.

IV

We talked as people have not talked in England since. We talked on trains, in bars, in canteens, in Lyons Corner Houses, on buses, as if our statements had to be made before it was too late. There are glimpses in my memory of walks, of talk — a walk in the park with Archibald MacLeish when he tells me that he has spent the rest of his life finding out that what he knew at eighteen was true, an officer from an English regiment who tells me he hates the bloody Yanks. One has stolen his girl.

An OSS officer from Hollywood tries to convince me that I must be a Communist. "But you do recognize the historic inevitability, don't you?" He sounds annoyed. The joke was then that the OSS and M15 spent more time following each other and all of us than on German spies.

I sat on the wall by Hyde Park Gate across from the hospital with a young American fighter pilot who flew P-38s. He had just been posted to a station in the south of England. On the way through New York on leave he had seen a wonderful new musical, and he sang to me, "Oh, What a Beautiful Morning." It was the first song I ever heard from *Oklahoma*. He was killed the next week.

I lived then in Gloucester Terrace, near Gloucester Road tube station, in a top floor flat that I had been sent to by the English Speaking Union, one of those nests of threadbare gentility that had survived all over Kensington, with ladies clinging to them, literally, for their dear lives, measured not in coffee spoons, but in patched linen, polished tables, and the eking out of rations in bone china cups.

Doreen Green, who hastened to tell me that she had been brought up in a large Georgian country house outside of Dublin, explained at once that it was not the money, but the duty that made her even consider letting a room, that she did, after all, have an income but it was, you know, in trust. She lived there with her fifteen-year-old son and one of those ancient splay-footed nannies left after the children were grown. I had first stayed there when I had come to London on leave, in uniform, but in the fall of 1943, there were evening dresses hanging in my cupboard in the genteel pastel bedroom with its embroidered runners and its pale rugs, and Victorian china knickknacks, all the thin fragility of the genteel poor. She had told me the first time I went there that she was divorced from a husband who had lived too long in France when he was young and had picked up beastly habits, you know, from those people.

If London had become drab and shabby, flats like this one were threadbare instead, for shabby has an air of neglect about it, but threadbare is worn down with care, with meticulous patching, with make do and make do. There was something of this in Doreen's small, pinched face, too, as if she would make do through the war as the others did, because she had to, and because the time was overwhelming except in the safety of the Irish antique furniture she had there, all that was left for her of what had been, at least in memory, a great Anglo-Irish house outside of Dublin. As with all of us, her safety was more psychic than real, since the flat was on the vulnerable top floor.

From time to time, several evenings a week, during the late fall and on into the winter, she gave us tea when I was there, dressed in her Air Raid Precaution uniform, ready to go on duty through the night, a woman too frail, it seemed, to survive an ordinary day. It was women like her, now forgotten in the more dramatic annals of the war, who sat all night, night after

night, on watch in the ARP stations, middle-class soldiers, dim
with worry that their homes would not be there when they went
off duty.

During the nights of the "little blitz" when the air raid warning went, we would gather in the tiny living room of the flat on
the ground floor, and pretend not to be afraid. The ancient
splay-footed nanny, who seemed as much of a fixture in such
homes as the dear antiques, the careworn and beautifully
patched linen, would say, as the ack-ack guns in Hyde Park
shook the house, "Is that one of theirs or one of ours?"

Dutifully Desmond or his mother would say, "Nanny, it's one
of ours."

That Christmas an ice storm turned the trees in Hyde Park
into a glittering parody of Christmas trees, and the children
picked up silver strips of foil in the street that had been dropped
by German aircraft to confuse our radar, and took them home
to decorate their houses.

Almost imperceptibly London moved out of winter into a
drab spring. The weather was cold, the days were gray, and
there was a sense of watching the sky, as a farmer watches it, to
read the future in it. At night, once in a while, if the sky was
clear, a German plane got through the defenses of the city, and
you could see it, a tiny bug pinned in the sky by the searchlights
that converged on it. I was told after the war by a Luftwaffe
pilot that they were sent over London alone as punishment.

V

I had been moved, in one of those decisions that seemed to have
been made for the sake of decision itself, down to the radio
section in Dean Street, Soho, to the broadcasting studios of both
"black" and "white" radio — black to the resistance in Europe
and white to whoever would risk their lives to listen to Aaron
Copland.

For two years there had been rain-soaked graffiti all over
London saying *Open the Second Front Now.* In early June, the
days were so long that we seemed always to be walking in twilight under a solid blanket of American and English bombers

across the sky all the way to the horizons. Some of the men I worked with and the correspondents got edgier and edgier, drank more, caroused more, fell into silences. If there had been not a single spy in London, the world would have known from the poised waiting, the draining out of London of troops, that at last what we all called then the Second Front was going to be opened.

Then, for forty-eight hours, day and night, in early June the loud drone of the planes overhead never ceased. I walked down to the station early one morning. For some reason neither I nor anyone else in the flat had been able to sleep. I walked in to the only other person there, who was sitting in her office watching the wall. I asked what was happening, and she snapped, "None of your business. Shut up." For some reason I still can't fathom she had been let in on the secret, and was sitting there vicariously invading Europe. It was the morning of June 6.

Everything changed in that day. London woke up, the pace was faster. I was assigned to the midnight briefings at the Ministry of Information in the London University building. They seemed futile, since correspondents and troops were already coming back and forth in an open corridor that made London seem like a part of the front itself.

Then, on June 13, in the middle of the night, the first buzz bomb flew over London, the engine cut, and it crashed into a house, killing six people. It was the first of Hitler's long-rumored secret weapons. They came, self-propelling bombs with little stubby wings. They looked like huge cigars, and they sounded like motorcycles in the air. The more that were shot down coming over the coast, the more came into London. We began to listen; we listened all the time, whether consciously or not, to the cutoff of the engines which meant that the buzz bomb would either crash straight down or glide.

Everyone thought their own part of London received the brunt of them, and there were rumors of targets that had been chosen. Nothing was chosen. They fell completely indiscriminately, ludicrously. I went home to Gloucester Terrace one evening to find Doreen sobbing. I thought after all the time she had forgotten how to cry. One of her best friends a few streets away had been wiped out with her whole family an hour before. She kept saying, "They were only getting ready to go to the theater," as if that had to do with their silly, useless deaths.

I walked down with her to watch the digging out of their bodies from the trash heap that smelled of dust and plaster that had been their home, and I made her go back to the flat and put sugar in her tea when I saw that they were about to bring out the first body. Usually she would pretend she didn't like sugar so that Desmond and Nanny could have more of the meager ration. She confided in me that she drank her tea with lots of sugar for energy when she was on duty, since it wasn't rationed at the ARP station. When I brought home the Mars Bars they seemed fond of, a present from the PX, she sliced them and served them for tea on Irish china so thin you could see her hand through it as she passed the plate. Somehow the memory of teatime with her and the death in the other house seem linked together, as they should be.

On a train coming in from a grand weekend in Wiltshire, I met an unattractive, shy young refugee from Germany who had been conscripted into the Pioneer Corps. But when he began to talk about music, his face took on a glow. He asked me if I would go with him to a prom concert in the Albert Hall. We climbed up to just below the great round glass roof. Away in the distance, a tiny figure, Myra Hess, played to the kind of silence she commanded from the huge crowd. In the middle of a Mozart cadenza a buzz bomb rode over the Albert Hall. We could see its faint shadow through the dirty glass. The pure, small sound of Mozart was the focus of a dead silence. Her fingers never faltered. We were hypnotized by her concentration, and the bomb exploded a hundred yards away across Kensington High Street in Kensington Gardens. She had kept us from a panic that could have killed many people. It was the last concert there until the war was over.

Late at night, after the last tube, sometimes I had to stay in the bomb shelter at the MOI. There was no way to get home. One evening after the midnight briefing, Gene Solo, who was a Hollywood script writer attached to the film division, said, "Don't sleep here. We all have a room at the Savoy and a car.

Come with us." I said I would come if I could have a quart of milk to drink.

When I got there, there was a poker game on a table that had been drawn up between two twin beds. It seemed to have been going on for some days. Dixie Tighe, William Saroyan, Gene Solo, Irwin Shaw, and a man from *Newsweek* were the people I remember. I lay down behind the safe broad backs of Solo and Saroyan, drank my two weeks' ration of milk in a room that reeked of gin and cigarettes, and went to sleep deeply for the first time since the buzz bombs had started and I had had to sleep in the shelter. I was waked in the morning by Saroyan throwing pound notes in the air and yelling, "I've won! I've won."

What made for a sense of safety so often was not true safety at all, but a psychic calm, Doreen Green sitting among her dear antiques from Ireland on the top floor of a London building saying, "This is nothing. You should have seen Dublin during the troubles. You could see the fires all the way from Balawly." She was remembering being sixteen, not the troubles.

I finally had found my own psychic safety, my own home away from home. I went like a pigeon to the cote to the top floor of a building in Soho, whose walls were a twenties décor of small glass mirrors which would have shattered into a million shards if we had been hit. But I had found my pub, my local — the kind of place you go to unthinking, that becomes habit almost as soon as you see it.

No place else had done this until I had met another refugee in the corridors of the OWI. We made friends as quickly as children. He was the most ridiculous GI I have ever seen. Chinless, popeyed, hair cut by Trumpers, already and impressively a published poet in his early twenties, newly graduated from Harvard, where he had been a protégé of Robert Hillyard, Dunstan Thompson made even the ill-fitting GI uniform of a private soldier look elegant. Someone had rescued him from the more useless service that he would have been given in the Army, as I had been rescued. He already knew every "literary" name in London. When I told him I was a writer, he accepted me completely as what I thought I was. He was already used to people who wrote and published, rather than those who still only wanted to, or those who posed. I think that it was this, and his acerbic teaching kindness that came so naturally to him, that made me really begin to write, not as a caprice but as a dedication. He also made me realize how ignorant I was, and I began to read contemporary work and classics, filling a great hunger like somebody who had been starving and didn't know it.

We drank at the Gargoyle Club, and we ate our jugged hare, and there were evenings I remember when Dylan Thomas was sitting on somebody's knee, when Robert Newton broke things, the names, Cyril and Stephen and Guy, were called across the floor, boyfriends quarreled in the men's room, and somebody's mistress vomited in the ladies'. I was having lunch with two journalists from Belgium when a buzz bomb stopped overhead. No one else stopped eating. The Belgians, who were not fools, took one look at the glass walls and went under the table. I suspect that everyone else wanted to, but there was a kind of noblesse oblige about it. One feared more than anything else being embarrassed in front of the others.

VI

Dunstan may have recognized me as a writer when I didn't deserve it, but Eric Hawkins, the editor of the *Paris Herald*, made me do some work, and I am always grateful to him for forcing me into a postgraduate course in journalism when I was hardly qualified for the first grade.

He gave me assignments and made me do them. He identified me from time to time. He looked around my door one day and said, "I know who your grandfather was — William Blake."

On another day, soon after I began to work for him, he stuck his head in the door and said, "Hey, kid, have you ever heard of the Grand Coulee Dam?" I stopped writing my wartime novel (long since lost) and said no. "Well, you better find out about it. I want five thousand words by next Wednesday." This article, for one of those OWI publications which seemed so tenuously connected with the war, scared me so that I still remember facts about the Grand Coulee Dam I would rather forget. I had never written anything five thousand words long.

He sent me to the British Museum, which had been bombed, and where the readers were relegated to a small back room. But it was my first visit to a place which would be a treasure house where later I would research and write three novels.

I had moved back to Carlos Place, and the news was pouring in day after day. There seemed to be some attempt, not at political censorship, but at not disturbing the American people more than they could take, like sitting upright when the buzz bombs halted over you so as not to disturb the others. When Belsen, the first of the concentration camps, was liberated, at first no one believed the evidence that was coming out. It was too much like the old "babies on bayonets" propaganda that too many people remembered from the First World War. A delegation of members of Parliament insisted on inspecting it to see if the news was true. One of them, a nice Conservative lady MP, Mrs. Smith, came back and put her head in the gas oven.

Then the first pictures came, and I was set to work as a kind of fuse. How much could people take? The pictures were shown me and if I retched, they were put to one side, to be censored. If I had no violent reaction, they were passed for publication. Alas, I soon got inured to them, as one gets used to anything, and I was less successful at the job of protecting the public from the truth that was like a yawning hole in any hope. Gradually the findings began to be believed, and we had the sense then that we had been in more than a conventional war. We had been in an invasion of a hell run by efficient clerks.

On the beaches of Normandy the Allied armies met such an international army of conscripts that they had to comb London for people who spoke obscure European languages and dialects in order to interrogate many of the prisoners, while Mark Blitzstein and I sat in an office and chose records from American composers to play on the loudspeaker systems of trucks when they weren't calling in German, "Surrender."

The war was running down, and we knew that it was nearly over. There was some naïve hope — a lot of it — that things would be "better" than they had been before the war. The Beveridge Plan had been debated in Parliament in an all-night session where Quentin Hogg had brought the members to their feet cheering at his words, "If you do not give the people social reform, they will give you social revolution!" When I asked another member about it, he said, "Oh, we always cheer when somebody uses two political clichés in the same sentence."

The Labour party was getting its slate ready for the first postwar election, and when I asked Harold Laski who they were choosing, he answered, in his little pinched professorial voice, "One third workers with the hands, and two thirds workers with the mind." Labour, of course, won by a landslide when the British went to the polls in July 1945.

Lovely Kay Kendall sang, "I'm going to get lit up when the lights go on in London," and we all cried, and John Armstrong, the painter, asked me, as a "young person" he said, when I was as old that day as I will be until I die, "What do you young people believe?"

"I, for one, have no communal hope," I told him, "only a recognition that individuals must become just, as Keats said, before the world becomes just. That belief is all that is left to me."

"If I thought that I would commit suicide," he told me. He was an older, sweet, left-winger I was ashamed of hurting, with his hope retained as romantically as Doreen Green's "before the war" in Ireland.

On the eighth of September I was walking with a friend in Soho when the ground under us heaved and then was still again. Six miles away the first V-2 had landed in Chiswick. In some vague attempt to keep the hit from the Germans the news was released that a gas main had exploded in Chiswick. For a while the V-2s were called Flying Gas Mains.

They were terrible, in all the classic sense of that misused word. There was no warning. If you heard the explosion you were safe. They killed hundreds more people than was ever admitted. Some of the shallower shelters became mass graves. It was a miracle that they weren't launched earlier. I believe that London could have panicked under too long a siege of them. It was an exhausted city by then, that deep brutal exhaustion that had seeped into our souls, our bodies, our relationships with each other, a kind of fatal disease of exhaustion that I believe had more to do with some older men killing themselves after the war, when the pressure ceased and they realized how little was left, than any personal problem.

That crack-up at the release of pressure was common. I saw it happen to more men in New York after they had come back from war than I ever saw under the pressures of London. I had thought that I paid little attention after a while to the V-1s and the V-2s, but some weeks after I came back to New York I went to see *Meet Me in St. Louis*. The short was called *V-One*. At the first sound of the familiar buzz bomb engine, I fainted and had to be carried out of the theater. I remember that my last thought before I passed out was, "This is ridiculous. I'm in New York. I'm safe."

It was the targetless, unaimed V-2s, even more than the atom bomb that was so far away, a tragedy read about, not suffered by us, that brought home the fact that war in the future was going to be nearly impossible, agonizing, and short. At least I thought so, but what humans can suffer and still survive in some kind of tatters in this bloody century has been seen over and over since.

Wernher von Braun's V-2s were the predecessors of those missiles that ever since have showered on the just and the unjust, without warning, without target, without hope, sold to whoever will pay for them.

In this brave new world, and this brave new kind of war, and still with the dim hope that something, at least, had changed after the terrible time, I came back to New York in the early spring of 1945. On the second day I was asked to dinner by Constantine Alajalov, the painter who painted so many prewar *New Yorker* covers. There were three other people at dinner, Alajalov, Tilly Losch, and an elegant Free French officer who had been sent in his beautifully cut uniform with his beautifully cut aristocratic face as a propaganda visitor. Recognizing that we Americans love a lord, it was his assignment to improve the image of the country that had been occupied since 1940, and obscure the truth that so many of its citizens had collaborated with Hitler or been passive under the Vichy regime.

He said at dinner, taking for granted in the company that it was an acceptable remark, "Well, at least Hitler did one thing for us. He got rid of the Jews in France."

I was too frozen with shock to move or speak. I felt drained of life. Despair can leave you too lost to resist seduction. The thing I had not known about what war can do I found out in that moment. You go along. I did not leave quickly enough. In short, I was polite.

But that, to them, casual moment has left me with something, when I think of it, like a darkness of soul, a cold recognition of the waste of the dead, the years of deprivation, of grayness, of dedicated uselessness. It has thrown the responsibility in any country straight onto a society that Turgenev called "the rich, the happy, and unjust."

It has taken me a long time since that night to realize that the war years were not wasted. I have had to face the fact that social change does not change evil people. There is only this difference. Their seduction is no longer officially tolerated in democracies. Evil men and evil prejudices are with us still; "nice" people belong to anti-Semitic country clubs, and their imitators drive pick-up trucks with gun racks and hate "niggers." The only thing that saves us is that such beliefs have been unacceptable to decent people since 1945. I know that "unacceptable" is a small word for this enormity, but the world runs on shallowness for the most part. We are left, at least, with a residue of social shame as a weapon.

ANNE CARSON

Kinds of Water

FROM GRAND STREET

St. Jean Pied de Port   20th of June

> *The good thing is we know the glasses are for
> drinking.*
>
> Machado

At the foot of the port of Roncesvalles, a small town bathes
itself. Thunderstorms come down from the mountains at evening. Balls of fire roll through the town. Air cracks apart like a
green fruit. Underneath my hotel window is a river (La Nive)
with a sizable waterfall. There is a dark shape at the edge of the
falls, as I look down, knocking this way and that in the force of
the current. It would seem to be a drowned dog. It *is* a drowned
dog. And I stand, mind burning, looking down. No one is noticing the dog. Should I mention it? I do not know the word for
"drowned." Am I on the verge of an ancient gaffe? Waiters
come and go on the terrace of the hotel bar, bending deeply
from the waist to serve *potage*. A fathom below them the dark
body slaps. At the foot of the falls, where water is rushing away,
a fisherman casts his line over it. What sense could there be in
things? I have come through countries, centuries of difficult
sleep and hard riding and still I do not know the sense of things
when I see it, when I stand with the pieces in my hands. Could
there be a sculpture of a drowned dog on the ledge of an ancient
waterfall? I watch and pass, hours pass. My mind a laughing-
stock. Evening falls, the shape is still there. Fisherman gone,

waiters whisking tablecloths on the terrace. What is it others know?

Pilgrims were people who loved a good riddle.

———————————

from St. Jean Pied de Port   21st of June

> *Presently, to a distant tinkling of bells, they*
> *turned and started off. The retreating figures*
> *made Kaname think of a line from the pilgrim's*
> *canticle they had practiced so earnestly with the*
> *innkeeper the evening before:*
> *Hopefully we take the path from afar*
> *to the temple where blooms*
> *the flower of the good law.*
>
>   Tanizaki

It rained during the night. We sit on the hotel terrace drinking coffee. Morning sparkles on us. I watch the dog. One soaked paw has moved over the ledge and is waving back and forth as water streams around it. The man I am traveling with peers vaguely towards it: "Ah!" and returns to eating bread. His concern is with the more historical aspects of pilgrimage. Pilgrims, for example, were traditionally gracious people and wore wide-brimmed hats in order that they might doff them to other pilgrims. The man I am traveling with demonstrates how this should be done. I think I will call him "My Cid." It speeds up the storytelling. Besides, he is one "who in a happy hour was born," as the famous poem says. You will see this as the journey proceeds, see him sailing through danger and smiling at wounds. Perhaps I — no, he is waiting for me. I doff my hat in the general direction of the waterfall, and we set off. Behold now this good fortune.

By afternoon it is darker, thunder comes down the hills. Presently we are in Spain. In the bar where we stop, a press of people, a small cup of coffee. I wipe the table with my hat: paws still dripping.

When is a pilgrim like a sieve? When he riddles.

———————————

Buergete   22nd of June

unmoved the melons
don't seem to recall
a drop
of last night's downpour

                                                        Sodo

  The small hotel of Buergete is made of water. Outside, rain streams all night. Roofs pour, the gutters float with frogs and snails. You would not see me — I lie in the dark listening, swirling. Walls of the hotel are filled with water. Plumbing booms and sluices. A water clock, embedded in the heart of the building, measures out our hours in huge drops. Wheels and gears turn in the walls, the roaring of lovers washes over the ceiling, the staircase is an aqueduct of cries. From below I can hear a man dreaming. A deep ravine goes down to the sea, he calls out, rushes over the edge. The mechanisms that keep us from drowning are so fragile: and why us?

  In the morning the hotel is dark, no sign of life, no smell of coffee. Old clock ticking in the deserted hall. Dining room empty, shutters drawn, napkins in glasses. Morning drifts on. I peer into the kitchen: still as a church. Everyone has been washed away in the night. We pile money on the table in the hall, leave without breakfast, without ado! as they say in my country. Outside is silent, street dissolving, far hills running down in streaks. We filter westward.

  Pilgrims were people who figured things out as they walked. On the road you can think forward, you can think back, you can make a list to remember to tell those at home.

---

to Pamplona   23rd of June

When he thought of the fragile O-hisa made over
to look like the winsome pilgrim of the Kabuki
and of the old man at her side ringing a
pilgrim's bell and intoning a canticle from one
holy place to the next, Kaname could not help
feeling a little envious. The old man chose his

*pleasures well. Kaname had heard that it was
not uncommon for men of taste in Osaka to dress
a favorite geisha as a pilgrim and do the Awaji
circuit with her every year. The old man, much
taken with the idea, announced that he would
make this the first of an annual series. Always
afraid of sunburn, O-hisa was less enthusiastic.
"How does it go? We sleep at Hachikenya, is it?
Where do you suppose Hachikenya is?"*

                                                    Tanizaki

Kinds of water drown us. Kinds of water do not. My water jar
splashes companionably on my back as I walk. A pool of
thoughts tilts this way and that in me. Socrates, after bathing,
came back to his cell unhurriedly and drank the hemlock. The
others wept. Swans swam in around him. And he began to talk
about the coming journey, to an unknown place far from their
tears, which he did not understand. People really understand
very little of one another. Sometimes when I speak to him, My
Cid looks very hard and straight into my face as if in search of
something (a city on a map?) like someone who has tumbled off
a star. But he is not the one who feels alien — ever, I think. He
lives in a small country of hope, which is his heart. Like Socrates
he fails to understand why travel should be such a challenge to
the muscles of the heart, for other people. Around every bend
of the road is a city of gold, isn't it?

I am the kind of person who thinks no, probably not. And we
walk, side by side, in different countries.

Pilgrims were people in scientific exile.

Puente la Reina   24th of June

*the world so unsure, unknowable
the world so unsure, unknowable
who knows — our griefs may hold
our greatest hopes*

                                                    Zeami

A bridge is a meeting point, where those who started out how
many, now how many nights ago? come together. Hearts uneasy

in their depths. It was in the medieval city of Puente la Reina
that all the pilgrims heading for Compostela, from France and
Spain and Italy and other points of origin, met at the crossing
of the River Arga. Except, in those days, there was no crossing.
Boatmen plied the river — many of them not honest men at all
but sordid assassins who took advantage of the pilgrims! Kinds
of water drown us. Evil boatmen threw many a pilgrim to his
watery death. Then an act of grace supervened. The queen of
Spain was moved to pity for the pilgrims' difficult situation. She
gave it some thought. How could she defend them? Why not
a bridge! A beautiful, antic, keyholed construction, washed by
gold shadows on the underside (photograph). She smiled, when
she saw it, out of the side of her eyes: *curva peligrosa* says the
sign on the bridge to this day. *Deadly slant.* There were stars in
the plane trees and stars in her eyes. There were pilgrims singing on the bridge. There were boatmen who turned to worse
crime. Such is the balance of human efforts.

Pilgrims were people wondering, wondering. Whom shall I
meet now?

Estella   25th of June

> *like lame-wheeled carriages*
> *we creep forth reluctantly*
> *on the journey from the capital*
>   Zeami

On dark mornings in Navarre the fall-off hills rise in masses,
flat on top. White clouds bite down on them like teeth. In my
country too it is morning now, they are making coffee, they are
getting out the black bread. No one eats black bread here. Spanish bread is the same color as the stones that lie along the roadside — gold. True, I often mistake stones for bread. Pilgrim's
hunger is a curious thing.

The road itself was built by the pilgrims of ancient times as
they walked. Each carried a stone and set it in place. As is clear
from the photographs, these were in general stones of quite
good size. While the pilgrims trudged, they would pretend the

stones were loaves of bread and, to keep spirits high, they sang songs about bread, or about the rock that was following them. *¡No me mates con tomate, mátame con bacalao!* You can hear this one still, in bars, some nights. *Don't kill me with tomato, kill me with cod!* What is it that keeps us from drowning in moments that rise and cover the heart?

Pilgrims were people whose recipes were simple.

---

to Nájera   27th of June

> we pick spring greens
> in the little field of Ikuta
> a sight so charming
> the traveler stops to watch
> foolishness! all these questions
>   Kan-ami

Rain during the night. No guests in the hotel except My Cid and me. Yet, just before dawn, someone made his way down the stairs and past our rooms to the bath. Much noise of taps and other facilities. A rough cough. I fell asleep, when I woke he was gone. In the plaza we find bars and shops already open, how surprising. We purchase blood oranges and eat them very fast. It is already late when you wake up inside a question. Rose petals are being swept from the church steps as we pass, and faces in the doorway are lit with vague regret. Someone has roused the town, not me. Someone has been gained and lost, someone of value. Are there two ways of knowing the world? a submissive and a devouring way. They end up roughly the same place.

Pilgrims were people who tried not to annoy the regular inhabitants.

Nájera   28th of June

> moon drifts in cloud
> I have a mind

to borrow
a small ripe melon

Shiki

We are moving on the edge of the Meseta. Hills are harsher, terraced, red soil shows through the green like sunburn. Small trees line up in spikes on the horizon. No more deep woods shaded for battle. No more long winds rolling down from Roland's eyes.

You see that uncertainty along the horizon (photograph)? Not rain. It is heat haze on the plain of León.

Water is less, and less.

In Nájera are buried the kings of Navarre. They lie on their tombs long-limbed and cool as water plants. The stone faces are full of faith but rather private, with a characteristic set to the lips: one straight incision across like the first cut made by a man peeling his orange with a knife. My Cid, as you know, prefers the speckled kind called blood oranges, which are quick to eat but slow to peel. Cleaning his knives reminds him of a story. There was once a pilgrim who carried a turnip all the way from France. A turnip of quite good size. He had in mind to feast his fellow pilgrims on the last hill outside Compostela and be king of their hearts for a while. Thieves broke his head open, just as he came to the top of the hill. The good man's name has not come down to us, but the hill is still there and is called Monte del Gozo. From where you are perhaps you can see it. Mountain of Joy. My Cid tells these old stories wonderfully well. He has two knives, for different sizes of oranges.

Pilgrims were people who carried knives but rarely found joy.

Santo Domingo de la Calzada   29th of June

waited for you along the road, I did —
silent, silent, walking alone
but today again the darkness falls

Gensei

As we move into Castile we are accompanied on either side of the road by aqueducts and other more modern systems of irrigation, for the water grows less. Like pastries of red lava the rocks rise in visible layers. Fields are no longer dark and edged close with woods but stretch out and roll away beneath the eye, sectioned in areas of ocher and amber and red. *Nine months of winter, three months of hell* is the proverbial description of climate on the Meseta. No dark green wheat riding in waves under the wind here, as there was all through Navarre. No wind at all. That smell is light, ready to fall on us. One day closer to the plain of León.

We live by waters breaking out of the heart.

My Cid loves heat and is very elated. He rarely gets thirsty. "I was born in the desert." Twice a day, at meals, he drinks a lot of wine, staring at the glass in genial amazement as it empties itself again and again. He grows heavier and heavier like a piece of bread soaking, or a fish that floats dreamily out of my fingers down deeper and deeper in the tank, turning round now and then to make dim motions at me with its fins, as if in recognition, but in fact it does not recognize me — gold shadows flash over it, out of reach, gone. Who is this man? I have no idea. The more I watch him, the less I know. What are we doing here, and why are our hearts invisible? Once last winter when we were mapping out the pilgrimage on his kitchen table, he said to me, "Well, what are you afraid of, then?" I said nothing. "Nothing." Not an answer. What would your answer be?

We think we live by keeping water caught in the trap of the heart. *Coger en un trampa* is a Spanish idiom meaning "to catch in a trap." *Coger por el buen camino* is another, constructed with the same verb, that means "to get the right road." And yet to ensnare is not necessarily to take the right road.

Afraid I don't love you enough to do this.

Pilgrims were people who got the right verb.

———

Villamayor del Río   30th of June

As I look back over the many years of my frivolous life, I remember at one time I coveted an official post with a tenure of land and at another time I was anxious to confine myself

*within the walls of a monastery. Yet I kept
aimlessly wandering on like a cloud in the wind.
. . . It is because I believe there is no place in this
world that is not an unreal dwellng. At this
point I abandoned the line of thinking and went
to sleep.*

Basho

The town of Villamayor del Río, My Cid observes, is three
ways a lie. "It is not a town, it is not big and there is no river."
The observations are correct. Notwithstanding, we lunch, and
over lunch a conversation — about action, in which he does not
believe. I would relate the conversation and outline the theory
of his belief but theories elude me unless I write them down at
the time. Instead, I was watching his dreamy half smile. It floats
up through his face from the inside, like water filling an aquarium, when he talks about God. For his conversations about action (we have had more than one) are all descriptions of God,
deep nervous lover's descriptions.

I should have taken photographs. A theory of action is hard
to catch, and I know only glimpses of his life — for instance, at
home he makes his own bread (on Saturday morning, very good
bread). He thought about being a priest (at one time). He could
have made a career on the concert stage, and instead built a
harpsichord (red) in the dining room. The harpsichord goes
unmentioned in Villamayor del Río. I am telling you this because a conversation is a journey, and what gives it value is fear.
You come to understand travel because you have had conversations, not vice versa. What is the fear inside language? No
accident of the body can make it stop burning.

---

to Burgos   2nd of July

*what does he do —
the man next door
in the abode in late autumn?*

Basho

"The land is lean indeed!" He quotes from the poem as we
begin our long, cold climb up the windswept plateau of Burgos.

Cold is the mountain road that goes curving up. Cold are the
woods where winds come roaring out at us as if we were enemies
— or birds, for here are tiny birds walking about on the road,
who have strolled out of their homes in the treetops now level
with the road as we ascend — and there is no one else. The
wind is too loud to talk. He walks ahead, eyes front.

In the city of Burgos lies El Cid himself — beside Ximena he
rests in an eternal conversation. Beneath the transept of Burgos
cathedral they have lain since 1921, and before that, in a burial
place in the city from the year 1835, and previously, seven
hundred years in the monastery of San Pedro outside the city
walls. By now she must know every word he is going to say. Yet
she kisses his mouth and the eyes of his face, she kisses his
hands, his truth, his marrow. What is the conversation of lovers?
Compared with ordinary talk, it is as bread to stone. My heart
gets dizzy. It is the most difficult photograph I have tried to take
so far: up the scaffolding, hand over hand and out onto the
pinnacles they blow, her hair like a red sail as they veer around
storks' nests in the wind and clutch wide at the railings, leaning out over the tiny city, its clockwork shadows so crazily far
below. One shriek goes flaring and flattening away down the
valley. Gone. She kisses him on the shoulder in the Moorish custom. They look at one another. They look into the light. They
jump.

There is no question I covet that conversation. There is no
question I am someone starving. There is no question I am
making this journey to find out what the appetite is. And I see
him free of it, as if he had simply crossed to the other side of a
bridge, I see desire set free in him like some ray of mysterious
light. Now tell me the truth, would you cross that bridge if you
came to it? And where, if you made the grave choice to give up
bread, would it take you? You see what I fear. One night I
dreamed of such a world. I rowed upon the surface of the moon
and there was no wind, there were no moments, for the moon
is as empty as the inside of an eye and not even the sound of a
shadow falling falls there. I know you want me to tell you that
hunger and silence can lead you to God, so I will say it, but I
awoke. As the nail is parted from the flesh, I awoke and I was
alone.

Ahead of me walks a man who knows the things I want to
know about bread, about God, about lovers' conversations, yet
mile after tapping mile goes by while I watch his heels rise and
fall in front of me and plant my feet in rhythm to his pilgrim's
staff as it strikes the road, white dust puffing up to cover each
step, left, right, left.

When is a pilgrim like a letter of the alphabet? When he cries
out.

———————————

from Burgos   3rd of July

> now I return to the burning house
> but where is the place I used to live?
>
> Kan-ami

Cold Burgos is beautiful to leave along the avenue of dark
plane trees that line the river. Whiteness floats on the water. At
the bend of the river a water bird stands on one long, chill leg.
He turns an eye. *Adiós.* Gladly and bravely we go — how surprising. Burgos was to have been for us a major interval, some
four days of luxury and recuperation, according to our original
itinerary. Instead, we stay just long enough to mend our trou-
sers and tie new straps on our hats. The cloud-moving wind
calls through our sleep: we rise too early, look at one another,
set off again. It is an open secret among pilgrims and other
theoreticians of this traveling life that you become addicted to
the horizon. There is a momentum of walking, hunger, roads,
empty bowl of thoughts that is more luxurious — more *civil,*
than any city. Even the earliest *Pilgrim's Guide,* published in A.D.
1130, contains remarks touching the dilemma of the pilgrim
who reaches his destination and cannot bear to stop. But that is
not my question, presently.

My questions, as you know, concern pilgrims' tradition. Animals ride on top of one another. Animals ensnare themselves in
plants and tendrils. These are two motifs that may be seen re-
peatedly in reliefs and other works of art along the pilgrim's
route. Signs are given to us like a voice within flesh, that is my
question. Signs point our virtue. I want to ask how is it this man

and I are riding on top of one another, and how ensnared, for it is not in the customary ways. We take separate rooms in hotels. Carnal interest is absent. Yet tendrils are not. A pilgrim is a person who is up to something. What is it? A pilgrim is a person who works out an attitude to tendrils and other things that trammel the feet, what should that be? Chop them as fast as they grow with my sharp pilgrim's knife? Or cherish them, hoarding drops of water of every kind to aid their struggle? Love is the mystery inside this walking. It runs ahead of us on the road like a dog, out of the photograph.

———————————

to Castrogeriz   4th of July

> *twisting up hemp*
> *I spin a thread that has no use*
> *the tears that fall*
> *are not beads for stringing*
>   Tsurayuki

We walk for hours through a single wheat field stretching as far as the eye can see in every direction to the sky. Hills come lower. Horizon flattens. Color begins to bleach out of the landscape as we move onto the Meseta. No more red clay. Where soil shows through the vegetation now it is white, or the porous grey of pumice, and powders off in the wind. Trees are short and clenched like fists in a Goya painting. No rivers at all today until just outside the town of Castrogeriz we cross the Río Odra, a dry gully.

My Cid has taken to wearing a goatskin bag (*odra*) for carrying water. He is rarely thirsty but likes the effect of it slung across his body like a gangster's gun, and he is perfecting the knack of shooting water from the goatskin into his mouth with one hand while reading a map in the other as he walks. Half smile. Very ordinary behavior can be striking when it plays in the shapes of things like a sage, or a child biting into a pear. In the photograph the two of us are bending over the map, looking for Castrogeriz which has been obscured by water drops. Here is an enlargement. You can see, within each drop, a horizon stretching, hard, in full wind. Enlarged further, faint dark shapes become visible, gathering on the edge of the plain of León. *¡Corazón arriba!*

Castrogeriz   4th of July

> *I will gaze at the moon*
> *and cleanse my heart*
>
> Zeami

Castrogeriz is a pile of history. It is layered upward from the dry ravine of the Odra to the ancient remains of a Roman camp high on top of the rock. This smashed Roman grin commands the rock and the town and the whole valley below. It stands behind every sound, like something dripping.

Why then, I wonder, in the town of Castrogeriz, do they turn the water off at night? Not only in each house, but in the fountain of the central square and also in all the fountains of the lesser plazas. A surprise, and a long dry night for me. I walk back to the hotel, hands hanging down. Surprises make a child of us: here is another. A moon rising, edge so sharp you can feel it in your back teeth. By the time she is full, there will be two grave children walking the plain of León. Unexpectedness moves us along. And the moon — so perfectly charted, never fails to surprise us, I wonder why. The moon makes a traveler hunger for something bitter in the world, what is it? I will vanish, others will come here, what is that? An old question.

Well, a pilgrim is like a Nō play. Each one has the same structure, a question mark.

---

to Frómista   5th of July

> *daybreak comes on distinctly*
> *with sounds of a punted boat*
> *does not the dissolving moon*
> *stay yet in the sky?*
>
> Shohaku

Every morning as I walk behind him, I gather a handful of flowers which My Cid pins to his hat. Flowers are banal between lovers but this is not that. Mine are much less an offering to My Cid than an entangling of him in an offering to the saint, which is in turn an entangling of the saint in an offering to God, as the pin snares the flower stalks and the hat gives occasion to the whole. As you know from the photographs, Saint James in his day was insouciance itself — with his great hat tilted low over one eye and his blue cloak unfurling around him like the first notes of paradise. Morning is clear. The hearths smoke. Distances go silent.

Pilgrims were debonair people.

———————

Frómista   7th of July

> *as one turns about the moon*
> *understands one's very heart*
>   Sozei

Hills continue to pale and scarify. They look shaved, like old heads of women in an asylum. What is the breaking point of the average pilgrim? I feel so lonely, like childhood again. What kind of ensnaring can touch the loneliness of animals? Nothing can touch it. No, maybe that is not altogether correct. This evening My Cid gave me a back rub and spoke to me, more kindly than he has before, about his mother, who suffers from a wasting disease. Once, when he first learned of her illness, his heart broke. Then he set about taking care of her, with back rubs and other attentions. A voice coming from behind your back can be different. Animals who ride on top of one another do not have to see each other's face. Sometimes that is better.

———————

Carrión de los Condes   7th of July

> *as usual with men who are blind*
> *my ears are sharp, you know*

you just called me "a man without feelings"
don't go on saying things like that!

Zeami

The morning is clear. The morning is immensely clear. Lower the lance and lean forward in the saddle. It is time to question him about the loneliness. His answer both surprises me and does not.

He has not been lonely since he was thirty, when he took the decision to channel his sadness into forms "more metaphysical." He began to think about penance. Like a blind poet of ancient times, he built his hut on a meeting slope, chose a small number of objects and waited for friends. Fish dart out of gold regions. His loves are deep, sudden services. And his delight is of a very particular kind. "You have a passion for people who are pelted, Dan," says Sir Hugo to Daniel Deronda in a novel I read once. My Cid lives this novel; his friends are ones in affliction. *She is someone who has known hardship,* he often begins. Has a bad back, father abandoned her, gives all her money away to the poor, history of lunacy, lost the whole family, royalty — fallen, nowhere to go. He loves these stories — they make people seem real. Nonetheless there are difficulties. People mistake his intentions, especially women, and some do drown.

For women may regard a story as the beginning of something, like a love affair. Serious mistake. For him it is already the end: *se abandona.* Persons studying the photographs from different angles may see different tendrils, but for him these entanglements are not a problem. It is you who are lonely.

And in the end, his tendency to rescue maidens is not something I can explain to you, nor dramatize — I am a pilgrim (not a novelist) and the only story I have to tell is the road itself. Besides, no one can write a novel about a road, any more than you can write a novel about God, simply because you cannot get round the back of it. A round character is one you can see round. He changes according to the company he keeps. He moves but your movements are always larger, and circumnavigate his. Inside the minds of other characters you see him flicker past, suddenly funny — or evil. Now I think it is true to say of the road, and also of God, that it does not move. At the same time, it is everywhere. It has a language, but not one I know. It has a story, but I am in it. So are you. And to realize this is a moment of some sadness. When we are denied a story, a light goes off — Daniel Deronda vanishes; do we vanish too? I am asking you to study the dark.

———————

Sahagún   8th of July

> *no wind, yet the windbells*
> *keep on ringing*
>   Shiren

The light is astounding, a hammer. Horizon no closer, ever. Hills again change color: gold and dark gold and darker gold. Whole fields are nothing but slabs of this gold soil, smashed up in chunks for cultivation, as if the massive altar at Castrogeriz had toppled straight across León. The pieces of bread that line the pilgrims' road have the color and shape of the round loaves of León, many show bites taken out. They were famished people who built this road.

My Cid and I have our first open anger today. It cut like glass. Animals entangle themselves in one another, and grow enraged. (What is rage?)

When I spoke to him about the loneliness I didn't mean out in the wheat fields. There is a loneliness that opens up between two people sitting in a bar, not in love with one another, not even certain they like the way they are entangled with one another, one taps a glass with a spoon, stops. There is a silence that pounds down on two people. More astounding than the light that hammers the plain of León, at least for those animals who choose to fear it. (Is it a choice?)

———————

El Burgo Ranero   9th of July

> *your autumn leaves —*
> *it is because they fall we love them*
> *so why not launch our Takase river boat?*
>   Shikibu

It would be an almost perfect love affair, wouldn't it? that between the pilgrim and the road. No mistake, it is a beautiful thing, the *camino*. It stretches away from you. It leads to real gold: look at the way it shines. And it asks only one thing. Which happens to be the one thing you long to give. You step forward. You shiver in the light. Nothing is left in you but desire for that perfect economy of action, using up the whole heart, no residue, no mistake: *camino*. It would be as simple as water, wouldn't it? If there were any such thing as simple action for animals like us.

Pilgrims were people glad to take off their clothing, which was on fire.

Mansilla de las Mulas   10th of July

> bones on the moor
> wind blows on them through my heart
> Basho

Meseta colder than expected. Distances crushing. Horizon beats on the eyes.

Everything is gold. I cannot describe the gold. I have shown you the photographs (or have I?) but they don't come near it. You get almost no warning. Something is coming along the edge of the wheat, drumming the plain like a horseman, you stop, listen, begin to turn — don't!

It is life taken over, *esa es la verdad*.

---

to León   11th of July

> the rumor is already
> in circulation
> yet when I began to love
> there was not a soul who knew
> Tadamine

Water abandons itself. Gold does not. Gold takes life over. There are drownings on the Meseta. I will show you the pho-

tographs if you like but, really, in this case they are not helpful.
Because the light is not something you *see,* exactly. You don't
look at it, or breathe, you feel a pressure but you don't look. It
is like being in the same room as a man you love. Other people
are in the room. He may be smoking a cigarette. And you know
you are not strong enough to look at him (yet) although the fact
that he is there, silent and absent beside a thin wisp of cigarette
smoke, hammers you. You rest your chin on your hand, like a
saint on a pillar. Moments elongate and drop. A radiance is
hitting your skin from somewhere, every nerve begins to burn
outward through the surface, your lungs float in a substance
like rage, sweet as rage, no! — don't look. Something falling
from your mouth like bits of rust.

Well, the photograph — after all it may give some idea of the
thing. From outside it all, looking down: two tiny figures moving
on the Meseta. Two animals enraged with one another. How
can you tell? Pay particular attention to the nerves. Every one is
visible. See, as they burn, you can look right down the heart's
core. See it crumble like old dry bread.

———————

to León   11th of July

> In the Nō play Obasute, *at the line "I feel*
> *ashamed to see the moon," there exists a moment*
> *when the acting can be so effective that (as they*
> *say) "gold is picked up in the middle of the*
> *road."*
>
>   Zeami

A baking hot morning. I can feel you watching. I shrug and go
on.

In allegorical renderings of the pilgrimage to Compostela,
days spent crossing the plain of León stand for the dark night
of the soul — how can it help being that way? Although we taste
everything and take on every animal, although your true love
exists (and maybe it does), we continue to behave more or less
like the people we are, even on a pilgrimage. No soul ever goes
dark enough for you. Look again at the photograph. Two fig-

ures moving on the Meseta, running slowly on a table of gold. Running with arms out, mouths open. Two small ensnared animals howling toward Finisterre.

You can lead a pilgrim to water.

León   12th of July

> *when in the clear water*
> *at Ausaka border*
> *it sees its reflection*
> *the tribute horse from Mochizuki*
> *will surely shy away*
>
>   Zeami

Various dangers come at you from water. We cross the top of the world and descend into the city of León in conditions much different than expected. Lashing rain and slate-grey winds, horizontal and cold as winter. Something is being prepared on the plain of León. The city itself is a bright animal, bustling, turning, restless to lie down. We find lodgings and fall asleep. Storms pass over the city. My Cid dreams of leviathans coming up out of the water to kill him. He impales one of them on his pilgrim's staff and hurls it back. Losing his staff (I point out). But the creature will (he feels sure) be purified on its journey downstream to the ends of the earth. A clean gold animal clambering ashore at the end of the world, isn't that so? I am the kind of person who says let's wait and see.

Arzoá   12th of July

> *she at once capped his verses*
>
>   Shikibu

My Cid and I are very polite with one another. At the same time, somewhat dialectical — that is, I contradict everything he says. I have been trying to curb this habit by picking up pieces of bread from along the roadside to gnaw as I walk. It must have been, in origin, for this purpose that pilgrims began to put the bread there.

An origin is not an action, although it occurs (perhaps loudly) at the very start and may open an action (as in breaking a gun). How long ago it seems we started out. In the photographs from this leg of the journey you will notice a certain absence of scale clues, so that a bullet-pocked rock seems to hold the heavens.

Pilgrims were people who took a surprisingly long time to cross the head of a pin.

———————————

Órbigo   13th of July

> *since my house burned down*
> *I now own*
> *a better view*
> *of the rising moon*
>
> Masahide

Color begins to return to the fields as we move towards the edge of the Meseta. There are green potato fields cut by canals. Avenues of poplar trees turn their bright soles to the wind. Horizon closing in. Behind the light, towards the west, (darkish) shadows are gathering. That would be animals on the rim of the plain. That would be the wolf.

The pieces of bread along the roadside are blacker now and more wildly bitten. At the same time, in some places you see whole loaves thrown down untouched. Curious. Insouciance may escalate to proportions of madness at this stage in the pilgrimage. Breaking points appear.

———————————

Astorga   14th of July

> *the dried sardine is broiled at noon*
> *but in this back country*
> *the use of coins is not yet heard of*
> *what a bother to travelers*
>
> Basho

Those things that cut across the time are what you remember, voices cutting across sleep.

"*¡Agua! ¡Agua!*" ripping through my siesta like a color.

Red. The color red speeds through the land as we move into the mountains again. Sections of brick-red soil mark out the green plantings of the hills as they rise. Poppies flash along the roadside, amid dark chunks of rusted bread. At noon, the cicadas let their red throats crack open. Red, My Cid informs me, is the only color wolves see: this is taken as clear testimony, in ancient Celtiberian belief, that they are genuinely royal animals.

It is over lunch that we talk of wolves, and My Cid has ordered trout. The scales and eyes are gold as it sizzles on the plate. He cuts in. The flesh is a deep rose color. After lunch we proceed to the museum to see a twelfth-century statue called *The Virgin of the Trout,* with wooden cheeks of the same rose color. Her smile an underwater bell. Ancient pilgrims traveled from far and wide, on delicately tinted feet, to visit her. And there is still more red, as we move from the museum to the cathedral, for the cathedral at Astorga wears a deep blush. Its porch of rose limestone is inscribed with scenes of shame: Christ expelling moneylenders from the temple, and others. Now we are close to the heart of the color. Shame. Look at the photograph. Yes, it is a picture of a hole in a wall.

The hole dates from medieval times. It is located in the west wall of the cathedral at a height of about two meters above the head of My Cid. Behind it is a pit opening into the wall and, in front, iron bars. Women once placed themselves inside the pit and lived there, taking as sustenance only what was offered by those passing by. Many a pilgrim on his way to Compostela shared his meager rations with the women, handing in water or pieces of bread or whatever he had. Others passed with their eyes on the road. Some tossed stones through the bars. It is a strange economy that shame set up, isn't it? almost as strange as that of honor. Pilgrims blush in broad daylight. Women blush in a hole. They trade morsels of gold through a grillwork and so all live to overcome another day. What is a blush?

Dum pudeo pereo (as I blush, I die) says an old love song. Blood rushes to the face, at the same time the heart seems to wither in on itself and snap, like the eye socket of a trout when it hits the hot oil. Shame is the presence of someone right up against me. Hot because her eyes are closer to me than my own honor. She is a woman in a pit in a wall with a stone hot as the midday sun in her hands: listen, footsteps go fading down the street. She is My Cid cut open by a word from me, him weeping within me. Kinds of water drown us.

The women in the wall were called *las emparedadas* (the walled-in ones). What is a pilgrim's life after he quits the *camino?* There is an ancient tradition: the afterlife of a pilgrim is three ways shame. Never hungry again. He will eat and eat and taste nothing. Never free again, according to the terms of the freedom he finds while bound to the road. Never angry again, with that kind of rage that scorches two animals ensnared on the Meseta. It is an anger hard to come back from as death, or so it seems to me now as I recollect the day near Sahagun when My Cid and I cut ourselves open on a moment of anger, and blasphemed your name. Let's take out those photographs again, *momentito*. There is something here that deserves to be studied, there is a sense of the excitement and danger of the night. And yet it was broad day: look.

————————

> *from today the dew*
> *will erase the inscription on my hat*
> *"I am one of two traveling together"*
> Basho

I have never felt life to be as slow and desperate as that day on the Meseta with the sky empty above us, hour after hour unmoving before us and a little wind whistling along the bone of my ear. Walking across the top of the world. Hours give no shade. Wind gives no shade.

Sky does not move. Sky crushes all that moves.

We had been out since sunrise, we were growing black. Then we saw water.

A plane tree in the middle of the desert with a spring beside it. We ran to it and drank, drank more, grew arrogant. Here I

am swaggering like a *torero* around the little oasis, or so it looks
(photograph), water all over my face. Now I ask My Cid a question — and what follows — well, it may seem to be nothing at
all. But in fact it was sackcloth of hair and the moon became
blood. He begins to answer the question (I don't remember what
it was). And he has a certain way of answering a question (as we
all do). And I know what he is going to say (as soon as he begins).
And all at once I am enraged. My sharp pilgrim's knife flashes
once. "*I know!*" right across his open face.

I know. I know what you say. I know who you are. I know all
that you mean. Why does it enrage an animal to be given what
it already knows? Speaking as someone who is as much in love
with knowledge as My Cid is in love with the light on the plain
of León, I would say that knowing is a road. The metaphor is
unoriginal but now you may set it beside the photographs of the
pit in the wall and see what it signifies to me.

You reach out your hand for bread and grasp a stone. You
touch stone, you feel sweat running down your body. Sweat
running, day going black, it is a moment that does not move.
How I did waste and exhaust my heart. Something darker
appears to be running down the body of the saint in the
photograph, but it is just an effect of the light filter we were
using on the Meseta. There is nothing darker (than the second
death).

Now that I study them, however, I have to confess the photographs of the *emparedadas* are something of an embarrassment. I tried to angle my lens so as to shoot through the bars
but the grillwork was too high. None of them printed properly.
Look at this one, for instance — it could be a picture of a woman
with something in her hands. It could be a drowned dog floating
in bits of stone. Can you make it out? The picture has been
taken looking directly into the light, a fundamental error. As I
was considering these matters, he had gone his way, footsteps
fading down the street like the last drops of water running
out of a basin. I hurry after him. Kinds of water drown us.
Kinds of water blister the negatives irremediably (prints look
burned). Perhaps I will have time to put these through again
later.

voice of wind in pines
makes the solitude familiar
who will do such waking for each dawn?

Sogi

Mountains. We have come over the mountains of León. It takes a whole day from light to light. The road goes winding, winding, winding up. The road goes plunging down. You understand these were *words* before: up, down. It is nearly my limit, nearly stupor, whereas he grows lighter and lighter as he walks. What is penance?

Up.

On top of the mountains of León is an iron cross. Here we stop. A wind whistles up one side of the mountains from early times, mornings, much too far away and still those mornings, down on the plain of León. "Somewhere down there we were hot," he says. Somewhere down there we were drowning. I fall over on a flat rock and fall asleep, while he watches. Wolves come and go, browsing at my back. At sunset we get up and start down the other side of the mountains.

Down.

Gorge after gorge, turning, turning. Caverns of sunset, falling, falling away — just a single vast gold air breathed out by beings — they must have been marvelous beings, those gold-breathers. Down. Purple and green islands. Cleft and groined and gigantically pocked like something left behind after all the oceans vanished one huge night: the mountains. Their hills fold and fold again, fold away, down. Folded into the dens and rocks of the hills are ghost towns. Broken streets end in them, like a sound, nowhere. Shadow is inside. We walk (oh quietly) even so — breaking lines of force, someone's. Houses stand in their stones. Each house an empty socket. Some streaked with red inside. Words once went on in there — no. I don't believe that. Words never went on there.

Down.

We circle, circle, circle again. Around each bend of the road, another, bending back. It is sunset. Look down: at the foot of the mountain something comes into view. Clustered on the water like wings, something, shining. Something, marveling, at the float of its wings around it on the water — how they change and turn gold! That is what an evening was in the beginning, you once told me. *Y la paloma volvió a él a la hora de la tarde.* The photograph has been taken with the light behind it so that the two figures stand out clear against the mountains, which crush them from behind. They appear to be running — not because of the wolves who, as you see, are merely watching from this peak or that in mild curiosity. An effect of immediacy has been achieved by showing the figures close up and cut off at the knees. *And the dove came into him in the evening.*

Pilgrims were people to whom things happened that happen only once.

———————

Trabadelo   17th of July

> *great moor*
> *answering heart*
> *oh do not forget*
> *the bounds of life keep shifting*
>
> Socho

All day we steer along the edge of the mountains, looking up: the massif of Galicia. Tomorrow, climb again. "We will strike them in the name of God and of Saint James!" He is blithe. I am not. With folded paws they watch us, wait.

———————

Cebreiro   18th of July

> *in the town of Kowata*
> *there were horses to hire*
> *but I loved you so much*
> *I walked barefoot all the way*
>
> Kan-ami

So we climb to the top of the world once more. Straight up a rocky goat track, teetering, panting, pouring with sweat, plastered in dust to the pass of Cebreiro. At the top the wind is suddenly wide open and cold as a river. Look back — now it all pulls away at our feet, a thousand miles straight down straight back to the morning we began, it was a good bright morning in the eleventh century and we must have been very young to judge from the photograph. So white was I when I went to harvest.

"I do not wish to sound Socratic," between angry bites of tortilla, "but what is your definition of penance?" He is annoyed with me today. He does not find my definition adequate. Pilgrims who go on foot but sleep in hotels (like us) are, in his view, more authentic than pilgrims who drive cars but sleep on the ground. Well, Galicia is a surprising place, is my view. And authenticity is surprisingly well defended here. For example, in this hotel, one huge white wolf guards us through the night. He has a huge, slow gaze and lies in the lettuces, still as a sculpture except for his huge, black eyes which rove tirelessly back and forth over the moon-washed grounds. Who would have thought we would reach the zone of greatest danger to find that the wolves are the hospitalers here? Penance can be a surprising study and pilgrims, even very authentic ones, raven in ways they do not expect. I have seen men die of the waters because they had learned to crave only wormwood. What sense could there be in that? What sense is there in pain at all — however we contrive it for ourselves as we cast about for ways to bind up the wound between us and God? The penitent in the act of binding up pain with pain is a photograph I have tried (unsuccessfully) a number of times to capture.

On the edge of the world is a black row of trees, shaking. Moon like a piece of skin above.

When is a pilgrim like a photograph? When the blend of acids and sentiment is just right.

———————

to Samos

> *ah, for her too, it is the midnight*
> *pilgrimage*
> *how many of them there are! is this*
> *the work of hell?*
>
> Chikamatsu

What is the relation of rage to penance? Of entanglement?
It is a room of women. The night is black. In the photograph
you can see an eyelid outlined in light from the street, here.
The wall streaked with darker moisture, there. We listen to each
other breathe. A cicada has got in here tonight and with his tiny
rasp is nicking our nerve ends open. Even among the living,
sometimes it seems a night will never end. A woman begins now
to shriek, softly. I am not one to interfere, but sadness is sadness. Maybe a little song — my mother used to sing to me, sometimes at night, old ballads from the civil war:

> as each hour passes Miguel my love
> you grow more dear:
> is that the reason Miguel my love
> you are not here?

Ah. The shrieking has stopped. The others are breathing.
The room grows quiet. Sometimes it is enough just to recognize
a *camino*. Your bitter heart heals my heart, oh stay with me.

Samos   19th of July

> *"Yes," he says, "for your sake."*
> *What is he saying?*
>
> Zeami

Penance is something broken off and thrown back, like a
sweetness that pierces your thoughts when all at once you re-

member someone you dreamed of last night. It was someone
unknown. Just at dawn he was there, gleaming, shuffling. It
makes the night transparent to think of. It makes the night
incomparable. You dreamed of black arms shaking on the edge
of the world. Reaching back for that, you drop through a freedom so clear it is simply pain. *Corazón nuevo* means "new heart."
It is a place you reach for through your skin, which goes silver,
through shame burned black on you, through a thirst that we
cannot describe, to where he is cooling his wings in the stars like
a pond, looking down at them trailing around him on the dark
water — look, there he is, vaguely marveling — oh beloved,
who could catch your eye?

———————

Palas del Rey   21st of July

> *two petals fall*
> *and the shape of the peony*
> *is wholly changed*
>
>   Shikibu

   Climbing and tracking through the bottomlands of Galicia in
deep fog. Shapes of life loom and vanish at us, grow grotesque.
Fog invents the imagination. We do not like to be surrounded
by meaningless grotesquerie, we are animals who take it upon
us to find form in the misshapen. There (photographs) is Veláz-
quez on a cabbage stalk, and the pine trees here a row of teeth?
a fortress? dice? and this fence post has the outline of the Dead
Sea, I believe.
   Shapes of life change as we look at them, change us for looking. Take wolves. You may think you know what a wolf looks
like: Queen Lupa thought so. For the countryside around Palas
del Rey was once thick with wolves and Lupa was their queen,
commanding them from a rough fort called the Castro Lupario.
Strange her yellow eyes should fasten one day on Saint James
himself.
   He had come through Galicia in the first century A.D. on his
way to Finisterre, bent on Christianizing the uttermost edge of
the known world, and returned some years later to Palestine to

be martyred. Whereupon his disciples took the body and em-
barked on a boat. They reached Galicia, within sight of the
Castro Lupario: see Lupa's eyes narrow. She goes to meet them
and offers them land to bury the saint. Her speech is fluent, her
face empty as a pocket and her plan is to kill them with death.
That very night she sends the holy men out with the body on a
cart. What are those animals yoked to the cart? Oxen, says Lupa.
They look somehow darker, but at night who can say? Of course
they are Lupa's own wolves — is this just a name? As they walk
through the dark the wolves become oxen and pull the cart to a
good high hill. There the apostles build their tomb and offer
thanks. Lupa's eyes widen. She studies the photographs under
various magnifying lenses and, in the end, converts to the new
religion.

Animals who ride on top of one another become entangled in
ways they do not expect. From behind its back you may see a
wolf as a queen, or a hill as a holy body, or action as a fact. But
facts form themselves this way and that, when we look for them
in photographs or historical accounts.

Penance is one form we find, one form we insist on.

———————

to Compostela   23rd of July

> it's not easy to tell which end
> is which of a resting snail
>
> Kyorai

Your voice I know. It had me terrified. When I hear it in
dreams, from time to time all my life, it sounds like a taunt —
but dreams distort sound, for they send it over many waters.
During these hard days I, a pilgrim, am giving my consideration
to this. I trudge along the bottom of the river and the questioning goes on in me. What are we made of but hunger and rage?
His heels rise and fall in front of me. How surprised I am to be
entangled in the knowledge of some other animal. I know the
animal. Does that mean I hand myself over? What is knowing?
That is the question no one was asking, although I went from
place to place and watched and listened to all that they said. I

began to suspect some code was in operation. It had me terrified. Why? It plunged me in a pit, why? Because it is your question.

Your question I leave to you. There is in it a life of love I can scarcely look at, except in dreams. Or from time to time in photographs. Here is an old picture of My Cid with his mother. He is reaching up to put his hat on her head. Even before her illness she disliked being exposed to the afternoon sun. Yet she never brought a hat, and I believe they walked most afternoons. "Must get a hat," she would say every time, bending her head. Half smile.

How is a pilgrim like a blacksmith? He bends iron. Love bends him.

———————

to Compostela   24th of July

why, my dear pilgrim hat
you must accompany me
to view the plum trees!

Basho

It takes a long time to arrive from not very far away. Just before the end we climb the small hill called Monte del Gozo. On achieving this height, from which the long-desired city can suddenly be seen half a league distant, ancient pilgrims would fall to their knees, shed tears of joy and begin to sing the Te Deum. "They felt like seafarers on reaching a haven after a tempest at sea," says one old account, which My Cid is reading aloud as he walks ahead of me. His voice is joy, his steps are joy, moved along like a water wheel in water. While for my part I feel I have broken in half. Every pilgrim hits the mark in his own way.

Stars are spitting out of the cathedral as we enter Compostela: the cathedral! No, it is not a mirage, this stupendous humming hulk of gold that stands as if run aground upon the plaza at the center of the city of Santiago. Built in the early years of the

twelfth century, it was embellished towards the end of that century by one Master Mateo, who added the Portal of Glory to
replace the original entrance. That was an act of grace. An
entrance is important to a pilgrim: there can be only one.

An entrance should be a door built as a kiss, so Master Mateo
understood it. All over his Portal are creatures in glory, harping
with the harps of God. Smiles and half smiles fall from them
like music. Animals and prophets, angels and the unnamed people of God raise their hands (surprised) and lean together in
joy. Some show a small blush on each cheek. Through this portal, since the twelfth century, pilgrims enter. Won and not
cheaply! They go straight in. They go to greet the Master of the
place, entering with hand outstretched — I did it too (photograph). You approach the tree of Jesse, carved on the main
column shaft by Master Mateo in 1195. You fit your hand into
the five hollows visible at shoulder height among the tendrils of
the tree. With your fingers in the hollows you can just lean down
and kiss the head of Master Mateo, who has sculpted himself
into the column base amid entangled leaves and animals. So
many pilgrims' lips have brushed the hard plane of the Master's
forehead that it has been worn into a convex pool, where rain-
water and other moistures collect. *Se abandona.* (I like this photograph of two hurried visitors mistaking Master Mateo for a
font.)

Stars, as I say, are shooting from the cathedral high into the
air as we make our way across the plaza. They drop to the
ground and lie in white fire. My Cid is bending down, in the
photograph, to see whether he has one lodged in the sole of his
sandal: in fact he does — problematic, you would think. But this
is an example of the way trials turn to joy for him. Since an
accident in childhood his legs have been of unequal length, but
now, with a star in his shoe he is walking evenly for the first
time in years. It has tripled his insouciance. He embraces a
statue of Saint James. He embraces me — and I fall over (I have
had several glasses today) — my good black beret rolling in the
dust. "Why, I'm drunk!" "Why, I know." Half smile. With a
certain flourish he replaces my beret.

Compostela   25th of July

since you are blind
your sense of poetry
can't be expected to show on your face
                                                Zeami

At midnight, fireworks in the plaza. No photographs — you know what fireworks are like. Tawdry, staggering, irresistible, like human love. Live stars fall on twenty thousand people massed in a darkened square. Some cry out, get burned, applaud. No star falls on me, although I try to position myself. Will you say you cannot make out my face in the dark? you heartless creature.

At the end of the fireworks we burn down the cathedral, as is traditional. So dazed with light and sulphur by now, there is no question it is the appropriate finale. Tomorrow morning, when we try to celebrate Saint James's solemn mass amid the charred ruins, we will think again. But fireworks are always now, aren't they? like human love. ¡Corazón arriba!

When is a pilgrim like the middle of the night? When he burns.

———————————

Compostela   25th of July

even I who have no lover
I love this time
of new kimonos
                                                Ontsura

Notwithstanding a rainy morning in Compostela, solemn mass in honor of Saint James is a debonair event. Pilgrims stand knee-deep in gold rubble, beneath swaying shreds of the high lantern, from which fire is still dropping in lit flakes. Soot and rain stream down on their shoulders unnoticed. The chancel is rumored to be a molten lake and small animals drowning in the side aisles, but we cannot see past a barrier of klieg lights and recording apparatus that has been set up in the central vault by National Spanish Television (the festival mass will be broadcast live, with excerpts for the six o'clock news). Camera crews, trying to string booms across the nave, dodge and curse as they wade on the glassy sea.

There are several fine moments, for example, just about midway through the Credo the central chandelier begins to short circuit — exploding a drizzle of stars over pilgrims in the front pews, quite spectacular. All applaud. But I see you peering hard at another photograph. Oh yes.

That solid silver asteroid is the *botafumeiro,* a vessel from which incense is dispensed at the close of the festival mass, to sanctify the crowds. It hangs straight down from the lantern of the church on a silver rope, about the size of a full-grown wolf. Beneath it, as you see, crowds of pilgrims are packed tight as fish all down the central aisle of the church, while the transepts are empty — why? It is to create a sort of runway: when the crowds are blessed, the *botafumeiro* is swung the whole width of the church — sixty-five meters from transept to transept — in great fuming swerves that carry our prayer up to God and drown the stench of new hearts as they burn below. Saint James tilts his brim: sixty-five meters across! Never was My Cid so happy.

Tomorrow, the ultimate absurdity. We will hire a car and drive to Finisterre.

————————

Compostela   26th of July

> the eye you see isn't
> an eye because you see it
> it's an eye because it sees you
> Machado

Just as no mountain ends at the top, so no pilgrim stops in Santiago. The city and the saint buried there are a point of thought, but the road goes on. It goes west: Finisterre. So, although a pilgrim arrives in Compostela thinking he wants nothing more than to stop, and although the city entangles his feet so that for a day or two days or a week he stands still, or walks from statue to statue kissing Saint James, or lies on a bed in a

dream, comes a day he awakens. Morning is cutting open its
blue eyes. Time is a road. Time to go: Finisterre.

It would not be amiss to mention here one or two things about
this place. The farthest western point of the land mass of Europe, a point sought by earliest Celtic inhabitants of the continent and made the object of pilgrimages centuries before Saint
James was born, it is located on a spit of the Atlantic coast of
Spain called *Cabo de Finisterre*. You can walk there. You can walk
no farther (west).

Why did pilgrims and others searching to pinpoint the end of
the world go always towards the west? For gold, says My Cid. As
you travel west, days are longer: gold, more gold, and still more
gold. However that may be, it is an endeavor as old as civilization to set out on a road that is supposed to take you to the very
end of things, if you keep going. What do you find there? That
is a good question. Who would you be if you knew the answer?
There is one way to find out. So a pilgrim sets off. One thing is
certain, one item is constant in the set of beliefs with which he
travels. It is simply this, that when you reach the place called
the end of the world, you fall off into the water. Some pilgrims
drown, some do not. *Claro.*

How is a pilgrim like a Nō play? His end is not the point. And
yet it is indispensable, to the honor and to the shame.

---

to Finisterre   26th of July

> *if we pick them*
> *we'll pick by guessing*
> *white chrysanthemums*
> *when first frost has settled*
> *and deceives the eye*
>   Mitsune

In all honesty I am, when the time comes, unenthusiastic
about proceeding to Finisterre. I slept heavily through the night
and dreamt I was a criminal on the run from the local authorities. When they corner me in a cellar I hurl at them with marrow
bones, which explode in the air like live stars. Now dark and

unshaven I crouch over my breakfast and jump! when My Cid comes up behind my back. Conversation is balky. He taps a glass with a spoon. I page through the guidebook and find no entry for Finisterre. Is it a place of any interest? He grasps his beard. "Perhaps not." Half smile. "There is nothing there except the end of the world." And so we go to Finisterre.

There is only one road out of Compostela and we take it. Fog closes over us as we drive west. Hours pass. Blurring. Whitening. Fog keeps folding in. Outside — there is no outside. No presence at all out there. Abruptly the road ends. We stop. Disembark. Lock the car. Start to walk. A path is visible now and again through rents in the fog. We make our way along it for some time. Suddenly the path vanishes. There is not a cry. Not a living thing. Just white. Boulders come forward. We begin to climb over them, down, slipping, clutching at roots and lichen. Until the rocks go no farther. We grope this way. That way. There is nowhere to go. Still, we are not at the end. Eyes sting with peering. Cold air from some ice age is pulsing up out of the raw lungs under the sea. Foghorns go round, go off. Distances pass each other, far out. And a cry of some animal — white. Cold. "Shall we go back?" We begin to retreat the way we came, hand over hand, up the rocks. Fog is still shifting in, white, burning. Nothing is visible. And by now we are utterly lost. Let me revise that. I am lost. Suddenly pressingly alert I look around. No one is here but me. And there is no road.

How is a pilgrim like an epigram? Ask me tomorrow.

———————

Finisterre

> *a dried salmon*
> *a pilgrim's gauntness*
> *both in the coldest season*
>
> Basho

There is a fearful ashy light falls on the end of the world. It makes the photographs slow. But you can see the scorched place and the immense hour. Eyes search the shore. There is no wind. There is no shadow. One flat event moves out in a ripple over the whole expanse of the water towards the line of the horizon. Still as watchers they stand, they look, moving their lips. They begin to approach. Now they are browsing at my back, where I have fallen at the edge of the water, knocking back and forth slightly in the force of the waves. They are leaning over me. What is it they are saying? Perhaps — no. Words never went on in me.

But one of them is bending closer. Fear shakes me. As it sometimes will just when we are about to be handed over. Your action is simple. You take hold of my paws and cross them on my breast: as a sign that I am one who has been to the holy city and tasted its waters, its kinds.

Pilgrims were people who carried little. They carried it balanced on their heart.

———————

¡E ultreja e sus eja Deus adiuva nos!

ALBERT GOLDBARTH

After Yitzl

FROM THE GEORGIA REVIEW

> It is not for nothing that a Soviet historian once remarked that
> the most difficult of a historian's tasks is to predict the past.
> — Bernard Lewis, *History*

I

THIS STORY BEGINS in bed, in one of those sleepy troughs between the crests of sex. I stroke the crests of you. The night is a
gray permissive color.

"Who do you think you were — do you think you were anyone, in an earlier life?"

In an earlier life, I think, though chance and bombs and the
saltgrain teeth in ocean air have destroyed all documents, I
farmed black bent-backed turnips in the hardpan of a *shtetl*
compound of equally black-garbed bent-backed grandmama
and rabbinic Jews.

My best friend there shoed horses. He had ribs like barrel
staves, his sweat was miniature glass pears. (I'm enjoying this
now.) On Saturday nights, when the Sabbath was folded back
with its pristine linens into drawers for another week, this Yitzl
played accordion at the *schnapps*-house. He was in love with a

Author's Note: In the writing of this essay/poem/story I drew on many rich sources
of information and inspiration, two of which deserve special mention: Douglas
Curran's *In Advance of the Landing: Folk Concepts of Outer Space* (1986) and Alex
Shoumatoff's *The Mountain of Names: An Informal History of Kinship* (1985).

woman, a counter girl, there. She kept to herself. She folded
paper roses in between serving; she never looked up. But Yitzl
could tell: she tapped her foot. One day the cousin from Milano,
who sent the accordion, sent new music to play — a little sheaf
with American writing on it. *Hot* polka. Yitzl took a break with
me in the corner — I was sipping sweet wine as dark as my
turnips and trying to write a poem — and when he returned to
his little grocer's crate of a stand, there was an open paper rose
on his accordion. So he knew, then.

In this story-*in*-my-story they say "I love you," and now I say
it in the external story, too: I stroke you slightly rougher as I
say it, as if underlining the words, or reaffirming you're here,
and I'm here, since the gray in the air is darker, and sight
insufficient. You murmur it back. We say it like anyone else —
in part because our death is bonded into us meiotically, from
before there was marrow or myelin, and we know it, even as
infants our scream is for more than the teat. We understand
the woodsmoke in a tree is aching to rise from the tree in its
shape, its green and nutritive damps are readying always for
joining the ether around it — any affirming clench of the roots
in soil, physical and deeper, is preventive for its partial inch of
a while.

So: genealogy. The family tree. Its roots. Its urgent suckings
among the cemeterial layers. The backsweep of teat under teat.
The way, once known, it orders the Present. A chief on the
island of Nios, off Sumatra, could stand in the kerosene light
of his plank hut and (this is on tape) recite — in a chant, the
names sung out between his betel-reddened teeth like ghosts
still shackled by hazy responsibility to the living — his ancestral
linkup, seventy generations deep; it took over an hour. The
genealogical record banks of the Mormon Church contain the
names and relationship data of 1½ to 2 billion of the planet's
dead, "in a climate-controlled and nuclear-bomb-proof repository" called Granite Mountain Vault, and these have been
processed through the church's IBM computer system, the
Genealogical Information and Names Tabulation, acronymed
GIANT.

Where we come from. How we need to know.

If necessary, we'll steal it — those dinosaur tracks two men removed from the bed of Cub Creek in Hays County, using a masonry saw, a jackhammer, and a truck disguised as an ice cream vendor's.

If necessary (two years after Yitzl died, I married his *schnapps*-house sweetie: it was mourning him that initially drew us together; and later, the intimacy of hiding from the Secret Police in the burlap-draped back corner of a fishmonger's van. The guts were heaped to our ankles and our first true sex in there, as we rattled like bagged bones over the countryside, was lubricated — for fear kept her dry — with fishes' slime: and, after . . . but that's another story) we'll make it up.

II

Which is what we did with love, you and I: invented it. We needed it, it wasn't here, and out of nothing in common we hammered a treehouse into the vee of a family tree, from zero, bogus planks, the bright but invisible nailheads of pure will. Some nights a passerby might spy us, while I was lazily flicking your nipple awake with my tongue, or you were fondling me into alertness, pleased in what we called bed, by the hue of an apricot moon, in what we called our life, by TV's dry-blue arctic light, two black silhouettes communing: and we were suspended in air. If the passerby yelled, we'd plummet.

Because each midnight the shears on the clock snip off another twenty-four hours. We're frightened, and rightfully so. Because glass is, we now know, a "slow liquid"; and we're slow dust. I've heard the universe howling — a conch from the beach is proof, but there are Ears Above for which the spiral nebulae must twist the same harrowing sound. Because pain, in even one cell, is an ant: it will bear a whole organ away. And a day is so huge — a Goliath; the tiny stones our eyes pick up in sleeping aren't enough to confront it. The marrow gives up. We have a spine, like a book's, and are also on loan with a due date. And the night is even more huge; what we call a day is only one struck match in an infinite darkness. This is knowledge we're born with, this is in the first cry. I've seen each friend I have, at one time or another, shake at thinking how susceptible and brief a person is: and whatever touching we do, whatever small narrative starring ourselves can bridge that unit of emptiness, is a triumph. "Tell me another story," you say with a yawn, "of life back then, with — what was her name?" "With Misheleh?" "Yes, with Misheleh." As if I can marry us backwards in time that way. As if it makes our own invented love more durable.

The Mormons marry backwards. "Sealing," they call it. In the sanctum of the Temple, with permission called a "temple recommend," a Mormon of pious state may bind somebody long dead (perhaps an ancestor of his own, perhaps a name provided by chance from a list of cleared names in the computer) — bind that person to the Mormon faith, and to the flow of Mormon generations, in a retroactive conversion good "for time and all eternity." (Though the dead, they add, have "free agency" up in Heaven to accept this or not.) A husband and wife might be "celestially married" this way, from out of their graves, and into the spun-sugar clouds of a Mormon Foreverness . . . from out of the Old World sod . . . from sand, from swampwater . . . Where does ancestry *stop*?

To pattern the present we'll fabricate the past from before there *was* fabric. Piltdown Man. On display in the British Museum. From sixty-five million years back — and later shown to be some forgery of human and orangutan lockings, the jawbone stained and abraded. Or, more openly and jubilant, the Civilization of Llhuros "from the recent excavations of Vanibo, Houndee, Draikum, and other sites" — in Ithaca, New York, Norman Daly, professor of art at Cornell and current "Director of Llhurosian Studies" has birthed an entire culture: its creatures (the Pruii bird, described in the article "Miticides of Coastal Llhuros"), its rites (". . . the Tokens of Holmeek are lowered into the Sacred Fires, and burned with the month-cloths of the Holy Whores"), its plaques and weapons and votive figurines, its myths and water clocks, its poems and urns and a "nasal flute." An elephant mask. An "early icon of Tal-Hax." Wall paintings. "Oxen bells." Maps. The catalogue I have is 48 pages — 135 entries. Some of the Llhuros artifacts are paintings or sculpture. Some are current garbage, given ancient life. Properly anachronismed, a five-and-dime on-sale orange juicer becomes a *trallib,* an "Oil container . . . Middle Period, found at Draikum." A clothes iron: "Late Archaic . . . that it may be a votive of the anchorite Ur Ur cannot be disregarded." Famous athletes. Textiles. "Fornicating gods."

Just open the mind, and the past it requires will surface. "Psychic archaeologists" have tranced themselves to the living worlds of the pyramids or the caves — one chipped flint scraper can be connection enough. When Edgar Cayce closed his eyes he opened them (inside his head, which had its eyes closed) in the undiluted afternoon light of dynastic Egypt: wind was playing a chafing song in the leaves of the palm and the persea, fishers were casting their nets. "His findings and methods tend to be dismissed by the orthodox scientific community," but Jeffrey Goodman meditates, and something — an invisible terraform diving bell of sorts — descends with his eyes to fully twenty feet below the sands of Flagstaff, Arizona: 100,000 B.C., his vision brailling happily as a mole's nose through the bones set in the darkness there like accent marks and commas.

Going back . . . The darkness . . . Closing your lids . . .

A wheel shocked into a pothole. Misheleh waking up, wild-eyed. Torches.

"We needed certain papers, proof that we were Jews, to be admitted to America. To pass the inspectors there. And yet if our van was stopped by the Secret Police and we were discovered in back, those papers would be our death warrant. Such a goat's dessert! — that's the expression we used then."

"And . . . ?"

"It comes from when two goats will fight for the same sweet morsel — each pulls a different direction."

"No, I mean that night, the escape — what *happened*?"

"The Secret Police stopped the van."

III

Earlier, I said "in a trough between crests" — sea imagery. I mean in part that dark, as it grows deeper, takes the world away, and a sleepless body will float all night in horrible separation from what it knows and where it's nurtured. Freedom is sweet; but nobody wants to be flotsam.

Ruth Norman, the eighty-two-year-old widow of Ernest L. Norman, is Uriel, an Archangel, to her fellow Unarian members

and is, in fact, the "Cosmic Generator" and Head of all Unarius
activities on Earth (which is an applicant for the "Intergalactic
Confederation" of thirty-two other planets — but we need to
pass a global test of "consciousness vibration"). In past lives,
Uriel has been Socrates, Confucius, Henry VIII, and Benjamin
Franklin — and has adventured on Vidus, Janus, Vulna, and
other planets. All Unarians know their former lives. Vaughn
Spaegel has been Charlemagne. And Ernest L. himself has been
Jesus (as proved by a pamphlet, *The Little Red Box*), and currently is Alta; from his ankh-shaped chair on Mars he commu-
nicates psychically and through a bank of jeweled buttons with
all the Confederation. Everyone works toward the day Earth
can join. The 1981 Conclave of Light, at the Town and Country
Convention Center in El Cajon, California, attracted over four
hundred Unarians, some from as far as New York and Toronto.
Neosha Mandragos, formerly a nun for twenty-seven years, was
there; and George, the shoe store clerk; and Dan, assistant manager of an ice cream parlor.

Uriel makes her long-awaited entrance following the *Bolero*-
backed procession of two girls dressed as peacocks, led by
golden chains, then two nymphs scattering petals from cornu-
copias, someone wearing a feathered bird's head, and various
sages. Four "Nubian slaves . . . wearing skin bronzer, head-
dresses, loincloths and gilded beach thongs" carry a palanquin
adorned with enormous white swans, atop which . . . Uriel! In
a black velvet gown falling eight feet wide at the hem, with a
wired-up universe of painted rubber balls, representing the
thirty-two worlds, that dangles out to her skirt's edge. According
to Douglas Curran, "the gown, the painted golden 'vortex' headdress, and the translucent elbow-length gloves with rapier nails
have tiny light bulbs snaked through the fabric. The bulbs explode into volleys of winking. Waves of light roll from bodice to
fingertips, Infinite Mind to planets." People weep. Their rich
remembered lives are a sudden brilliance over their nerves, like
ambulance flashers on chicken wire, like . . . like fire approach-
ing divinity. Nobody's worrying here over last week's sales of
butter pecan parfait.

We'll sham it. We need it. It's not that we lie. It's that we *make*
the truth. The Japanese have a word especially for it: *nisekeizu,*

false genealogies. Ruling-class Japan was obsessed with lineage and descent, and these connived links to the Sewangezi line of the Fugiwaras qualified one — were indeed the only qualification of the time — for holding office. "High birth." "Pedigree." It's no less likely in Europe. In the seventeenth century, Countess Alexandrine von Taxis "hired genealogists to fabricate a descent from the Torriani, a clan of warriors who ruled Lombardy until 1311."

European Jews, who by late in the 1700s needed to take on surnames in order to cross a national border, often invented family names that spoke of lush green woods and open fields — this from a people traipsing from one cramped dingy urban ghetto to another. Greenblatt. Tannenbaum. Now a child born choking on soot could be heir to a name saying miles of mild air across meadows. Flowers. Mossy knolls.

Misheleh's name was Rosenblum. I never asked but always imagined this explained the trail of paper roses she'd left through Yitzl's life. My name then was Schvartzeit, reference to my many-thousand-year heritage of black beets. The name on our papers, though, was Kaufman — "merchant." This is what you had to do, to survive.

I remember: they were rough with us, also with the driver of the van. But we pretended being offended, like any good citizens. It could have gone worse. This was luckily early in the times of the atrocities, and these officers — they were hounds set out to kill, but they went by the book. A hound is honest in his pursuit. The rat and the slippery eel — later on, more officers were like that.

They might have dragged us away just for being in back of the van at all. But we said we were workers. In this, the driver backed us up. And the papers that shouted out *Jew?* My Misheleh stuffed them up a salmon. Later, after the Secret Police were gone, and we clumped across the border, we were on our knees with a child's doll's knife slicing the bellies of maybe a hundred fish until we found them! Covered in pearly offal and roe. We had them framed when we came to America. Pretty. A little cherrywood frame with cherubim puffing a trump in each corner. We were happy, then. A very lovely frame around an ugliness.

"And you loved each other."

Every day, in our hearts. Some nights, in our bodies. I'll tell you this about sex: it's like genealogy. Yes. It takes you back, to the source. That's one small bit of why some people relish wallowing there. A burrowing, completely and beastly, back to where we came from. It tastes and smells "fishy" in every language I know. It takes us down to when the blood was the ocean, down the rivers of the live flesh to the ocean, to the original beating fecundity. It's as close as we'll ever get.

And this I'll tell you, about the smell of fish. For our earliest years, when I was starting the dry goods store and worrying every bolt of gabardine or every bucket of nails was eating another poem out of my soul — which I think is true — we lived over a fish store. Kipper, flounder, herring, the odors reached up like great gray leaves through our floorboards. And every night we lived there, Misheleh cried for a while. After the van, you see? She could never be around raw fish again, without panic.

But on the whole we were happy. There was security of a kind, and friends — even a social club in a patchy back room near the train tracks that we decorated once a month with red and yellow crepe festoons and paper lanterns pouring out a buttery light.

Once every year she and I, we visited the cemetery. A private ritual: we pretended Yitzl was buried there. Because he'd brought us together, and we wanted him with us yet. For the hour it took, we always hired a street accordionist — it wasn't an uncommon instrument then. Like guitar now. Play a polka, we told him — *hot*. It drove the other cemetery visitors crazy! And always, Misheleh left a paper rose at the cemetery gates.

We heard that accordion music and a whole world came back, already better and worse than it was in its own time. Harsher. Gentler. Coarser. Little things — our *shtetl* dogs. Or big things too, the way we floated our sins away on toy-sized cork rafts once each spring, and everybody walking home singing . . . All of the world was keeping its shape but growing more and more transparent for us. Like the glass slipper in the fairy tale. The past was becoming a fairy tale. In it, the slipper predicates a certain foot and so a certain future.

At night I'd walk in my store. The moon like a dew on the barrel heaped with bolts, and the milky bodies of lamps, and the pen nibs, and shovels . . . Kaufman. Merchant.

IV

Within a year after death we have what Jewish tradition calls "the unveiling" — the gravestone dedication ceremony. September 14, 1986: I arrived in Chicago, joining my mother, sister, two aunts, and perhaps thirty others, including the rabbi, at the grave of my father, Irving Goldbarth, his stone wrapped in a foolish square of cheesecloth. A stingy fringe of grass around the fresh mound. The burial had taken place in bitter city winter, the earth (in my memory) opening with the crack of axed oak. Now it was warmer, blurrier, everything soft. My mother's tears.

The rabbi spoke, his voice soft: to the Jews a cemetery is a "house of graves" . . . but also a "house of eternal life." The same in other faiths, I thought. There are as many dead now as alive. A kind of balance along the ground's two sides. That permeable membrane. Always new dead in the making, and always the long dead reappearing over our shoulders and in our dreams. Sometimes a face, like a coin rubbed nearly smooth, in a photo. We're supposed to be afraid of ghosts but every culture has them, conjures them, won't let go. Our smoky ropes of attachment to the past. Our anti-umbilici . . . My mind wandering. Then, the eldest and only son, I'm reciting the *kaddish*. "Yisgadahl v'yiskadash sh'may rahbo . . . " In back, my father's father's grave, the man I'm named for. Staring hard and lost at the chiseling, ALBERT GOLDBARTH. My name. His dates.

In 1893 "Albert Goldbarth An Alien personally appeared in open Court and prayed to be admitted to become a Citizen of the United States . . . " — I have that paper, that and a sad, saved handful of others: September 15, 1904, he "attained the third degree" in the "Treue Bruder Lodge of the Independent Order of Odd Fellows." Five days after, J. B. Johnson, general sales agent of the Southern Cotton Oil Company, wrote a letter recommending "Mr. Goldbarth to whomsoever he may apply, as an honest and hardworking Salesman, leaving us of his own accord." That was 24 Broad Street, New York. In two years, in Cleveland, Ohio, John H. Silliman, secretary, was signing a notice certifying Mr. Albert Goldbarth as an agent of the American Accident Insurance Company. And, from 1924: "$55 Dollars, in hand paid," purchasing Lot Number 703 — this, from the envelope he labeled in pencil "Paid Deed from Semetery Lot from Hibrew Progresif Benefit Sociaty." I'm standing there now. I'm reading this stone that's the absolute last of his documents.

There aren't many stories. Just two photographs. And he was dead before I was born. A hundred times, I've tried inventing the calluses, small betrayals, tasseled mantle lamps, day-shaping waves of anger, flicked switches, impossible giving of love in the face of no love, dirty jokes, shirked burdens, flowerpots, loyalties, gold-shot silk page markers for the family Bible, violin strings, sweet bodystinks from the creases, knickknacks, lees of tea, and morning-alchemized trolley tracks declaring themselves as bright script in the sooted-over paving bricks — everything that makes a life, which is his life, and buried.

And why am I busy repeating that fantastical list . . . ? We're "mountain gorillas" (this is from Alex Shoumatoff's wonderful study of kinship, *The Mountain of Names*) who "drag around moribund members of their troop and try to get them to stand, and after they have died" (above my grandfather's grave, imagining bouts of passion with imaginary Misheleh over my grandfather's grave now) "masturbate on them and try to get some reaction from them." An offering, maybe. A trying to read life backwards into that text of dead tongues. Give us any fabric scrap, we'll dream the prayer shawl it came from. Give us any worthless handful of excavated soil, we'll dream the scrap. The prayer. The loom the shawl took fragile shape on, in the setting *shtetl* hill-light. The immigrant ships they arrived in, the port, the year. We'll give that year whatever version of semen is appropriate, in homage and resuscitory ritual. We'll breathe into, rub, and luster that year.

1641: On a journey in Ecuador, a Portuguese Jew, Antonio de Montezinos, discovered — after a week-long, brush-clogged hell trek through the hinterlands — a hidden Jewish colony, and heard them wailing holy writ in Hebrew. Yes, there in the

wild domain of anaconda and peccary — or so he told the Jewish scholar and eminent friend of Rembrandt, Menasseh ben
Israel. Or so Menasseh claimed, who had his own damn savvy
purposes; and based on his claim 'that the Ten Lost Tribes of
Israel were now found in the New World, and their global equi-
dispersion near complete — as the Bible foretells will usher in
an Age of Salvation — Britain's Puritan leaders readmitted
their country's exiled Jews, the better to speed the whole world
on its prophesied way to Redemption. (Maybe Rembrandt was
an earlier body of Ernest L. Norman? Maybe the massed Confederation planets were holding their astrocollective breath
even then, as destiny wound like spoolthread on the windmills.
And maybe, in the same Dutch-sunset oranges and mauves he
let collect like puddled honey in his painted-dusk skies, Rembrandt helped Menasseh finagle this plot on behalf of a troubled
people, tipped a flagon of Burgundy in a room of laundered
varnish rags, and plotted as the radiotelescope Monitor Maids
of planet Vidus lounged about in their gold lamé uniforms,
listening . . .)
    Maybe. Always a maybe. Always someone forcing the scat-
tered timbers of history into a sensible bridge. The Lost Tribes:
China. The Lost Tribes: Egypt. The Lost Tribes: Africa. India.
Japan. They formed a kingdom near "a terrible river of crashing stones" that roared six days a week "but on the Jewish Sabbath did cease." Lord Kingsborough emptied the family fortune, won three stays in debtor's prison, "in order to publish a
series of sumptuously illustrated volumes proving the Mexican
Indians . . . " Ethiopians. Eskimos. The Mormons have them
reaching America's shores as early as "Tower of Babylon times"
and later again, about 600 B.C., becoming tipi dwellers, hunters
of lynx and buffalo, children of Fire and Water Spirits . . .
Maybe. But today I think these caskets in Chicago soil are voyage enough. The moon's not that far.
    We visit the other family graves: Auntie Regina (brain cancer)
. . . Uncle Jake (drank; slipped me butterscotch candies) . . .
Miles square and unguessably old, this cemetery's a city, dis-
tricted, netted by streets and their side roads, overpopulated,
undercared. Dead Jews dead Jews dead Jews. *Ruth Dale Nopar-
stak ★ Age 2 Weeks ★ 1944* — death about the size of a cigar box.

My mother says to Aunt Sally (a stage whisper): "You'll see, Albert's going to write a poem about this." Later, trying to help that endeavor: "Albert, you see these stones on the graves? Jews leave stones on the graves to show they've visited." Not flowers? Why not flowers? . . . *I think I farmed black bent-backed turnips in the hardpan of a* shtetl *compound of equally black-garbed bent-backed grandmama and rabbinic Jews.*

My mother's parents are here in the Moghileff section, "Organized 1901." "You see the people here? They came from a town called Moghileff, in Russia — or it was a village. Sally, was Moghileff a town or a village? — you know, a little place where all the Jews lived. And those who came to Chicago, when they died, they were all buried here. Right next to your Grandma and Grandpa's graves, you see? — Dave and Natalie? — they were Grandma and Grandpa's neighbors in Moghileff, and they promised each other that they'd stay neighbors forever, here."

"Your Grandma Rosie belonged to the Moghileff Sisterhood. She was Chairlady of Relief. That meant, when somebody had a stillbirth, or was out of a job, or was beat in an alley, she'd go around to the members with an empty can and collect five dollars." Sobbing now. "Five dollars."

On our way out there's a lavish mausoleum lording it over this ghetto of small gray tenanted stones. My Uncle Lou says, still in his Yiddish-flecked English: "And *dis* one?" Pauses. "Gotta be a gengster."

V

The Mormons marry backwards, "Sealing," they call it.
"Is that the end of your story of Misheleh and you?"
The story of marrying backwards never ends.
In Singapore not long ago, the parents of a Miss Cheeh, who had been stillborn twenty-seven years before, were troubled by ghosts in their dreams, and consulted a spirit medium. Independently, the parents of a Mr. Poon consulted her too — their son had been stillborn thirty-six years earlier and, recently, ghosts were waking them out of slumber. "And the medium, diagnosing the two ghosts' problem as loneliness, acted as their marriage broker." The Poons and the Cheehs were introduced,

a traditional bride price paid, and dolls representing the couple were fashioned out of paper, along with a miniature one-story house with manservant, car and chauffeur, a table with teacups and pot, and a bed with bolster and pillows. Presumably, on some plane of invisible, viable, ectoplasmic endeavor, connubial bliss was enabled. Who knows?—one day soon, they may wake in their version of that paper bed (his arm around her sex-dampened nape, a knock at the door . . .) and be given the chance to be Mormon, to have always been Mormon, and ever-lastingly Mormon. They'll laugh, but graciously. She'll rise and start the tea . . .

These ghosts. Our smoky ropes of attachment. And our reel-ing them in.

Eventually Misheleh and I prospered. The store did well, then there were two stores. We grew fat on pickled herring in cream, and love. I suppose we looked jolly. Though you could see in the eyes, up close, there was a sadness: where our families died in the Camps, where I was never able to find time for the poetry — those things. Even so, the days and nights were good. The children never lacked a sweet after meals (but only if they cleaned their plates), or a little sailor suit, or kewpie blouse, or whatever silliness was in fashion. Before bed, I'd tell them a story. *Once, your mother and I, we lived in another country. A friend introduced us. He was a famous musician. Your mother danced to his songs and a thousand people applauded. I wrote poems about her, every-one read them. Gentlemen flung her roses . . .*

I died. It happens. I died and I entered the kingdom of Worm and of God, and what happens then isn't part of this story, there aren't any words for it. And what I became on Earth — here, in the memory of the living . . . ? — isn't over yet, it never ends, and now I'm me and I love you.

Because the ash is in this paper on which I'm writing (and in the page you're reading) and has been from the start. Because the blood is almost the chemical composition of the ocean, the heart is a swimmer, a very sturdy swimmer, but shore is never in sight. Because of entropy. Because of the nightly news. Be-cause the stars care even less for us than we do for the stars. Because the only feeling a bone can send us is pain. Because the

more years that we have, the less we have — the schools don't
teach this Tragic Math but we know it; twiddling the fingers is
how we count it off. Because because because. And so somebody
wakes from an ether sleep: the surgeons have made him Elvis,
he can play third-rate Las Vegas bars. And so someone revises
the raven on top of the clan pole to a salmon-bearing eagle: now
his people have a totem-progenitor giving them certain territorial privileges that the spirits ordained on the First Day of Creation. So. Because.

In *He Done Her Wrong*, the "Great American Novel — in pictures — and not a word in it" that the brilliant cartoonist Milt
Gross published in 1930, the stalwart square-jawed backwoods
hero and his valiant corn-blond sweetheart are torn from each
other's arms by a dastardly mustachioed villain of oily glance
and scowling brow, then seemingly endless deprivations begin:
fistfights, impoverishment, unbearable loneliness, the crazed
ride down a sawmill tied to one of its logs . . . And when they're
reunited, as if that weren't enough, what cinches it as a happy
ending is uncinched buskskin pants: the hero suddenly has a
strawberry birthmark beaming from his tush, and is known for
the billionaire sawmill owner's rightful heir . . .

Because it will save us.

The story-in-my-story is over: Misheleh and the children walk
home from the cemetery. She's left a stone and a paper rose.
We never would have understood it fifty years earlier, sweated
with sex, but this is also love.

The story is over, too: the "I" is done talking, the "you" is
nearly asleep, they lazily doodle each other's skin. We met them,
it seems a long while ago, in what I called "a trough between
crests." Let their bed be a raft, and let the currents of sleep be
calm ones.

Outside the story, I'm writing this sentence, and whether
someone is a model for the "you" and waiting to see me put my
pen down and toe to the bedroom — or even if I'm just lonely,
between one "you" and the next — is none of your business.
The "outside" is never the proper business between a writer and
a reader, but this I'll tell you: tonight the rains strafed in, then

quit, and the small symphonic saws of the crickets are swelling the night. This writing is almost over.

But nothing is ever over — or, if it is, then the impulse is wanting to *make* it over: "over" not as in "done," but "again." "Redo." Re-synapse. Re-nova.

I need to say "I love you" to someone and feel it flow down the root of her, through the raw minerals, over the lip of the falls, and back, without limit, into the pulse of the all-recombinant waters.

I meet Carolyn for lunch. She's with Edward, her old friend, who's been living in the heart of Mexico all of these years:

> Our maid, Rosalita, she must be over 70. She had "female troubles" she said. She needed surgery. But, listen: she's from the hills, some small collection of huts that doesn't even bear a name, so she hasn't any papers at all — absolutely no identification. There isn't a single professional clinic that can accept you that way. There isn't any means for obtaining insurance or public aid.
>
> So we went to a Records Division. I slipped the agent *dinero*. He knew what I was doing. It's everywhere. It's the way Mexico works. And when we left, Rosalita was somebody else. She had somebody else's birth certificate, working papers — everything.
>
> She had somebody else's life from the beginning, and she could go on with her own.

WILLIAM MANCHESTER

Okinawa: The Bloodiest Battle of All

FROM THE NEW YORK TIMES MAGAZINE

ON OKINAWA TODAY, Flag Day will be observed with an extraordinary ceremony: two groups of elderly men, one Japanese, the other American, will gather for a solemn rite.

They could scarcely have less in common. Their motives are mirror images; each group honors the memory of men who tried to slay the men honored by those opposite them. But theirs is a common grief. After forty-two years the ache is still there. They are really united by death, the one great victor in modern war.

They have come to Okinawa to dedicate a lovely monument in remembrance of the Americans, Japanese and Okinawans killed there in the last and bloodiest battle of the Pacific war. More than 200,000 perished in the 82-day struggle — twice the number of Japanese lost at Hiroshima and more American blood than had been shed at Gettysburg. My own regiment — I was a sergeant in the 29th Marines — lost more than 80 percent of the men who had landed on April 1, 1945. Before the battle was over, both the Japanese and American commanding generals lay in shallow graves.

Okinawa lies 330 miles southwest of the southernmost Japanese island of Kyushu; before the war, it was Japanese soil. Had there been no atom bombs — and at that time the most powerful Americans, in Washington and at the Pentagon, doubted that the device would work — the invasion of the Nipponese homeland would have been staged from Okinawa, beginning with a landing on Kyushu to take place November 1. The six Marine divisions, storming ashore abreast, would lead the way. President Truman asked General Douglas MacArthur, whose estimates of casualties on the eve of battles had proved uncannily accurate, about Kyushu. The general predicted a million Americans would die in that first phase.

Given the assumption that nuclear weapons would contribute nothing to victory, the battle of Okinawa had to be fought. No one doubted the need to bring Japan to its knees. But some Americans came to hate the things we had to do, even when convinced that doing them was absolutely necessary; they had never understood the bestial, monstrous and vile means required to reach the objective — an unconditional Japanese surrender. As for me, I could not reconcile the romanticized view of war that runs like a red streak through our literature — and the glowing aura of selfless patriotism that had led us to put our lives at forfeit — with the wet, green hell from which I had barely escaped. Today, I understand. I was there, and was twice wounded. This is the story of what I knew and when I knew it.

To our astonishment, the Marine landing on April 1 was uncontested. The enemy had set a trap. Japanese strategy called first for kamikazes to destroy our fleet, cutting us off from supply ships; then Japanese troops would methodically annihilate the men stranded ashore using the trench-warfare tactics of World War I — cutting the Americans down as they charged heavily fortified positions. One hundred and ten thousand Japanese troops were waiting on the southern tip of the island. Intricate entrenchments, connected by tunnels, formed the enemy's defense line, which ran across the waist of Okinawa from the Pacific Ocean to the East China Sea.

By May 8, after more than five weeks of fighting, it became clear that the anchor of this line was a knoll of coral and volcanic ash, which the Marines christened Sugar Loaf Hill. My role in mastering it — the crest changed hands more than eleven times — was the central experience of my youth, and of all the military bric-a-brac that I put away after the war, I cherish most the Commendation from General Lemuel C. Shepherd, Jr.,

U.S.M.C., our splendid division commander, citing me for "gallantry in action and extraordinary achievement," adding, "Your courage was a constant source of inspiration . . . and your conduct throughout was in keeping with the highest tradition of the United States Naval Service."

The struggle for Sugar Loaf lasted ten days; we fought under the worst possible conditions — a driving rain that never seemed to slacken, day or night. (I remember wondering, in an idiotic moment — no man in combat is really sane — whether the battle could be called off, or at least postponed, because of bad weather.)

Newsweek called Sugar Loaf "the most critical local battle of the war." *Time* described a company of Marines — 270 men — assaulting the hill. They failed; fewer than 30 returned. Fletcher Pratt, the military historian, wrote that the battle was unmatched in the Pacific war for "closeness and desperation." Casualties were almost unbelievable. In the 22d and 29th Marine regiments, two out of every three men fell. The struggle for the dominance of Sugar Loaf was probably the costliest engagement in the history of the Marine Corps. But by early evening on May 18, as night thickened over the embattled armies, the 29th Marines had taken Sugar Loaf, this time for keeps.

On Okinawa today, the ceremony will be dignified, solemn, seemly. It will also be anachronistic. If the Japanese dead of 1945 were resurrected to witness it, they would be appalled by the acceptance of defeat, the humiliation of their emperor — the very idea of burying Japanese near the barbarians from across the sea and then mourning them together. Americans, meanwhile, risen from their graves, would ponder the evolution of their own society, and might wonder, What ever happened to patriotism?

When I was a child, a bracket was screwed to the sill of a front attic window; its sole purpose was to hold the family flag. At first light, on all legal holidays — including Election Day, July 4, Memorial Day and, of course, Flag Day — I would scamper up to show it. The holidays remain, but mostly they mean long weekends.

In the late 1920s, during my childhood, the whole town of

Attleboro, Massachusetts, would turn out to cheer the procession on Memorial Day. The policemen always came first, wearing their number-one uniforms and keeping perfect step. Behind them was a two-man vanguard — the mayor and, at his side, my father, hero of the 5th Marines and Belleau Wood, wearing his immaculate dress blues and looking like a poster of a Marine, with one magnificent flaw: the right sleeve of his uniform was empty. He had lost the arm in the Argonne. I now think that, as I watched him pass by, my own military future was already determined.

The main body of the parade was led by five or six survivors of the Civil War, too old to march but sitting upright in open Pierce-Arrows and Packards, wearing their blue uniforms and broad-brimmed hats. Then, in perfect step, came a contingent of men in their fifties, with their blanket rolls sloping diagonally from shoulder to hip — the Spanish-American War veterans. After these — and anticipated by a great roar from the crowd — came the doughboys of World War I, some still in their late twenties. They were acclaimed in part because theirs had been the most recent conflict, but also because they had fought in the war that — we then thought — had ended all wars.

Americans still march in Memorial Day parades, but attendance is light. One war has led to another and another and yet another, and the cruel fact is that few men, however they die, are remembered beyond the lifetimes of their closest relatives and friends. In the early 1940s, one of the forces that kept us on the line, under heavy enemy fire, was the conviction that this battle was of immense historical import, and that those of us who survived it would be forever cherished in the hearts of Americans. It was rather diminishing to return in 1945 and discover that your own parents couldn't even pronounce the names of the islands you had conquered.

But what of those who *do* remain faithful to patriotic holidays? What are they commemorating? Very rarely are they honoring what actually happened, because only a handful know, and it's not their favorite topic of conversation. In World War II, 16 million Americans entered the armed forces. Of these, fewer than a million saw action. Logistically, it took nineteen men to back up one man in combat. All who wore uniforms are called veterans, but more than 90 percent of them are as uninformed about the killing zones as those on the home front.

If all Americans understood the nature of battle, they might be vulnerable to truth. But the myths of warfare are embedded deep in our ancestral memories. By the time children have reached the age of awareness, they regard uniforms, decorations and Sousa marches as exalted, and those who argue otherwise are regarded as unpatriotic.

General MacArthur, quoting Plato, said: "Only the dead have seen the end of war." One hopes he was wrong, for war, as it had existed for over four thousand years, is now obsolete. As late as the spring of 1945, it was possible for one man, with a rifle, to make a difference, however infinitesimal, in the struggle to defeat an enemy who had attacked us and threatened our West Coast. The bomb dropped on Hiroshima made the man ludicrous, even pitiful. Soldiering has been relegated to Sartre's theater of the absurd. The image of the man as protector and defender of the home has been destroyed (and I suggest that that seed of thought eventually led women to re-examine their own role in society).

Until nuclear weapons arrived, the glorifying of militarism was the nation's hidden asset. Without it, we would almost certainly have been defeated by the Japanese, probably by 1943. In 1941 American youth was isolationist and pacifist. Then war planes from Imperial Japan destroyed our fleet at Pearl Harbor on December 7, and on December 8 recruiting stations were packed. Some of us later found fighting rather different from what had been advertised. Yet in combat these men risked their lives — and often lost them — in hope of winning medals. There is an old soldier's saying: "A man won't sell you his life, but he'll give it to you for a piece of colored ribbon."

Most of the men who hit the beaches came to scorn eloquence. They preferred the 130-year-old "Word of Cambronne." As dusk darkened the Waterloo battlefield, with the French in full retreat, the British sent word to General Pierre Cambronne, commander of the Old Guard. His position, they pointed out, was hopeless, and they suggested he capitulate. Every French textbook reports his reply as "The Old Guard dies but never surrenders." What he actually said was "*Merde*."

If you mention this incident to members of the U.S. 101st Airborne Division, they will immediately understand. "Nuts" was not Brigadier General Anthony C. McAuliffe's answer to the Nazi demand that he hoist a white flag over Bastogne. Instead, he quoted Cambronne.

The character of combat has always been determined by the weapons available to men when their battles were fought. In the beginning they were limited to hand weapons — clubs, rocks, swords, lances. At the Battle of Camlann in 539, England's Arthur — a great warrior, not a king — led a charge that slew 930 Saxons, including their leader.

It is important to grasp the fact that those 930 men were not killed by snipers, grenades or shells. The dead were bludgeoned or stabbed to death, and we have a pretty good idea how this was done. One of the facts withheld from civilians during World War II was that Kabar fighting knives, with seven-inch blades honed to such precision that you could shave with them, were issued to Marines and that we were taught to use them. You never cut downward. You drove the point of your blade into a man's lower belly and ripped upward. In the process, you yourself became soaked in the other man's gore. After that charge at Camlann, Arthur must have been half drowned in blood.

The Battle of Agincourt, fought nearly one thousand years later, represented a slight technical advance: crossbows and long bows had appeared. All the same, Arthur would have recognized the battle. Like all engagements of the time, this one was short. Killing by hand is hard work, and hot work. It is so exhausting that even men in peak condition collapse once the issue of triumph or defeat is settled. And Henry V's spear carriers and archers were drawn from social classes that had been undernourished for as long as anyone could remember. The duration of medieval battles could have been measured in hours, even minutes.

The Battle of Waterloo, fought exactly four hundred years later, is another matter. By 1815, the Industrial Revolution had begun cranking out appliances of death, primitive by today's standards, but revolutionary for infantrymen of that time. And Napoleon had formed mass armies, pressing every available man into service. It was a long step toward total war, and its impact was immense. Infantrymen on both sides fought with single-missile weapons — muskets or rifles — and were supported by (and were the target of) artillery firing cannonballs.

The fighting at Waterloo continued for three days; for a given regiment, however, it usually lasted one full day, much longer than medieval warfare. A half century later, Gettysburg lasted three days and cost 43,497 men. Then came the marathon slaughters of 1914–1918, lasting as long as ten months (Verdun) and producing hundreds of thousands of corpses lying, as F. Scott Fitzgerald wrote afterward, "like a million bloody rugs." Winston Churchill, who had been a dashing young cavalry officer when Victoria was queen, said of the new combat: "War, which was cruel and magnificent, has become cruel and squalid."

It may be said that the history of war is one of men packed together, getting closer and closer to the ground and then deeper and deeper into it. In the densest combat of World War I, battalion frontage — the length of the line into which the 1,000-odd men were squeezed — had been 800 yards. On Okinawa, on the Japanese fortified line, it was less than 600 yards — about 18 inches per man. We were there and deadlocked for more than a week in the relentless rain. During those weeks we lost nearly 4,000 men.

And now it is time to set down what this modern battlefield was like.

All greenery had vanished; as far as one could see, heavy shellfire had denuded the scene of shrubbery. What was left resembled a cratered moonscape. But the craters were vanishing, because the rain had transformed the earth into a thin porridge — too thin even to dig foxholes. At night you lay on a poncho as a precaution against drowning during the barrages. All night, every night, shells erupted close enough to shake the mud beneath you at the rate of five or six a minute. You could hear the cries of the dying but could do nothing. Japanese infiltration was always imminent, so the order was to stay put. Any man who stood up was cut in half by machine guns manned by fellow Marines.

By day, the mud was hip deep; no vehicles could reach us. As you moved up the slope of the hill, artillery and mortar shells were bursting all around you, and, if you were fortunate enough to reach the top, you encountered the Japanese defenders, almost face to face, a few feet away. To me, they looked like badly wrapped brown paper parcels someone had soaked in a tub. Their eyes seemed glazed. So, I suppose, did ours.

Japanese bayonets were fixed; ours weren't. We used the knives, or, in my case, a .45 revolver and M1 carbine. The mud beneath our feet was deeply veined with blood. It was slippery. Blood is very slippery. So you skidded around, in deep shock, fighting as best you could until one side outnumbered the other. The outnumbered side would withdraw for reinforcements and then counterattack.

During those ten days I ate half a candy bar. I couldn't keep anything down. Everyone had dysentery, and this brings up an aspect of war even Robert Graves, Siegfried Sassoon, Edmund Blunden and Ernest Hemingway avoided. If you put more than a quarter million men in a line for three weeks, with no facilities for the disposal of human waste, you are going to confront a disgusting problem. We were fighting and sleeping in one vast cesspool. Mingled with that stench was another — the corrupt and corrupting odor of rotting human flesh.

My luck ran out on June 5, more than two weeks after we had taken Sugar Loaf Hill and killed the seven thousand Japanese soldiers defending it. I had suffered a slight gunshot wound above the right knee on June 2, and had rejoined my regiment to make an amphibious landing on Oroku Peninsula behind enemy lines. The next morning several of us were standing in a stone enclosure outside some Okinawan tombs when a six-inch rocket mortar shell landed among us.

The best man in my section was blown to pieces, and the slime of his viscera enveloped me. His body had cushioned the blow, saving my life; I still carry a piece of his shinbone in my chest. But I collapsed, and was left for dead. Hours later corpsmen found me still breathing, though blind and deaf, with my back and chest a junkyard of iron fragments — including, besides the piece of shinbone, four pieces of shrapnel too close to the heart to be removed. (They were not dangerous, a Navy surgeon assured me, but they still set off the metal detector at the Buffalo airport.)

Between June and November I underwent four major operations and was discharged as 100 percent disabled. But the young have strong recuperative powers. The blindness was caused by shock, and my vision returned. I grew new eardrums. In three years I was physically fit. The invisible wounds remain.

Most of those who were closest to me in the early 1940s had left New England campuses to join the Marines, knowing it was the most dangerous branch of the service. I remember them as bright, physically strong and inspired by an idealism and love of country they would have been too embarrassed to acknowledge. All of us despised the pompousness and pretentiousness of senior officers. It helped that, almost without exception, we admired and respected our commander in chief. But despite our enormous pride in being Marines, we saw through the scam that had lured so many of us to recruiting stations.

Once we polled a rifle company, asking each man why he had joined the Marines. A majority cited *To the Shores of Tripoli,* a marshmallow of a movie starring John Payne, Randolph Scott and Maureen O'Hara. Throughout the film the uniform of the day was dress blues; requests for liberty were always granted. The implication was that combat would be a lark, and when you returned, spangled with decorations, a Navy nurse like Maureen O'Hara would be waiting in your sack. It was peacetime again when John Wayne appeared on the silver screen as Sergeant Stryker in *Sands of Iwo Jima,* but that film underscores the point; I went to see it with another ex-Marine, and we were asked to leave the theater because we couldn't stop laughing.

After my evacuation from Okinawa, I had the enormous pleasure of seeing Wayne humiliated in person at Aiea Heights Naval Hospital in Hawaii. Only the most gravely wounded, the litter cases, were sent there. The hospital was packed, the halls lined with beds. Between Iwo Jima and Okinawa, the Marine Corps was being bled white.

Each evening, Navy corpsmen would carry litters down to the hospital theater so the men could watch a movie. One night they had a surprise for us. Before the film the curtains parted and out stepped John Wayne, wearing a cowboy outfit — ten-gallon hat, bandanna, checkered shirt, two pistols, chaps, boots and spurs. He grinned his aw-shucks grin, passed a hand over his face and said, "Hi ya, guys!" He was greeted by a stony silence. Then somebody booed. Suddenly everyone was booing.

This man was a symbol of the fake machismo we had come to hate, and we weren't going to listen to him. He tried and tried to make himself heard, but we drowned him out, and eventually he quit and left. If you liked *Sands of Iwo Jima*, I suggest you be careful. Don't tell it to the Marines.

And so we weren't macho. Yet we never doubted the justice of our cause. If we had failed — if we had lost Guadalcanal, and the Navy's pilots had lost the Battle of Midway — the Japanese would have invaded Australia and Hawaii, and California would have been in grave danger. In 1942 the possibility of an Axis victory was very real. It is possible for me to loathe war — and with reason — yet still honor the brave men, many of them boys, really, who fought with me and died beside me. I have been haunted by their loss these forty-two years, and I shall mourn them until my own death releases me. It does not seem too much to ask that they be remembered on one day each year. After all, they sacrificed their futures that you might have yours.

Yet I will not be on Okinawa for the dedication today. I would enjoy being with Marines; the ceremony will be moving, and we would be solemn, remembering our youth and the beloved friends who died there.

Few, if any, of the Japanese survivors agreed to attend the ceremony. However, Edward L. Fox, chairman of the Okinawa Memorial Shrine Committee, capped almost six years' campaigning for a monument when he heard about a former Japanese naval officer, Yoshio Yazaki — a meteorologist who had belonged to a four-thousand-man force led by Rear Admiral Minoru Ota — and persuaded him to attend.

On March 31, 1945, Yazaki-san had been recalled to Tokyo, and thus missed the battle of Okinawa. Ten weeks later — exactly forty-two years ago today — Admiral Ota and his men committed seppuku, killing themselves rather than face surrender. Ever since then Yazaki has been tormented by the thought that his comrades have joined their ancestors and he is here, not there.

Finding Yazaki was a great stroke of luck for Fox, for whom an Okinawa memorial had become an obsession. His own division commander tried to discourage him. The Japanese could hardly be expected to back a memorial on the site of their last great military defeat. But Yazaki made a solution possible.

If Yazaki can attend, why can't I? I played a role in the early stages of Buzz Fox's campaign and helped write the tribute to the Marines that is engraved on the monument. But when I learned that Japanese were also participating, I quietly withdrew. There are too many graves between us, too much gore, too many memories of too many atrocities.

In 1978, revisiting Guadalcanal, I encountered a Japanese businessman who had volunteered to become a kamikaze pilot in 1945 and was turned down at the last minute. Mutual friends suggested that we meet. I had expected no difficulty; neither, I think, did he. But when we confronted each other, we froze.

I trembled, suppressing the sudden, startling surge of primitive rage within. And I could see, from his expression, that this was difficult for him, too. Nations may make peace. It is harder for fighting men. On simultaneous impulse we both turned and walked away.

I set this down in neither pride nor shame. The fact is that some wounds never heal. Yazaki, unlike Fox, is dreading the ceremony. He does not expect to be shriven of his guilt. He knows he must be there but can't say why. Men are irrational, he explains, and adds that he feels very sad.

So do I, Yazaki-san, so do I.

SAMUEL HYNES

The Feeling of Flying

FROM THE SEWANEE REVIEW

*Between 1943 and 1946 I learned to fly in the U.S. Navy, and did a
tour of duty as a Marine pilot in the Pacific theater—first at Ulithi in
the Western Carolines and later at Okinawa. This very ordinary military
career provided me with my first skill and my first experience of the adult
world. The war was always there, as the thing we were all training for,
but the experience that remains in the memory mostly involves planes
and the feeling of flying, and has very little to do with combat. In this
fragment of a memoir I have tried to put what remains of the way it felt
to be young and a flier in those times.*

1. Beginnings

Denton, Texas, spring 1943. In March 1943 I was sent by the Navy
to a small town in north Texas. I was to begin learning to fly
there — not at a proper naval establishment but at a civilian
flying school. It wasn't much of a school: its staff was a couple
of local crop-dusters, and its airport was a pasture on the edge
of town, which we shared with the sheep. It had no runway,
only grass, which the sheep kept trimmed. It was not even flat
— it sank in the middle, and rose steeply at the far side, where
it ended in a grove of scrubby trees. At the corner of the field
by the road was a small hangar, and a shed that was called the
Flight Office; beside the hangar four or five Piper Cubs were
parked. That was all the equipment there was, except for a
windsock, once red and yellow but faded now to an almost invisible gray, which drooped on a staff near the fence. There was

nothing impressive or even substantial-looking about the place; but I took my first flight there, and soloed there, and I have the same sort of blurred affection for it that I have for other beginnings — for the first girl, the first car, the first drink.

First flight: what images remain? I am in the rear seat of a Cub, and my instructor is taxiing to the takeoff position. The wheels of the plane are small, and it rides very low, so that I seem to be sitting almost on the ground, and I feel every bump and hollow of the field as we taxi. The wings flap with the bumps, and the whole machine seems too small, too fragile, too casually put together to be trusted.

The instructor turns into the wind and runs up the engine, and I feel the quick life of the plane. It begins to roll, bumpily at first, as though we are still taxiing. The nose is high, I can't see around it, and I have a panicky feeling that we are rushing toward something — a tree or a sheep or another plane; and then the flow of air begins to lift the wings, the tail comes up, and the plane moves with a new grace, dancing, touching the rough field lightly, and then not touching it, skimming the grass, which is still so close that I can see each blade, and I am flying, lifted and carried by the streaming air.

At the end of the field the grove of trees is first a wall, a dark limit; and then it sinks and slides, foreshortening to a green island passing below us; the plane banks, and I can see the town — but *below* me, all roofs and treetops — and beyond it there is distance, more and more distance, blue-hazy and flat and empty stretching away to the indistinct remote horizon. The world is enormous: the size of the earth increases around me, and so does the size of the air; space expands, is a tall dome filled with a pale clean light, into which we are climbing.

Below me the houses, each in its own place, look small and vulnerable perched on the largeness of the earth. I stare down at first like a voyeur, looking into other people's lives. A truck drives along a road and turns into a yard; a woman is hanging out clothes; she stops and runs to the truck. Should I be watching? Does she feel me there above her life? The world below exposes itself to me — I am flying, I can see everything!

I don't remember doing any flying myself on that first flight. I must have tried, and I could invent what the instructor said and what I did, but I don't remember it. What I remember is the way the world changed from the familiar, comfortable space I had always lived in to the vast empty flier's world.

The Piper Cub, with its large square wings and slender fuselage, resembles a kite with a small engine in it; it will float on an air current, settle lightly to the ground with no power at all, and bounce forgivingly away from a bad landing to give you a chance to try again. In heavier planes the engine dominates, pulling the plane along, but in a Cub it is the wings; the engine seems to do no more than hold you hovering in space. It was a wonderful plane to begin with, friendly and safe.

At first we did simple things — turns and climbs and gentle glides. I was all right while the plane was flying straight and level, but I felt insecure and vulnerable when it banked, and I could feel myself leaning away from the turn, trying to keep my body vertical to the ground, as though I might get some support from the earth if I stayed loyal to it. Then the instructor would tell me to relax, and lean with the plane; and gradually I learned to do that, instinctively, and to let the world tilt as it would. For once you are really flying it is the world that tilts, not the plane; it's the horizon that tips up when you turn, and settles back when you roll out, sinks when you climb, and rises when you dive. The plane remains a steady thing, a part of yourself, and you are not flying the plane — you are flying the world.

II. *The World Upside Down*

Memphis, autumn 1943. Memories of flying are almost always memories of landscape. It isn't that you think, *I am flying over this state or that one,* but that you are moving above a landscape pierced by a mountain, or patched with woodlands, or edged by the sea. The earth is always there below, apart and beautiful (no land is ugly from the air), revealing its private features in a way that it never does to the traveler on its surface. I suppose this knowledge of the earth's face is a part of the feeling of dominion that a pilot feels when his plane reaches a commanding altitude, and he looks down on the world that stretches out beneath him.

At the naval air station at Memphis, where I went after leaving Texas, there was most of all the river, a broad presence lying to the west of the airfield: black in the morning light, a vast reflector at sunset, gray when the sky was gray, but always there. The impression it gave, from the air, was of absolute flatness — an odd impression, for what would you expect a river to be except flat? Still, the earth from the air retains its contours and remains three dimensional (it never looks like a map or a patchwork quilt); but the river was relentlessly two dimensional. It didn't seem to move, or to have any irregularities at all — it just lay there, like an old mirror, revealing nothing, only reflecting.

Beside the river the air station looked temporary, raw, and ugly. A year before it had been a Tennessee farm, with a big old frame house surrounded by oaks, and a pond where cattle stood and drank. Bulldozers had come in, and the trees and the pond were gone. In their place were rows of insubstantial gray buildings and two circular landing mats, and around the whole station ran a high wire fence, along which military police patrolled with guard dogs. It was a place without a single thing to please the eye, and I was always glad to escape from it, and to see the river and the farmland outside it.

Life at the air station was lived in the constant presence of planes — the sound of engines testing, warming up, taking off. There were planes overhead all day, and at night, as you walked back from a movie or a beer at the Slop Chute, red and green running lights passed in the dark sky, and the exhaust flames flickered. You went to sleep to the sound of flying, and woke to the first morning takeoffs. Planes became a part of your subliminal life, only thrusting up into consciousness when an engine faltered, and you rushed to a window or stepped into the street to look up at trouble.

The planes at Memphis were Stearman N2Ss, open-cockpit biplanes that were painted yellow and were known as Yellow Perils. In fact they were anything but perilous: they were probably the safest and strongest airplanes ever built. They could be flown through acrobatic maneuvers that would disintegrate a fighter; they could be dropped to a landing from a stall twenty feet in the air; they could be ground-looped with no more damage than a bit of scraped paint. I did all of these things, and the planes (and I) survived. And in the process I learned a bit more about flying.

What I learned, first of all, was the intense delight of flying an open plane. I'm not sure that I can explain why it is so different from a closed cockpit, but it must come from the intimate presence of the air itself, the medium that you fly in, streaming past and around you. You can thrust your whole arm out into the slipstream, and press back against the flow of air; you can lean to the side, and the air will force tears from your eyes and rush into your lungs. And you can look straight into space, down to the earth, and up to the sky, with nothing between you and the whole world. The plane is not a protective shell, as an automobile is, but an extension of your body, moving as you move, and your head is the brain of the whole stretched and vibrating organism. Flying alone in an open plane is the purest experience of flight possible.

That pure experience is felt at its most intense in acrobatic flying, when you are upside down, or pointed at the sky or at the earth, and moving in ways that you can only in the unsubstantial medium of the air. Acrobatic flying is a useless skill in its particulars — nobody *needs* to do a loop or a roll, not even a fighter pilot — but this skill extends your control of the plane and yourself and makes extreme actions in the sky comfortable. In acrobatics the sense of flying is extended to its extreme limit; flying a plane through a loop or a Cuban-eight is the farthest thing possible from simply driving it. When you reach the top of a loop, upside down and engine at full throttle, and tilt your head back to pick up the horizon line behind you, you are as far outside instinctive human behavior as you can go — hanging in space, the sky below you and the earth above, inscribing a circle on emptiness. And then the nose drops across the horizon; your speed increases, and the plane scoops through into normal flight, and you are back in the normal world, with the earth put back in its place. The going out and coming back are what makes a loop so satisfying.

After a while, that is. At first it was terrifying, like being invited to a suicide that you didn't want to commit. "This is a

loop," my instructor said casually. He lowered the plane's nose
to gain airspeed, and then pulled sharply up. The earth, and
my stomach, fell away from me; and we were upside down, and
I could feel gravity clawing at me, pulling me out into the mile
of empty space between me and the ground. I grabbed at the
sides of the cockpit and hung on until gravity was on my side
again. Of course I knew that I had a safety belt that would hold
me in my seat; but my body didn't know it — *If you're upside
down in space,* my body said, *don't be a fool, hang on!*

"You seemed a little nervous that time," the instructor said
when the plane was right side up again. "You've got to have
confidence in that seat belt, or you'll never do a decent loop. So
this time, when we get on top, I want you to put both arms out
of the cockpit." And I did it. It was like stepping off a bridge,
but I did it, and the belt held, and the plane came round. And
after that I could fly a loop. It was, as I said, satisfying.

III. *Night*

There was only one natural threat left — the night. In darkness
instincts weaken: the horizon is scarcely there, up is less certainly up, and down may not be exactly down. The earth, which
by daylight offers a comforting variety of possible emergency
landing fields, at night becomes threatening: darkness hides
hills and trees and swallows every flat surface. There is no hope
for you down there at night, and it is reasonable that you should
feel fear, flying in darkness.

I didn't know anything about that kind of fear when I reported for night flying at Memphis: it was just one more test to
take, one more obstacle to get past on the way to becoming a
real pilot. The exercise was simple — anyone could do it. You
simply took off between rows of lights, followed the taillight of
the plane ahead of you around the traffic pattern, and landed.
Then you taxied back to takeoff position and did it again. The
only trouble was that you did it in the dark, and so everything
had to be learned anew. The cockpit, which by day had become
a familiar secure place, at night was a black hole; engine instruments showed only as dim greenish lines of phosphorescence;
switches were invisible, and had to be found by touch. Just get-

ting the engine started was a new and difficult process, and taxiing was a game of blindman's buff. Then you had to take off without swerving into a runway light, and find and follow the taillight ahead of you. But the night sky is full of lights, and if you chose a star instead of a taillight (and occasionally someone did), you would fly in a straight line forever, waiting for it to turn.

On my first night flight the darkness seemed immense and hostile, and the dots of light scattered across it trivial and distant; even the red and green running lights at my wing tips were separate from me, and a long way off. Memphis was a dim halo that seemed to come out of the earth itself, the airport beacon was a throbbing pulse, and on the dark earth below me each solitary light that was a house seemed lonely and apart. There were no certain distances, either on the earth or in the air; I wasn't sure where I was, and the plane was a stranger that made odd noises that it didn't make in daylight. I was eager to be back on the ground.

Not eager to land, though; landing at night was the worst part of night flying. It was like jumping into a dark pool, when you just have to take it on faith that there is really water down there. The runway — the hard, paved, comforting reality — was invisible: there were only the two rows of lights, and a black space between them. As you turn into your final landing approach, the lights run together and form two perspective lines, and you thump down between them; but for me that last moment, when I cut the throttle and waited for the thump, was a moment of complete despair. My confidence as a flier fell from me. I wasn't flying the plane, and I didn't know where the ground was; the plane would just have to get down on its own.

When I first came to Memphis it was late summer, and the fields lying eastward from the river were green. The cotton was being picked, and bits of white lay along the roadsides like blown snow. The sun was hot on the landing mat, and even high in the air it was warm. As I went through the training program autumn came, the fields turned brown and wet, and the days grew shorter. At the end of my time there, in November, darkness fell so early that it overtook the last flight of the afternoon. It was on one of those late flights that I learned a new thing about flying — that it makes the approach of night different. It was late as I flew back from some practice solo, and the sun was nearly set, but the air was still warm and bright. The flight must have gone well, and I was feeling at ease with the plane and, in spite of the engine's steady racket, quiet and peaceful. Below me lights began to come on in houses and farms, and everything that was not a light became dark and indistinct, so that the ground was almost like a night sky. But I still flew on in sunlight. The surface of the plane seemed to absorb and hold the light and color of the sunset; brightness surrounded me. It was as though the earth had died, and I alone was left alive. A sense of my own aliveness filled me. I would never die. I would go on flying forever.

IV. *Guns, Bombs, Emptiness*

Pensacola, winter and early spring 1944. At Bronson Field, west of Pensacola near the Alabama line, I learned to fly SNJs — training planes that were like real combat fighters, but slower, smaller, and safer. They had, most important, retractable landing gear. When a plane takes off and the wheels come up, it casts off its connection with the earth and becomes adapted to the air (birds do the same thing with their legs). The pilot can't see that the wheels are up, but just knowing it makes a difference. The SNJ also had a closed cockpit like a fighter's, and it could be mounted with a machine gun, and could carry toylike practice bombs. Because it had a variable-pitch propeller, it even sounded like a fighter — it took off with a whine that faded in the air to a sort of stammering whisper — *wh-wh-wh-wh*. Flying SNJs was like trying on an officer's uniform; it made one feel almost like an adult.

I flew then in a flight of six — always the same six cadets — and that changed the feeling of flying too, and made us all feel more like a squadron, a collective identity, and less like students doing exercises. The sudden Gulf Coast spring came as we began to fly together. Wisteria bloomed on the houses in the little towns, and the air was soft. We seem, in memory, always to have been high in a sky of tropical blueness, with perhaps some bright fair-weather clouds below us; we are making gun-

nery runs on a towed sleeve, or diving on a target at the edge of
the sea, or we are tail chasing, playing like children or birds, up
the sides of tall clouds that are blinding-white in the sunlight. I
remember flying among cumulus clouds on a fine day, and
hearing two of the Mexican students who also trained at Pensacola talking on the radio, one calling, "Hey, Cisco, where are
you?" and Cisco: "I'm over here, behind thees leetle cloud, come
chase me!" It was all like that, like play, *Come chase me;* it was
games, and we were children. Gunnery and bombing were only
follow the leader — you kept score, and somebody won and
somebody lost, but nobody got hurt.

In the game of gunnery practice, one member of the flight
took off towing a canvas sleeve at the end of a long cable. The
rest followed him to a proper altitude, and made attacks on the
sleeve, as though it were an enemy plane. A gunnery run is a
beautiful gesture, a long descending S curve from a position
above and to the side of the target that brings you into position,
and ends in a burst of firing. As plane after plane repeats it, it
seems as graceful, as symmetrical, as choreographed as a movement in a ballet.

Bombing was another kind of game, a sport like throwing
darts — the same target of concentric rings, the same scoring
according to how close you came to the bull's-eye. You approached the target in a steep glide, weight against your seat
belt, the plane bucking as it accelerated, wind whistling a higher
note as the speed increased, earth rising toward you. As you
dived you had to bring the target into your bombsight, jerking
the plane over with stick and rudder, holding it for an instant
to drop your bomb, and then pull up in a steep bank, to look
back and see where your bomb had hit. The dive was like taking
a dare, and the pullout was safety — the dare taken, another
test passed.

That spring at Bronson was full of games; flying, we seemed
possessors of the bright empty air. But the emptiness was not
always joyous. Once, flying alone, I wandered above a bank of
cloud, and learned how it feels to be separated completely from
the earth, how anonymous and signless clouds are, and how
uncomforting the sun is when it shines down on unbroken
trackless whiteness. This kind of experience, of separation from

the comfortable and the familiar, is a part of the price of flying. The pilot has to accept the stretches of loneliness and isolation, when the earth is erased by cloud or darkness, or is facelessly strange or hostile, when his will to fly has taken him into void space.

I felt this separation most intensely on the navigation flights that constituted part of the final training program. The first was a solitary flight inland — a triangular pattern that took me to one town, across to another, and back to the field. No doubt the solitariness was part of the flight's strange feeling, but it was more than that. I was flying over the pine woods of Florida and south Alabama, a surface as flat and featureless as the sea, that stretched unbroken to the horizon. Once I had flown out of sight of the Gulf behind me, I felt as though I had flown out of measurable space into the boredom of infinity.

I could see the shadow of my plane sliding along below me on the tops of the trees, and its insubstantial, steady movement seemed a part of the emptiness. Occasionally a railroad line appeared, diagonally cutting across the pines; but railroads are as identical as pine trees, and it did nothing to alter my mood. I checked the calculations on my plotting board, and I watched the clock on the instrument panel, and at the predicted time the right town appeared, an island of tin roofs and a water tower floating in the sea of pine trees. But I could feel no necessity in that appearance; it might as well have been some other town, or no town at all. I turned, found the second landmark, and headed back south. When I could see the Gulf once more beyond the trees, I felt that I was re-entering the real, distinguishable world.

The other flight was south, out over the Gulf in the same triangular pattern, and I felt then the same feeling of separation, and something else that was disquieting too — the feeling you get when the last bit of land disappears behind you, of the shapelessness and endlessness of space. Below you is the flat and uninformative sea; all around you the air extends its emptiness. Why go one way rather than another, when it is all the same, and goes on forever? People have committed suicide by flying straight out to sea, and I can understand that it might have the right feeling, that it would be a gesture that would be a way of expressing the feeling of suicide, as well as a way of dying.

v. *Flying in a War*

Ulithi, early spring 1945. I had been flying for two years by 1945, and it had all been a game. But at the end of the game there was always the war; that's what we wanted — to join a squadron, to fly in combat, to see the antiaircraft fire rising to meet us as we dived, and the smoke billowing up from the sunken ships and the wrecked airfields. That kind of flying would be an experience that would confer something special on us — maturity, or perhaps heroism, something that would transform us from the boys of the training game into men.

When the combat flying came at last, it wasn't at all like that. I had joined my first real squadron, of torpedo bombers, at Ulithi, an atoll in the Western Carolines that was an important fleet anchorage. There the ships were assembled that would attack Okinawa in the last battle of the war. My squadron was based at Ulithi, on a tiny island scarcely large enough to land a plane on; its job was to protect the ships at anchor there.

That sounds heroic, but it was in fact boring. Protect them from what? Perhaps from Japanese submarines: and so we flew endless patrols, looking for submarines that never appeared. Or perhaps from the enemy nearby. The only Japanese known to be within striking distance were those on Yap, an island a hundred miles to the west. Yap had been bypassed when the army took Ulithi on MacArthur's island-hopping campaign, and was considered of no importance, except for its airstrip. Still they were the only enemies we could reach, and so occasionally the squadron flew a strike against Yap. That seemed better than not attacking anybody.

My logbook of my first strike against Yap reads: "Strike on Yap — pier and shore installations — strafing — 4 × 500" (that last bit means four 500-pound bombs). Our intelligence officers, peering at aerial photographs of the island, had persuaded themselves that in an inlet there might be facilities for docking submarines. We sent twelve planes to destroy the dock, and to strafe whatever was seen on the ground.

I flew at the tail end of the flight, out over the fleet and beyond, until Ulithi was lost behind us; and there was nothing in sight but the water and the empty air. Without visual references we seemed to hang motionless above the sea, which seemed motionless below us, while the minutes passed. Then an island appeared, first a low darkness on the horizon, then a green mass. We reached it and circled, looking for the target, and the greenness became palm trees, each one a green asterisk on a lighter ground.

The island had been bombed again and again, and in among the trees where bombs had fallen there were spots of exposed white sand, like pockmarks on dark skin. The airstrip was a string of craters, and looked abandoned and desolate, a place where planes had once flown. Along the sides were the remains of wrecked and burnt-out planes, and one or two that seemed to be dummies, knocked together to tempt strafing planes down to where the waiting guns could find them.

Nothing moved below us; nothing suggested any life at all there: I saw no installation, no people, not a hut or a kitchen garden. The island seemed uninhabited and forlorn. We flew lower, across the inlet that Intelligence had marked. I thought I saw a fence strung across it — a few strands of barbed wire, perhaps — but nothing else. We circled again, and made our bombing runs. As I dropped my bombs, I could hear my two crewmen's machine guns firing — the hard rattle of the two fifty-calibers in the ball turret, and the high tinny popping of the radioman's thirty. What the hell were they shooting at, I wondered. Just shooting, because they were in combat now.

I pulled up and away from the island, and joined the rest of the formation. That was my first attack on an enemy, and I felt sour disappointment. Was this all there was to combat flying? No antiaircraft fire, no fierce defenders at their guns, nothing exploding, no columns of smoke visible for miles. I had expected flame and ruin, but even our own bombs had gone off squashily, blowing up mud and water, and destroying nothing (except maybe a barbed-wire fence). I didn't feel any different; I hadn't been initiated into manhood; I hadn't even seen the enemy. I flew disconsolately back to Ulithi.

(The enemy was there, though; there were both men and guns on Yap. They bided their time, and only took the easy shots, but they were there. The week after my first strike they shot a wing off one of our strafing planes, and it crashed and burned near the other wrecks along the ruined airstrip.)

VI. *Night Again*

Okinawa, August 1945. The next month the squadron flew north, up the islands to Tinian and Iwo Jima, and into Okinawa, where the invasion had just begun. The air war was livelier there, and I saw enough columns of smoke, and enough antiaircraft fire, to last me; but I have written about those days elsewhere, and this is a memory of flying, not fighting.

The most memorable, and the worst, flying at Okinawa came after the war ended in August. The war might have been over, but the flying wasn't; there were still Japanese submarines at sea, and the Navy's PBY flying boats, which had been doing antisub patrols around the island at night, had gone to Japan to evacuate prisoners of war. We were given their job, with instructions to fly armed, but not to attack unless fired upon, and not to take shots at Japanese planes or attack ground targets. It was odd, halfway in and halfway out of a war.

Night searching was a gloomy, fearful business. The weather had turned hot and stormy, the way it does sometimes in August; and every night there were squalls and thunderheads over the sea. The nights were black, without moon or stars or horizon line; even the lightning, which illuminated the piled clouds with a cold white light, didn't reach the darkness of the sea.

My sector was a long triangle over the China Sea — west toward China, then north, then back to the island. As soon as the plane was airborne the lights of the island disappeared, and I entered the blackness. I reported by radio that I was on station, and the voice of the controller came back, but so broken by crashing static that though it was audibly human, it spoke in meaningless syllables: "Hel . . . four . . . ver . . ."

I flew among thunderheads like mountains, watching ahead when the lightning flashed, altering course to avoid the moun-

tains and fly the valleys. (A tall thunderhead is full of violent
vertical current; it will tear a plane apart, hurl the pieces up and
down, and then scatter them over the sea.) Behind me, in the
body of the plane, my radar operator scanned the area around
us for submarines, but among such storms it was a useless exercise: only the thunderheads appeared on his scope. In that
electric atmosphere the plane itself became charged, and balls
of Saint Elmo's fire rolled up and down the wings, and whirled
on the propeller. Lightning flashed, and for a time after each
flash I could not read my instruments, and had to fly blindly,
holding the plane on its course by feel until sight returned.

I was more afraid then than I had ever been in the air, or
ever was again. Fear is probably always there, subliminally, in
an experienced pilot's mind; it is a source of that attentiveness
that keeps you alive. But only rarely does it thrust itself into
your consciousness. This never happened to me on a strike — I
felt keyed up, tense, abnormally aware of the plane, but not
exactly afraid; but it happened on those night patrols over the
China Sea. I felt fear then; but I also felt something else —
resentment, outrage that I was out there, with the war over,
alone and half-blinded with lightning and blackness, that I
might die out there, on a pointless exercise in the dark.

I flew my last night patrol on my birthday, August 29th.
When I got back, toward midnight, we had a party, and I got
very drunk. I was twenty-one, I kept explaining to everyone,
and I was old enough to drink. I had come of age, and the war
was over, and I would never have to fly at night in a storm
again.

VII. *Ending*

Pensacola, autumn 1945. In November I returned to the States,
and was told that I could report to any naval station I chose, to
be discharged from active duty. I chose Pensacola.

Why Pensacola? I think I wanted to return, just once, just for
a few days, to that place where I had learned the only skill I
had, and where I had been happy in the game of flying, before
the dying began. Perhaps the impulse to return is a sign that
one has grown up, an acknowledgment of the way the good

times pass us. We go back in space because we can't go back in time.

Pensacola was peaceful-looking in the winter sunshine; everything was bright with sun, the white-painted buildings, the sandy earth, the palm trees, the quiet waters of the bay. In that mild stillness the sound of planes was as distant and as natural as the buzzing of insects on a summer afternoon. The whole place seemed to know that the war was over, that there was nothing urgent left to be done.

I was still on flight orders, entitled to flight pay if I flew four hours in a month; so when I had reported in I went over to the hangar at the airfield to look for a plane. There I found another Marine pilot on the same errand, and one plane — an N2S trainer, the kind I had learned to fly in, back at Memphis. One tank of gas would last, if we stretched it, for just about four hours. We didn't know each other; neither had any particular reason to trust the other's flying; we had nothing to do and barely enough gas to do it, but we took off together to fly somewhere, anywhere, for four hours.

My companion climbed carefully over the lagoon and took a cautious level course north, over the pine woods. It was the same featureless landscape over which I had navigated two years before, and I felt the same withdrawal from the actual world. He flew on for an hour, made a careful turn, and flew back toward the field. When it came in sight I took over the controls and headed back out over the pines again. Time passed with excruciating slowness; there was nothing to see but the lengthening shadows of the pines, and we could not communicate from one cockpit to the other, even if we had had anything to say. The plane didn't seem to move, neither of us moved, we simply sat there, suspended in space in a Yellow Peril, while one slow minute succeeded another. It wasn't flying, it wasn't skillful, it wasn't fun; it was simply a way of wasting time, for money.

As the end of the four hours approached, I turned toward the field, checking my watch nervously against the fuel gauge. It looked as though we could make it, but without much gas to spare. I circled the field, using up the last few minutes. By then it was evening; the hangar cast a long shadow across the landing mat, and the water of the lagoon was dark. I began an approach to landing, letting down out of the last late sun into the twilight, and landed in shadow, and taxied to the parking ramp and shut down the engine. We both got out and walked silently to the hangar, and separated with scarcely a word. I think we must have had the same feelings; it was all over now: we had come to the end of the game.

ARTHUR C. DANTO

Gettysburg

FROM GRAND STREET

Then the whole of things might be different
From what it was thought to be in the beginning,
    before an angel bandaged the field glasses.

                                        John Ashbery

PITY-AND-TERROR, the classically prescribed emotional response
to tragic representation, was narrowly restricted to drama by
the ancient authorities. In my view, tragedy has a wider reference by far, and pity-and-terror is aroused in me by works of
art immeasurably less grand than those which unfold the cosmic
undoings of Oedipus and Agamemnon, Antigone, Medea, and
the women of Troy. The standard Civil War memorial, for example, is artistically banal by almost any criterion, and yet I am
subject to pity-and-terror whenever I reflect upon the dense
ironies it embodies. I am touched that the same figures appear
and reappear in much the same monument from village to village, from commons to green to public square, across the American landscape. The sameness only deepens the conveyed tragedy, for it is evidence that those who subscribed funds for
memorials, who ordered their bronze or cast-iron cement effi-
gies from catalogues or from traveling sales representatives, so
that the same soldier, carrying the same musket, flanked by the
same cannons and set off by the same floral or patriotic decorations, were blind to the tragedy that is, for me, the most palpable quality of these cenotaphs. That blindness is a component
of the tragedy inherent in the terrible juxtaposition of the most

deadly armaments and ordnance known up to that time, with
what, under those conditions, was the most vulnerably clad sol-
diery in history.

The Civil War infantryman is portrayed in his smart tunic
and foraging cap. Take away the musket, the bayonet and the
cartridge case, and he would be some uniformed functionary —
messenger, conductor, bellhop, doorman. This was the uniform
he fought in, as we know from countless drawings and photographs that have come down to us from the Civil War. Armed,
carrying a knapsack, he moved across the battlefield as though
on dress parade. But the weapons he faced were closer in design
and cold effectiveness to those standard in the First World War,
fifty years in his future, than to those confronted by Napoleon's
troops at the Battle of Waterloo, fifty years in his past. What
moves me is the contradiction between the code of military conduct, symbolically present in his garments but absent from his
gun. We see, instead of the chivalry and romanticism of war as
a form of art, the chill implacable indifference to any consideration other than maiming and death, typical of the kind of total
combat the Civil War became. That contradiction was invisible
when the memorials were raised, and it is its invisibility today
that moves me to pity-and-terror.

The rifled musket — one with a helically grooved bore giving
a stabilizing spin to the bullet and making possible a flat trajectory — was known in the eighteenth century, but it was used
then primarily for hunting. The smooth-bore musket was military issue. There is an affecting Yankee pragmatism in the fact
that the citizen-soldiers of the American Revolution should have
used their hunting weapons to such effect against the celebrated
"Brown Bess" — a smooth-bore musket with its barrel short-
ened and browned — that the rifled musket had to be adopted
by British and European armies. But the Brown Bess had been
Wellington's weapon in Belgium, in the style of warfare conducted on the classical battlefield, with disciplined infantry firing in ranks at short distance: a row of blasts from these
muskets, as from deadly popguns, could be pretty effective in
stopping or driving back an opposed line. Even the rifled musket, at that time, used the round ball. The elongated, cylindro-
conoidal bullet was invented only afterward, by Captain John

ARTHUR C. DANTO   101

Norton, in 1823, and though it has been acclaimed as the greatest military invention since the flintlock, Wellington could not see how it improved on the Brown Bess, as indeed it did not if battle were conducted as Wellington understood it. The elongated bullet, with its lowered wind resistance making its charge much more powerful, was understood by Sir William Napier as profoundly altering the nature of infantry, turning the infantry soldier into a "long-range assassin." Napier intuited that a change in the conduct of battle at any point would entail a change at every point — like what Heidegger calls a *Zeugganzes* — a complex of instruments, men and arms forming a total system which functions *as* a totality. Napier's objection implies the very code that the Civil War uniform embodies, and defines a certain moral boundary, the other side of which is not war so much as slaughter. Rifling, the Norton bullet and the percussion cap, established as superior to the flintlock by 1839, certainly changed the face of warfare. There was no room in the new complex for the cavalry charge, as had to be learned in the Charge of the Light Brigade in 1854, and relearned in the Civil War. In any case, the standard Civil War issue was the 1861-model Springfield rifle: percussion lock, muzzle-loading, .58 caliber, shooting a 480-grain conical Minié bullet. It was effective at a thousand yards, deadly accurate at three hundred. The smooth-bore was of limited effectiveness at one hundred to one hundred twenty yards. Civil War soldiers faced the kind of fire that made obsolete the way they were used by generals who learned about battle at West Point and had studied the Napoleonic paradigms. The guns faithfully depicted in the Civil War memorial statue made the style and gallantry of the men who carried them obsolete. Even the brass button would be a point of vulnerability in battles to come.

The 1903 and 1917 Springfield models were used by American infantry in the First World War. Increased muzzle velocity flattened trajectory; the ammunition clip, easy to change, speeded charging the magazine. But those rifles were fired over the cusp of trenches and the steel helmets protected the riflemen's heads. Of course, helmets have existed since ancient times and, in fact, were worn by Prussian and Austrian observers at Gettysburg, though more for ostentation than protection. They

were brightly polished. "The sword carries greater honor than
the shield" could be repeated by a military historian in very
recent years, giving a reason why Robert E. Lee should have
achieved greater honor through losing glamorously than his
opponent, George Meade, earned through winning stolidly, by
fighting a defensive battle. Lee had been mocked as "The King
of Spades" when he used entrenchments at Chancellorsville.
The steel helmet reduced injuries in the First World War by
about seventy-five percent. The casualties at Gettysburg, for the
three days of the battle, totaled about 51,000, of which 7,058
were outright deaths. The Roman legions were better protected,
and their sanitary conditions were better than those prevailing
in the 1860s. A wound in the July heat festered and went gan-
grenous quickly. There were 33,264 wounded. The wagon train
that carried the Confederate wounded away under driving rains
on July 5 was seventeen miles long. Over 10,000 were unac-
counted for, and I suppose their bones would still be turned up
at Gettysburg had the battlefield not become a military park. In
any case I am uncertain they would have worn helmets if they
had had them, for they were men who lived and died by an
exalted concept of honor. You went to your death like a soldier,
head held high under your jaunty cap. "As he passed me he
rode gracefully," Longstreet wrote, years after, of Pickett leading his stupendous charge, "with his jaunty cap raked well over
on his right ear and his long auburn locks, nicely dressed, hanging almost to his shoulders. He seemed rather a holiday soldier
than the general at the head of a column which was about to
make one of the grandest, most desperate assaults recorded in
the annals of war." Longstreet thought the great charge a terrible mistake. He thought Lee wrong from the start at Gettysburg.
Lee was deaf to Longstreet for the same reason that mourners
and patriots across America were blind to the message of their
memorials. Longstreet is my hero.

I recently trudged the battle lines at Gettysburg. The scene of
that great collision had, according to the architectural historian
Vincent Scully, been transformed by the National Park Service
into a work of art, and I was curious to see, in the first instance,
how the locus of agony and glory should have been preserved

and transfigured under the glass bell of aesthetic distance into a memorial object. An interest in memorial art and in the moral boundaries of war would have sufficed to move me as a pilgrim to what, since the Gettysburg Address, we have thought of as consecrated ground. But I had also been enough unsettled by a recent remark of Gore Vidal's that had come up in the civil strife between *Commentary* and *The Nation,* in regard to Norman Podhoretz's patriotism, to want to think out for myself whether, as Vidal claimed, the American Civil War is our Trojan War. Podhoretz had pretended to a greater interest in the Wars of the Roses than in the Civil War, and this had greatly exercised Vidal, whose family had participated on both sides and thus had internalized the antagonisms that divided the nation. The Trojan War was not of course a civil conflict. A better paradigm might have been the epic wars between the Pandavas and Kauravas, as recounted in the *Mahabharata* and given moral urgency in the *Bhagavad Gita,* where the fact that it is a *civil* war was deemed by the great warrior Arjuna — until he was persuaded otherwise by the god Krishna — a compelling reason not to fight. No one's remembered ancestors participated in the Trojan War when it in fact was their Trojan War in the sense Vidal must have intended, when the Homeric poems had emerged out of the mists to define the meaning of life, strife, love and honor for a whole civilization. The Civil War, if it were to be our Trojan War in that sense, would have to be so even for those whose families were elsewhere and indifferent when it took place. It has not received literary embodiment of the right sort to affect American consciousness as the *Iliad* affected Greek consciousness (Troy affected Roman consciousness through the *Aeneid*). And so a further question that directed me was whether the artistic embodiment of a battlefield into a military park might serve to make it our Trojan War in the required way, where one could not pretend an indifference to it because it was now the matrix of our minds and our beings.

Like Tewkesbury, where the climactic battle of the Wars of the Roses took place in 1471, the name Gettysburg has an irresistibly comic sound, good for a giggle in music hall or vaudeville. It could, like Podunk, serve as everyone's name for Nowheresville, the boondocks, the sticks. It was one of hundreds

of "-burgs" and "-villes" named after forgotten worthies
(James Gettys had been given the site by William Penn), indicat-
ing, before the place "became terrible" — Bruce Catton's phrase
— simply where life went on. Gettysburg in 1863 was the seat
of Adams County and a poky grove of Academe, with a college
and a seminary. But Gettysburg was no Troy: the battle was *at*
but not *for* Gettysburg. When Lee withdrew on July 5, its 2,400
inhabitants had ten times that number of dead and wounded to
deal with, not to mention mounds of shattered horses: the
miasma of putrefaction hung over the town until winter. Gettysburg became host to a cemetery large in proportion to its size,
though there is a strikingly prophetic Romanesque gatehouse at
Evergreen Cemetery, which gave its name to Cemetery Hill and
Cemetery Ridge, and which seemed waiting to welcome the
alien dead: you can see artillery emplacements in front of it in
a surviving photograph. You can count the houses in Gettysburg in another photograph of the time, looking east from Seminary Ridge. That the battle was there, between Cemetery Ridge
and Seminary Ridge, was an artifact of the war. Gettysburg was
not somebody's prize. Longstreet called it "ground of no value."
It was a good place for a battle, but though it is clear that there
had to be a battle someplace soon, it could have happened in
any number of other burgs or villes. Meade, knowing there was
to be a battle, would have preferred Pipes Creek as its site. Lee
was heading for Harrisburg, a serious city and the capital of the
state, and decided to *accept* battle instead, knowing he would
have to do so somewhere, and Gettysburg, by geological accident, was as good a place as any to fight.

In his novel *Lincoln,* Gore Vidal puts Mary Lincoln in the War
Room with her husband. She is supposed to have had, according
to the novel, a certain military intuition, and Vidal describes her
looking at a map, pointing to the many roads leading in and out
of Gettysburg, and saying, in effect, My goodness — whoever
controls Gettysburg controls everything. Perhaps this in fact is
intended to underscore Mary Lincoln's acute frivolity: if it
meant, really, to show how the mind of a general got lodged in
the pretty head of the President's wife, it simply shows the limits
of Vidal's own military intuition. Gettysburg was not that kind
of place. It was not, for example, like Monte Cassino, anchoring

a line because it controlled roads up the Italian peninsula, so
that when it fell, its defenders were obliged to fall back to the
next line of defense. Gettysburg really *was* nowhere, of no importance and no consequence: like Waterloo it was illuminated
by the sheer *Geworfenheit* of war. The essence of war is accident.

This is how it happened to happen there. It was known in
Washington in late June that Lee was somewhere in Pennsylvania, but not known where he was exactly. Despite the telegraph
and the *New York Times,* there is a sense in which men were as
much in the dark in regard to one another's whereabouts as
they might have been in England in the fifteenth century, fighting the Wars of the Roses. Lee had heard rumors that the Army
of the Potomac was somewhere east of him, but he had no clear
idea of where. This, too, was a matter of accident. In classical
warfare, the cavalry served as the eyes of the army. But Lee's
glamorous and vain cavalry leader, Jeb Stuart, was off on a toot
of his own, seeking personal glory. He turned up only on the
last day of the battle of Gettysburg, trailing some useless tro-
phies. Buford, a Union cavalry general, sent out to look for the
suspected Confederate troops, more or less bumped into General Pettigrew's brigade marching along the Chambersburg Pike
into Gettysburg to requisition shoes. They collided, as it were,
in the fog, and each sent word that the enemy was near. Buford
perceived that it was good ground for a battle and sent for
reinforcements. Lee perceived that it was a good *moment* for
battle and began to concentrate his forces. It happened very
fast: the next day was the first day of the engagement, July 1.

Here is Longstreet's description of the site:

> Gettysburg lies partly between Seminary Ridge on the West and
> Cemetery Ridge on the South-east, a distance of about fourteen
> hundred yards dividing the crests of the two ridges.

This is a soldier's description, not the imagined description of a
novelist's personage: you can deduce the necessary orders to
infantry and artillery from Longstreet's single sentence. The
battle seethed and boiled between the two ridges, as if they were
its containing walls. Gettysburg had the bad luck to lie partly
between the ridges. It had the good luck to lie between them

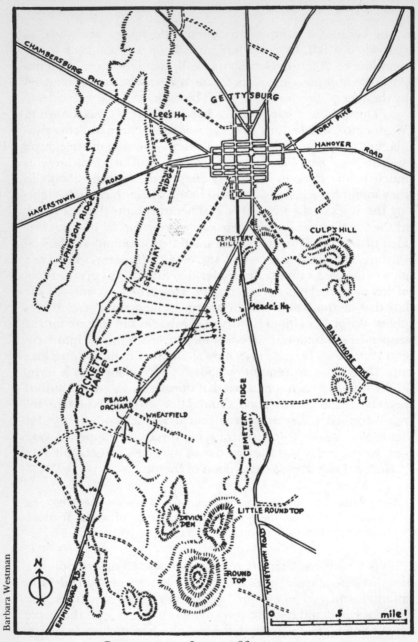

CHAMBERSBURG PIKE

GETTYSBURG

Lee's Hq.

YORK PIKE

HANOVER ROAD

HAGERSTOWN ROAD

McPHERSON RIDGE

SEMINARY RIDGE

CULP'S HILL

CEMETERY HILL

Meade's Hq.

BALTIMORE PIKE

PICKETT'S CHARGE

PEACH ORCHARD

WHEATFIELD

CEMETERY RIDGE

DEVIL'S DEN

LITTLE ROUND TOP

ROUND TOP

EMMITSBURG RD.

TANEYTOWN ROAD

N

Barbara Westman

0 .5 mile 1

GETTYSBURG • JULY 3, 1863 • 2:30 P.M.

partly. There was only one accidental, civilian death: the battle took place, mainly, to the south of the village. The ridges formed two facing natural ramparts, as though two feudal lords had built their walls within catapult distance of each other.

To visualize the terrain, draw a vertical line and label it Seminary Ridge. This is where the Confederate Army formed its line, along the crest. They seized it after a heated battle with Buford's forces, which, despite reinforcements, were driven fourteen hundred yards east to Cemetery Ridge. Now draw a line parallel and to the right of Seminary Ridge, only curve it to the right at the top, to form a sort of fishhook. This was the shape of the Union line, indeed called "The Fish-hook," on July 2 and 3. (Gettysburg is a dot between the lines, just about where the hook begins its curve.) Where the barb would be is Culp's Hill. Farther back along the shaft is Cemetery Hill. At the eye of the hook is Big Round Top, at a distance of about four miles from Cemetery Hill. About half its height, and upshaft, is Little Round Top. The four hills served as battle towers. The rampart itself slopes to the west to form what is designated a *glacis* in the vocabulary of fortification. It was a formidable defensive position, but Seminary Ridge too would have been a formidable defensive position. "If we could only take position here and have them attack us through this open ground!" Lee's chief of artillery, Porter Alexander, recalled having thought. "We were in no such luck — the boot, in fact, being upon the other foot." A defensive war was not what had brought Lee north and onto enemy territory. He had to attack if there was to be battle.

Longstreet did not think there needed to be battle. Standing beside Lee, he surveyed the Union position with his field glasses for a very long time, turned to Lee and said,

> If we could have chosen a point to meet our plans of operation, I do not think we could have found a better one than that upon which they are now concentrating. All we have to do is throw our army around by their left, and we shall interpose between the Federal Army and Washington. We can get a strong position and wait, and if they fail to attack us we shall have everything in condition to move back tomorrow night in the direction of Washington.

"No," said General Lee — the words are famous and fateful —
"the enemy is there and I am going to attack him there."

Perhaps Longstreet was wrong: Meade was as cautious a man
as he. Why need Meade have attacked them, even though between Washington and its army? Lee's supply line was long and
vulnerable, and Meade might have ringed any position he
would take and wait out a siege. Still, wars are fought not so
much by generals as by governments, and Longstreet knew that
Washington would pressure Meade to attack, needing a victory
and in fear for Washington itself. And Lee was probably right:
if he could crush Meade's army here, where it was, he would
have free access to Washington or Baltimore or Philadelphia.
He needed or thought he needed a *brilliant* victory. He had
invaded the North not for conquest but to astonish. And he
could sustain a defeat as Meade could not. If Meade were defeated, pressure to negotiate would be exerted on Lincoln by
the Peace Party in the Union. There might be foreign recognition. And morale would have been disastrously lowered since
the Union had just undergone a series of brutal defeats. He
might, on the symbolic date of July Fourth, achieve independence for the South. Whereas if he lost at Getttysburg, well, he
could have swaggered back to his own territory, as after a dashing raid, trailing glory. Besides, rounding the Federal left would
have baffled his troops, who had driven the enemy back to that
position. Morale is a precious factor, a form of power. Lee
would have to *smash* the Union left. He would have to take Little
Round Top, as he nearly succeeded in doing on the second day
of battle.

A battlefield has something of the metaphysical complexity of a
work of art: it stands to the terrain on which it is spread as a
work of art stands to the physical object to which it belongs. Not
every part of the physical object is really a part of the work of
art — we do not take the weave of canvas into consideration in
identifying the meaning of a picture, for example, since there is
no coherent way in which we can read the roughness of his
surfaces into, say, the iconographic program of Tintoretto's
Scuola di San Rocco. We rarely consider the fact that a surface
is dry when interpreting a painting. Richard Wollheim, in his

recent Mellon Lectures, borrowed from phenomenology the useful term "thematization," and would use it to say that not every part or property of the physical object is "thematized" by the work. Doubtless the concept can be taken further — I am seeking to thematize the contradiction, which most would not even see as there, in Civil War memorial statuary. But what I want to say here is that battle thematizes certain features of the terrain, transforming them into what soldiers call "ground." At Gettysburg, the flanking hills of the Federal line were thematized in this sense on the second day of battle; Cemetery Hill and the sweep of field and meadow between the ridges were thematized on the third and last day. It is doubtful the two ridges would have been so thematized in an imagined encounter between Napoleon and Wellington: their artillery would not have reached far enough, and besides, the explosive shell had not been invented in 1815. (Its invention meant the end of the wooden battleship.) What would be the point of lobbing cannon balls across the fields? One follows the structure of battle by grasping successive thematizations. War is a deadly artist. A battlefield is already more than halfway to a work of art.

On July 2, Lee strove to take either or both Culp's Hill and Little Round Top. Meade's defensive line along Cemetery Ridge would have been untenable had Lee succeeded: he would have had to draw back to Pipes Creek, and it would have been a defeat. The fighting that afternoon was fierce but uncoordinated — each commander had difficulties with his generals — and the outcome of the engagement was sufficiently ambiguous that Lee could interpret it as a victory. Still, no thanks to General Daniel Sickles, the tempestuous Federal general who had left Little Round Top undefended, both the contested hills remained, it may have seemed precariously, in Union hands. Had Meade's engineering chief, Gouverneur Warren, not happened to see that no one was holding the crest at Little Round Top and on his own authority diverted troops to its defense in the very nick of time, the outcome of that day's fighting would have been different.

It is worth contemplating Little Round Top from the perspective of weaponry. Little Round Top was called "the Rocky Hill" by the Confederates — armies improvise a nomenclature with their thematizations. Its slopes are strewn with heavy boulders of the kind that, piled up, gave the name "Devil's Den" to an adjacent site. It is full of ad hoc shelters and one-man fortresses, and offers an object lesson in the military imagination. It cried out for a kind of weapon — the grenade — which was to be indispensable to infantry in the World Wars but which was considered extinct at the time of the Civil War because of the increase in range and accuracy of muzzled arms. Grenades had been intensely employed in seventeenth-century tactics (when a grenadier was a special physical type, like a shot-putter). It came into its own again in the Russo-Japanese war. The field mortar, with its high trajectory, would also have done wonders at Devil's Den, with its freestone breastworks and God-given sniper nests. Civil War battle seems to have been imagined as something that takes place on a field, between massed armies. The grenade and mortar, conceived of as suited to storming fortresses, were inscrutable in 1863, even though all the technology was in place for the manufacture of the lightweight grenades that re-entered the armory half a century later. The weaponry determined the order of thematization, and particularly the field between the ridges on which Pickett's charge was to take place on July 3 was something generals understood or thought they understood. Longstreet knew they did not.

On July 3, Lee had determined to attack Meade's center. This was his reasoning: Meade, he believed, would infer that Lee was seeking to turn his flanks and would renew the attack on the anchoring hills. So Meade would move reinforcements to right and left, leaving the center weak. Meade's reasoning was this: Lee would reason as he in fact reasoned, so the right thing was to reinforce the center. In classical warfare there is a kind of language — armies communicate through guns (as the United States and the Soviet Union today communicate through nuclear testing): a cannonade announces a charge. All that morning the Federal officers and men watched the enemy concentrate its artillery — 150 guns focused on the Union center. "A magnificent sight," according to Henry Hunt, chief of artillery on the Union side: "Never before had such a sight been witnessed on this continent, and rarely, if ever, abroad." The

Union employed about 200 pieces in that battle, and a duel opened up at about 1 P.M. that lasted nearly two hours: nothing on that scale had ever taken place before. But the state of explosive chemistry in the mid-nineteenth century raised severe cognitive problems for the Confederate force. What was used then was black gunpowder, which created dense smoke. The exploding shells cast a smoke screen over Cemetery Ridge, concealing from Confederate artillery chief Porter Alexander that he was shooting too high, and that his shells were falling behind the Union line. By accident, he hit a dozen caissons of ammunition to Meade's rear. Union Major General Hunt decided to conserve ammunition for the attack to come, and ordered fire to cease. Alexander took this as a sign that he had silenced the Federal guns, and signaled Pickett to move forward. Smoke still hung blackly over Cemetery Ridge, but at a certain moment of no return a breeze lifted it and Pickett's men saw, in Allan Nevins's words, "the full panoply of Union strength in its terrifying grandeur, a double line of infantry in front, guns frowning beside them, and reserves in thick platoons further back." Until that moment, none of Lee's officers had any real idea of what power had been building up behind the sullen ridge. Had his cavalry been operative, Lee would not have charged. He fought blind.

It was in Pickett's grand charge up the slopes of Cemetery Ridge that the tragic contradiction between arms and uniform became palpable. Pickett's superb veterans, fresh in this battle, marched according to a magnificent code into a wall of fire. It was the brutal end to an era of warfare, the last massed charge. The triumph of slaughter over chivalry gave rise to Sherman's horrifying march through Georgia and South Carolina, to total war, to the firebombing of Dresden, to Hiroshima and Nagasaki, to the rolled grenade in the full jetliner. "It was the most beautiful thing I ever saw," exclaimed Colonel Fremantle, a British observer at Longstreet's side. The sentiment was widely shared. Pickett's charge was what war was all about in that era; it had the kind of beauty that made Lee remark, at the Battle of Fredericksburg, "It is well that war is so terrible — we should grow too fond of it." Longstreet wrote: "That day at Gettysburg

was one of the saddest in my life." I think he was more or less
alone in this feeling. I do not think Gettysburg was perceived as
the awful defeat it was by the South, at least not then, since news
of Grant's victory at Vicksburg had not yet come, nor do I think
it was received as a great victory, least of all in Washington, or
by Lincoln, who cared only that Meade should press his advantage. What no one could see, just because the doors of the future
always are closed, was that beauty on that occasion was only the
beginning of terror.

The bodies were rolled into shallow trenches, and the armies
moved off to other encounters. Some 3,500 Union dead are
today neatly buried in concentric arcs alongside Evergreen
Cemetery. Seventeen acres were set aside for this, weeks after
the battle, and it was here, before the landscaping was altogether completed, that Lincoln delivered the address which is
so enshrined in the national consciousness today that it requires
an effort of severe deconstruction to perceive it as a cry of
victory as gloating as anything that issued from the coarse throat
of Ajax. The Gettysburg Battlefield Memorial Association was
chartered in 1864 and began acquiring land which was absorbed
into the National Military Park established, without debate so
far as I can discover, by an act of Congress in 1895. In 1933 it
came under the jurisdiction of the National Park Service, which
transformed it in an unforgiving way. There is an historical
preservation I applaud but a political overlay that distresses me.
    It is always moving to visit a battlefield when the traces of war
itself have been erased by nature or transfigured by art, and to
stand amid memorial weapons, which grow inevitably quaint
and ornamental with the evolution of armamentary technology,
mellowing under patinas and used, now, to punctuate the fading thematizations of strife. The first cannon to be fired at the
Battle of Gettysburg stands by the memorial to Buford near
MacPherson's Farm, like a capital letter to mark the beginning
of a ferocious sentence. Four cannons form Cushing's battery
stand, like four exclamation points, to mark its end at the point
where Pickett's men penetrated the Union line only to be surrounded. General Francis Walker uses a Homeric metaphor to
describe Pickett's charge:

As the spear of Menelaus pierced the shield of his antagonist, cut through the shining breastplate, but spared the life, so the division of Pickett, launched from Seminary Ridge, broke through the Union defense, and for the moment thrust its head of column within our lines, threatening destruction to the Army of the Potomac.

When I was a soldier, I was often struck, as by a paradox, that at the very moment that artillery was pounding somewhere, somewhere else men and women in soft clothing were touching glasses and carrying on flirtations; and that before and after this moment, but in this place, the peaceful pursuit of human purposes would go innocently forward, that families would picnic where men were being killed. And I was overwhelmed after the war by the thick peace that had settled back over places I had seen sharded: Salerno, Velletri, Cassino, Anzio. There is that sense today at Gettysburg, as tourists consult their maps and point across to not very distant hills and ridges, or listen to patient guides rehearse the drama of those three days in July 1863. The statue of General Lee, on his elegant horse, Traveller, stands just where Lee himself stood, and faces, across the open field traversed by Pickett's division, to where an appropriately less flamboyant effigy of Meade looks west from Cemetery Ridge. The copse of trees that Lee had singled out as the point to head for still stands not far from Meade's statue, segregated by an iron fence, as if a sacred grove. Ranks of cannons point across, from ridge to ridge, and the sites are strewn with touching, simple monuments, placed by the units that were there so that it would always be remembered that they were there. The most florid monument celebrates the Pennsylvania presence (there are 537 Pennsylvanians buried in the National Cemetery, and 867 New Yorkers — the largest representation by state there). There is an art history of Gettysburg to be written, but the meaning that comes through, even without it, is that a momentous collision occurred here, and that it was connected with the high and generous feelings that are appropriate, after a battle, between those who fought it.

The Park Service's pamphlet of 1950 recommends an itinerary with fourteen stops — it maps onto the Stations of the Cross if you have an appetite for numerical correspondences. It is

chronological. You begin where the battle began, at Mac-
Pherson's Ridge at 8 A.M. on July 1. You now follow a trail south
along Seminary Ridge, and you may pause in front of Lee's
statue and recite the thought Faulkner insisted was in the breast
of every Southern boy: it is, there, eternally "still not yet two
o'clock on that July afternoon in 1863." Edging the Peach Orchard, where Sickles formed a reckless salient and lost a leg, you
mount Round Top and head north to The Copse of Trees and
Meade's headquarters. You pause at the cemetery and end, not
quite appropriately, at Culp's Hill. In 1950, as today, you would
leave 1863 from time to time and enter the present, for the
acreage of the Battle Park is intersected, here and there, with
fragments of mere unthematized Pennsylvania, along whose
roads tractors and trucks drive past restaurants and service stations on one or another civilian errand. The almost cubist inter-
penetration of past and present, war and peace, is semiotically
moving in its own right.

The itinerary of 1950 was dropped from revised editions of
the pamphlet, in 1954 and 1962, and today the visit has a different structure. Today you enter the park, amidst many monuments, along "High-Water Mark Trail." There are no Confederate markers among the celebratory monuments: instead,
there is "High-Water Mark Monument," erected by "us" to show
how far "they" reached. It was not really a high-water mark.
There was no flood: this was not Genghis Khan, but one of the
gentlest occupations the world has ever seen. It was, exactly as
General Walker put it, a spear point which penetrated but did
not slay — a Homeric poet would have supposed a god or god-
dess deflected the weapon. Lee was the spearman — Menelaus,
if the analogy appeals (except Menelaus triumphed). If we con-
strue the Military Park as a monumentary text, it now reads *not*
as the history of a great battle between heroic adversaries, but
as the victory of the Union. The text begins where the victory
was won. As a text, the park is now a translation into historical
landscape of the Gettysburg Address. Small wonder it "fell like
a wet blanket," as Lincoln afterward said. Small wonder the
Harrisburg Patriot editorialized the "silly remarks" this way: "For
the credit of the Nation we are willing that the veil of oblivion
shall be dropped and that they shall be no more repeated or

thought of." Half the men who fell there did not fight for what Lincoln said was achieved there, and of those who might have, Lincoln's were not in every case the reasons they were there. It was an inappropriate political speech on an occasion that called for generosity, vaunting and confessional. The language is concealingly beautiful, evidence that Auden is after all right that time worships language "and forgives / Everyone by whom it lives."

I can understand, or might be able to understand, how a literary scholar, though patriotic, might find the Wars of the Roses of greater interest than the American Civil War, even if he should have no special concern with the ambitions of Lancaster and York. Henry VI, the subject of an early tragedy of Shakespeare, founded Kings College, Cambridge. But the main reason, I should think, for being interested in the civil wars of the fifteenth century in England is connected with one main reason for being interested in our Civil War. The Wars of the Roses were of an unparalleled brutality and were fought by mercenaries. It was total warfare, and the sickening experience of having one's land run over by one's countrymen but acting like brigands and in the royal pay lingered for centuries in British consciousness. Henry VI also founded Eton, on whose playing fields the British Empire is said to have been won by practices governed by the rules of fair combat and respect for the opponent. The unspeakable conduct of battle on the Continent — think of the Thirty Years War — until the eighteenth century, when Anglicization began to define the moral outlines of military conduct, must have confirmed the legacy of the Wars of the Roses in the English mind.

My sense is that the high-minded perception of the soldierly vocation is embodied in the uniform, the insignia, the flags and the vulnerability of the militia depicted in sculpture of the Civil War. The other form of war is embodied in the weapons. If there is a high-water mark in the history of modern war, it was in Pickett's gallant and foregone assault. It has been growing darker and darker ever since. I am not certain this is a basis for seeing the Civil War as "our" Trojan War. In a sense, something is not a Trojan War if it is *ours:* the Trojan War speaks to what is universal and human, regardless of political division and national culture. I am not certain that the idea of Union has any more meaning than or as much meaning as Helen of Troy, as justification for pitched combat. If the Civil War is to address humanity as the Trojan War does, it must itself be addressed at a different level than any that has so far been reached. Gettysburg is a good place to begin.

WILLIAM KITTREDGE

Home

FROM OWNING IT ALL (GRAYWOLF PRESS)

IN THE LONG-AGO land of my childhood we clearly understood the high desert country of southeastern Oregon as the actual world. The rest of creation was distant as news on the radio.

In 1945, the summer I turned thirteen, my grandfather sentenced his chuckwagon cow outfit to a month of haying on the IXL, a little ranch he had leased from the Sheldon Antelope Refuge in Nevada. Along in August we came in to lunch one noontime, and found the cook, a woman named Hannah, flabbergasted by news that some bomb had just blown up a whole city in Japan. Everybody figured she had been into the vanilla extract, a frailty of cooks in those days. As we know, it was no joke. Nagasaki and then V-J Day. We all listened to that radio. Great changes and possibilities floated and cut in the air. But such far-off strange events remained the concern of people who lived in cities. We might get drunk and celebrate, but we knew such news really had nothing to do with us. Not in the far outback of southeastern Oregon.

When I came home from the Air Force in 1958, I found our backland country rich with television from the Great World. But that old attitude from my childhood, the notion that my people live in a separate kingdom where they own it all, secure from the world, is still powerful and troublesome. When people ask where I'm from I still say southeastern Oregon, expecting them to understand my obvious pride.

*

Jack Ray was one of the heroes of my boyhood. A slope-shoul-
dered balding little man, Jack dominated the late roughhouse
craziness at our mid-July country dances. The Harvest Moon
Ball.

"He can hit like a mule kicking," my father used to say after
those dances, winking at us kids and grinning at my mother's
back while she served up a very late Sunday breakfast of steak
and fried mush and biscuits and thick sausage gravy.

At that time I was maybe five or six years old, and I would
have been asleep in the back seat of our car for a couple of
hours when the shouting and fighting started around midnight.
So I recall those scenes with a newly awakened child's kind of
strobe-light clarity, a flash here and there, all illuminated in the
headlights of 1930s automobiles. The ranch women would be
crowded outside on the porch where they could see, some wife
weeping, the men out closer to the battle in the parking lot,
passing bottles.

But what I see mainly is Jack Ray getting up off the ground,
wiping a little trickle of blood from the corner of his mouth,
glancing down at the smear on his hand, his eyes gone hard
while some sweating farm boy moved at him again; and torn
shirts, the little puffs of dust their feet kicked there in the headlights. At that point my memory goes fragile. There is some
quick slippery violence, and the farm boy is on his knees. Jack
Ray is standing above him, waiting, wheezing as he breathes.

It's over, everybody knows, and soon it is. Two more grunting
punches, and the farm boy is down again, and Jack Ray steps
back, his eyes gone soft and almost bewildered in the light as a
little shudder moves though the crowd, and someone shouts,
and the bottles pass again. I see Jack Ray, there in those headlights, smiling like a child now that it's finished, the farm boy up
on his knees, shaking his head.

No harm done, the air clear. I see it over and over, summer
dance after summer dance. I see the kind of heroism my boyhood educated me to understand and respect.

And I hate the part that comes next. I grew up and ran the
haying and combine crews on our ranch, and there eventually
came a time when I hired Jack Ray to work for me. He had
worked a lot of seasons for my father, and such men always had

a job with us. Jack was maybe fifty by that time, and crippled by his life, the magic gone, a peaceable man who seemed to have turned a little simple. He did what he could, chores around the cook house, and once in a while he drank. After a bout in town which earned him some time in the county jail, he would show up grinning in the bunk house. "Well, hell, Jack," I would say, "it's a new day."

"Kid," he would say, "she's a new world every morning."

Looking backward is one of our main hobbies here in the American West, as we age. And we are aging, which could mean we are growing up. Or not. It's a difficult process for a culture which has always been so insistently boyish. Jack Ray has been dead a long time now. As my father said, he drank his liver right into the ground. "But, by God," my father said, "he was something once."

Possibility is the oldest American story. Head west for freedom and the chance of inventing a spanking new life for yourself. Our citizens are always leaping the traces when their territory gets too small and cramped.

Back in the late fifties, living with my wife and our small children in our little cattle-ranch house, when things would get too tight on a rainy Sunday afternoon in November I always had the excuse of work. "I got to go out," I would say, and I would duck away to the peacefulness of driving the muddy fields and levee banks in my old Ford pickup. Or, if the roads were too bad, I would go down to the blacksmith shop and bang on some damned thing.

Whenever I find myself growing grim about the mouth; whenever it is damp, drizzly November in my soul; whenever I find myself involuntarily pausing before coffin warehouses, and bringing up the rear of every funeral I meet . . . Then he runs away to sea. *Ishmael.*

". . . lighting out for territory," says Huckleberry Finn, with his broken-hearted optimism, right at the end of his getaway down the Mississippi.

And it wasn't just the runaway boys in books. John Colter left Ohio at the age of thirty, to head up the Missouri with Lewis and Clark in 1804. He stayed west another five years, earning his keep as a fur trapper in pursuit of the beaver. One fearsome

Montana winter he took a legendary walk from Fort Lisa on the Yellowstone, traveling through what is Yellowstone Park to circumnavigate the Tetons — about a thousand miles on snowshoes through country where no white man had ever been before. A thing both wondrous and powerful drove him. Maybe it was a need so simple as being out, away.

Imagine those shining snowy mountains burning against the sheltering endless bowl of clean sky, and Colter alone there in Jackson Hole. We will not see such things again, not any of us, ever. It's gone. We know it is. Only one man ever got to be Colter. Not even Bridger or Joe Meek or Jedediah Smith had a world so absolutely to themselves. Except for some natives, who maybe never thought they were alone.

In 1836 Narcissa and Marcus Whitman came west with Eliza and Henry Spalding. The first white women had crossed the Rockies. Along the way they witnessed one of the last fur-trapper rendezvous, on the Green River in Wyoming. Think of those Presbyterian women among the inhabitants of wilderness. Less than ten years later Marcus Whitman was leading one of the first wagon trains west from St. Louis to the Oregon country.

The New York newspaper editor Horace Greeley worried about the exodus, wondering what those families could be seeking, leaving behind the best of climates and agricultural lands, schools and churches and markets: "For what, then, do they brave the desert, the wilderness, the savage, the snowy precipices of the Rocky Mountains, the early summer march, the storm-drenched bivouac, and the gnawings of famine? Only to fulfill their destiny! There is probably not one among them whose outward circumstances will be improved by this perilous pilgrimage."

Anybody sensible, Greeley suggested, would stop "this side of the jumping-off place." The only practice stupider than such migration, he said, was suicide.

It's easy to understand his puzzlement. The wagon trains were predominantly middle-class ventures. Poor folks couldn't afford a wagon, much less provisions. The basic outfitting cost up toward a thousand dollars. And in those long-gone days that was some real money. But seemingly sensible people persisted in selling their good farms and heading west.

Imagine half the population of Ohio picking up sticks, selling out, and heading for one of our latter-day mythological frontiers, Alaska or Australia. Greeley was right, it was crazy, it was a mania.

What was pushing them? Lots of things. Among them a quite legitimate fear of mortal corruption and death. Cholera. By the spring of 1849 an epidemic had reached St. Louis. Ten percent of the population died of the disease. The road west from Independence was likened to traveling through a graveyard.

But mostly, we have to believe, they were lured west by promises. Promises of paradise for the taking. Free land, crystalline water, great herds of game roaming the natural meadowlands, good fishing, gold, all in unfettered abundance, a new world every morning.

What compelled men to believe promises of paradise on earth with such simpleminded devotion? Well, for openers, a gut yearning for the chance of becoming someone else, and freedom from the terrible weight of responsibilities, freedom too often equaling free, without cost.

My own great-grandfather on my father's side left Michigan in 1849 to travel down the Mississippi and across to Panama, where he hiked west through the jungles on the route Balboa had blazed, and caught a ship north to California and the gold camps. After a long and bootless career of chasing mineral trace in the mountain streams, first in the central Sierra and then up around the foothills of Mount Shasta, he gave it up and turned to ranching and school teaching in one place after another around the Northwest, until in 1897 he died white-trash poor in the sagebrush backlands near Silver Lake, Oregon, leaving a family determined to shake his suicidal despair.

It wasn't just the gold that he never found — such instant boomer riches were to have been only the beginning. The green and easy dreamland fields of some home place were to have been the ultimate reward for his searching, the grape arbor beside the white house he would own outright, where he could rest out some last serene years while the hordes of grandchildren played down across the lawns by the sod-banked pond where the tame ducks swam and fed and squawked in their happy, idiot way. The pastoral heaven on this earth — some particular secret and heart's-desire version of it — has time and again proved to be the absolute heart in American dreams. All this we promise you.

2

Childhood, it has been said, is always partly a lie of poetry. When I was maybe eight years old, in the fall of the year, I would have to go out in the garden after school with damp burlap sacks and cover the long rows of cucumber and tomato plants, so they wouldn't freeze.

It was a hated, cold-handed job which had to be done every evening. I daydreamed along in a halfhearted, distracted way, flopping the sacks onto the plants, sorry for myself and angry because I was alone at my boring work. No doubt my younger brother and sister were in the house and warm. Eating cookies.

But then a great strutting bird appeared out from the dry remnants of our corn, black tail feathers flaring and a monstrous yellow-orange air sac pulsating from its white breast, its throat croaking with popping sounds like rust in a joint.

The bird looked to be stalking me with grave slow intensity, coming after me from a place I could not understand as real, and yet quite recognizable, the sort of terrifying creature which would sometimes spawn in the incoherent world of my night dreams. In my story, now, I say it looked like death, come to say hello. Then, it was simply an apparition.

The moment demanded all my boyish courage, but I stood my ground, holding one of those wet sacks out before me like a shield, stepping slowly backwards, listening as the terrible creature croaked, its bright preposterous throat pulsating — and then the great bird flapped its wings in an angry way, raising a little commonplace dust.

It was the dust, I think, that did it, convincing me that this could not be a dream. My fear collapsed, and I felt foolish as I understood this was a creature I had heard my father talk about, a courting sage grouse, we called them prairie chickens. This was only a bird, and not much interested in me at all. But for an instant it had been both phantom and real, the thing I deserved, come to punish me for my anger.

For that childhood moment I believed the world to be absolutely inhabited by an otherness which was utterly demonic and natural, not of my own making. But soon as that bird was enclosed in a story which defined it as a commonplace prairie chicken, I was no longer frightened. It is a skill we learn early, the art of inventing stories to explain away the fearful sacred strangeness of the world. Storytelling and make-believe, like war and agriculture, are among the arts of self-defense, and all of them are ways of enclosing otherness and claiming ownership.

Such emblematic memories continue to surface, as I grow older and find ways to accept them into the fiction of myself. One of the earliest, from a time before I ever went to school, is of studying the worn oiled softwood flooring in the Warner Valley store where my mother took me when she picked up the mail three times a week. I have no idea how many years that floor had been tromped and dirtied and swept, but by the time I recall it was worn into a topography of swales and buttes, traffic patterns and hard knots, much like the land, if you will, under the wear of a glacier. For a child, as his mother gossiped with the postmistress, it was a place, high ground and valleys, prospects and sanctuaries, and I in my boredom could invent stories about it—finding a coherency I loved, a place which was mine. They tore up that floor somewhere around the time I started school, and I had the sense to grieve.

The coherency I found worn into those floorboards was mirrored a few years later, just before the war began, when I was seven or eight, in the summertime play of my brother and sister and cousins and myself, as we laid out roads to drive and rectangular fields to work with our toy trucks in the dirt under the huge old box elder which also functioned as a swing tree near the kitchen door to our house. It was a little play world we made for ourselves, and it was, we believed, just like the vast world beyond. In it we imitated the kind of ordering we watched each spring while our father laid out the garden with such measured precision, and the kind of planning we could not help but sense while riding with him along the levee banks in his dusty Chevrolet pickup truck. All the world we knew was visible from the front porch of our house, inside the valley, and all the work he

did was directed toward making it orderly, functional, and productive — and of course that work seemed sacred.

Our play ended when a small rattlesnake showed up in our
midst, undulating in sweeping little curving lines across our
dusty make-believe fields. A young woman who cooked for my
mother killed the snake in a matter-of-fact way with a shovel.
But the next spring my mother insisted, and my father hauled
in topsoil and planted the packed dirt, where we had played at
our toylike world of fields, into a lawn where rattlesnakes would
never come. We hated him for it.

These stories suggest reasons why, during childhood winters
through the Second World War, such an important segment of
my imagination lived amid maps of Europe and the Pacific.
Maps delineated the dimensions of that dream which was the
war for me, maps and traced drawings of aircraft camouflaged
for combat. I collected them like peacetime city boys collect
baseball cards, and I colored them in with crayons, my far South
Pacific and Europe invaded and shaped by dreams and invisible
forces I could not hope to make sense of in any other way.

In the spring of 1942, just before I turned ten years old, we
opened every first-period class in our one-room Warner Valley
schoolhouse singing "Praise the Lord and Pass the Ammunition." We embraced the war. We heard it every morning on the
Zenith Trans-Oceanic radio while we got ready for school, and
during recess we ran endless games of gunfighter pursuit and
justifiably merciless death in the playgrounds. Mostly we killed
Hitler and Mister Tojo.

Fall down, you're dead.

When it came your turn to play Nazi, you were honor bound
eventually to fall killed through the long adult agony, twisting
and staggering to heedless collapse in the dirt. Out in our land-
locked, end-of-the-road, rancher valley, the air was bright and
clean with purpose.

Always, at least in memory, those running battles involve my
cousins and my younger brother and my even younger sister,
and a black-and-white dog named Victory. Out back of the
house in the summer of 1942 we circled and shot our ways
through groves of wild plum in heavy fruit, and we swung to

ambush from gnarled limbs in the apple orchard where the blue flies and the yellowjackets were mostly interested in having their way with the rotting fallen fruit: yellowjackets flitting to a hive in the hollow trunk of a Lombardy poplar along the irrigation ditch, burning the air with their going, and near to the secret, stinging, irreligious heart of *my* paradise.

In late September our dog named Victory was crushed under the rear duals of a semi truck flatbed hauling one-hundred-pound burlap sacks of my father's newly combined oats across forty twisting miles of gravel road over the Warner Mountains to town and the railroad. My sister ran shrieking to the kitchen door, and my mother came to the roadside in her apron, and I was stoic and tough-minded as that poor animal panted and died. *Beyond the crystal sea, undreamed shores, precious angels.*

This was a time when our national life was gone to war against U-boats and Bataan and the death march, betrayal reeking everywhere. The death of that dog with cockleburrs matted into his coat must have shimmered with significance past heartbreak. We were American and proud, and we were steeled to deal with these matters.

So we unearthed a shallow grave in the good loam soil at the upper end of the huge rancher garden my father laid out each spring in those days, before it became cheaper to feed our crews from truckloads of canned goods bought wholesale in the cities. We gathered late-blooming flowers from the border beneath my mother's bedroom window, we loaded the stiffening carcass of that dead dog on a red wagon, and we staged a funeral with full symbolic honors.

My older cousin blew taps through his fist, my brother hid his face, and my six-year-old sister wept openly, which was all right since she was a little child. I waved a leafy bough of willow over the slope-sided grave while my other cousins shoveled the loose dry soil down on the corpse.

It is impossible to know what the child who was myself felt, gazing east across the valley which I can still envision so clearly — the ordered garden and the sage-covered slope running down to the slough-cut meadows of the Thompson Field, willows there concealing secret hideaway places where I would burrow away from the world for hours, imagining I was some animal, hidden and watching the stock cows graze the open islands of meadow grass.

On the far side of the valley lay the great level distances of the plow-ground fields which had so recently been tule swamps, reaching to the rise of barren eastern ridges. That enclosed valley is the home I imagine walking when someday I fall into the dream which is my death. My real, particular, vivid and populated solace for that irrevocable moment of utter loss when the mind stops forever. The chill of that remembered September evening feels right as I imagine that heartbreakingly distant boy.

It's hard for me to know where I got the notion of waving that willow branch over our burial of that poor dog unless I find it in this other memory, from about the same time. A Paiute girl of roughly my own age died of measles in the ramshackle encampment her people maintained alongside the irrigation ditch which eventually led to our vast garden. A dozen or so people lived there, and true or not, I keep thinking of them as in touch with some remnant memories of hunting and gathering forebears who summered so many generations in the valley we had so recently come to own.

In the fall of 1890 a man named James Mooney went west under the auspices of the Bureau of Ethnology to investigate the rise of Native American religious fervor which culminated in the massacre at Wounded Knee on December 29. In Mooney's report, *The Ghost Dance Religion and the Sioux Outbreak of 1890,* there is a statement delivered by a Paiute man named Captain Dick at Fort Bidwell in Surprise Valley — right in the home territory I am talking about, at the junction on maps where California and Nevada come together at the Oregon border.

All Indians must dance, everywhere, keep on dancing. Pretty soon in the next spring Big Man come. He bring back game of every kind. The game be thick everywhere. All dead Indians come back and live again. They all be strong just like young men, be young again. Old blind Indians see again and get young and have fine time. When the

Old Man comes this way, the all the Indians go to the mountains, high up away from the whites. Whites can't hurt the Indians then. Then while Indians way up high, big flood comes like water and all white people die, get drowned. After that water go away and then nobody but Indians everywhere game all kinds thick. Then medicine-man tell Indians to send word to all Indians to keep up dancing and the good time will come. Indians who don't dance, who don't believe in this word, will grow little, just about a foot high, and stay that way. Some of them will turn into wood and will be burned in the fire.

In the 1950s and '60s a Paiute named Conlan Dick lived in a cabin on our ranch in Warner Valley, and helped to look after the irrigation and fences. Conlan was reputed to be a kind of medicine man in our local mythology, related to the man who delivered that statement. His wife, whose name I cannot recall, did ironing for women in the valley. And there was a son, a young man named Virgil Dick, who sometimes came to Warner for a few weeks and helped his father with the field work.

In the early 1960s my cousin, the one who blew taps through his fist in 1942, was riding horseback across the swampy spring meadows alongside Conlan. He asked if Virgil was Conlan's only child.

Conlan grinned. "Naw," he said. "But you know, those kids, they play outside, and they get sick and they die."

Story after story. Is it possible to claim that proceeding through some incidents in this free-associative manner is in fact a technique, a way of discovery? Probably. One of our model narrators these days is the patient spinning and respinning the past and trying to resolve it into a story that makes sense.

". . . they get sick and they die." Once I had the romance in me to think that this was the mature comment of a man who had grown up healed into wholeness and connection with the ways of nature to a degree I would never understand. Now I think it was more likely the statement of a man trying to forget his wounds—so many of which were inflicted by schoolyard warriors like us. A healthy culture could never have taught him to forgo sorrow.

In any event, Captain Dick's magic was dead.

All these stories are part of my own story about a place called

Home, and a time in which I imagined we owned it all. The girl
who died was named Pearl. I recall her name with that particular exactness which occasionally hovers in memories. She was of
enormous interest to us because she so obviously disdained our
foolish play with make-believe weapons and miniature trucks.
Or so it seemed. Maybe she was only shy, or had been warned
away from us. But to our minds she lived with adults and shared
in the realities of adult lives in ways we did not, and now she
was being paid the attention of burial.

Try to imagine their singing that spring morning. I cannot. I
like to think our running brigade of warrior children might
have been touched by dim sorrow-filled wailing in the crystalline
brightness of her morning, but the memory is silent.

Maybe it's enough to recall the sight of people she loved,
carrying her elaborately clothed body in an open home-built
casket. Not that we saw it up close, or that we ever really saw a
body, clothed or unclothed.

They were making their slow parade up a sandy path through
the sagebrush to her burial in the brushy plot, loosely fenced
with barbed wire, which we knew as the "Indian Graveyard." I
see them high on the banking sand-hill behind our house, and
beyond them the abrupt two-thousand-foot lift of rimrock
which forms the great western lip of our Warner Valley. That
rim is always there, the table of lava flow at the top breaking
so abruptly, dropping through long scree slopes clustered with
juniper. As I grow older it is always at my back. The sun sets
there, summer and winter. I can turn and squint my eyes, and
see it.

From the flowering trees in the homesteader's orchard behind our house we watched that astonishing processional
through my father's binoculars, and then we ran out through
the brush beyond the garden, tasting the perfect spring morning and leaping along the small animal trails, filled with thrilling
purpose, and silent and urgent. We had to be closer.

The procession was just above us on the sandy trail when we
halted, those people paying us no mind but frightening us anyway, mourning men and women in their dark castaway clothing
and bright blankets and strange robes made of animal skins,
clutching at spring blossoms and sweeping at the air with thick

sheaves of willow in new leaf. It is now that I would like to hear the faint singsong of their chanting. I would like to think we studied them through the dancing waves of oncoming heat, and found in them the only models we had ever had for such primal ceremonies.

But this keeps becoming fiction. Ours was a rising class of agricultural people, new to that part of the world, too preoccupied with an endless ambition toward perfection in their work to care at all for any tradition of religion. No one in our immediate families had ever died, and no one ever would so far as we knew. None of us, in those days, had any interest in religion or ritual.

So I have this story of those shrouded people proceeding through my imagination. I feel them celebrating as that young girl entered into the ripe fruit of another paradise, lamenting the dole-food exigencies of their own lives, some of them likely thinking she was lucky to have escaped.

But I don't really have much idea what was going on behind the story I've made of that morning. It was as if those people were trailing along that sandy path toward tomorrow-morrow land themselves. Some of them, somewhere, are likely still alive.

In a book called *Shoshone*, the poet Ed Dorn tells of interviewing an ancient man and woman in a trailer house on the Duck Valley Reservation, a couple of hundred miles east of us but still deep in the high basin and range desert, along the border between Idaho and Nevada. They were both more than one hundred years old, and told Dorn they had never heard of white men until past the age of thirty. Which is possible.

It's easy to imagine those ancient people grinning in what looks to be a toothless old way in their aluminum-sided trailer house, with screens on the windows, on the Duck Valley Reservation. They must have understood the value of stories. Dorn says they demanded cartons of cigarettes before they allowed themselves to be photographed. The point is, they were willing to be part of any make-believe anybody could invent for them, willing to tell their stories and let us make of them what we could. But not for nothing. Stories are valuable precisely to the degree that they are for the moment useful in our ongoing task of finding coherency in the world, and those old people must have known that whatever story Dorn was imagining was worth at least the price of some smokes.

My father's catskinners bulldozed the shacktown Indian camp with its willow-roofed ramada into a pile of old posts and lumber, and burned it, after the last of those people had gone to wherever they went. Our children? In the fall of 1942, the same year that girl named Pearl was buried, they learned something about the emotional thrust of a warrior code as the news from the Zenith Trans-Oceanic radio was translated into singing in first-period music class, and they loaded that dead dog named Victory in a red wagon, and trailed him toward burial at the upper end of the garden. And I waved sweeps of willow over the ceremony while my cousin blew taps through his fist.

JAMES McCONKEY

Heroes Among the Barbarians

FROM SHENANDOAH

FIFTEEN YEARS AGO, an alienated fellow citizen, a Vietnam veteran living in a rusty trailer several miles from my Finger Lakes farmhouse, gave me, in return for my payment of his fine for shoplifting several cans of tuna fish from an Ithaca supermarket, a four-volume set of *The Documentary History of the State of New-York* that had belonged to his mother, now dead. The books were published in 1850–51, the documents arranged by E. B. O'Callaghan, M.D., under the direction of the Honorable Christopher Morgan, secretary of state. Here I found English translations of the papers relating to Frontenac's 1696 expedition into my region (a piece of land jutting into Cayuga Lake not far from my home is named for that French count and colonial governor in North America). His campaign was directed against the Iroquois; the translated accounts were written by young French aristocrats and others from the field, and presumably were sent back to the French court. "The Count is already advised," begins the opening paper, perhaps written to Frontenac during one of his sojourns to France,

by despatches at the departure of last year's ships, of the preparations for a considerable expedition against the Iroquois and principally against the Onnontagues which is the chief nation, where the councils of the other five are held, the most devoted to the English, and the most strenuously opposed to the negociations for peace of preceding years. It became of importance to crush them, and it appeared to many more advantageous to do so during the winter inasmuch as it was certain, said they, to find in the Village at least all the women and children who being destroyed or captured would draw down ruin on the warriors or oblige them to surrender to us.

How rational, how brutally cold, such calculations! I first read these accounts on a winter evening, sitting before a log fire in the living room of my Greek Revival farmhouse; the warmth of the fire, as well as the distance separating me from the struggle for colonial domination by European powers in the French and Indian Wars, permitted me the luxury of irony toward the scribes, those refined young men who doubly protected their sensibilities: first by giving to informed opinion the responsibility for the slaughter or enslavement of women and children while the warriors (I supposed) were off hunting, and then (as was obvious from other papers) by referring to all Indians, regardless of the side they supported, as savages or barbarians. The scribes found it painfully difficult to acknowledge that an Iroquois, even one whose behavior they admired, might possess the nobility or courage of a Frenchman, as the following account of the capture of an Onondaga fort reveals:

> The grain and the rest of the booty consisting of pots, guns, axes, stuffs, wampum belts, and some peltries were plundered by our Frenchmen and Savages. The destruction of the Indian corn was commenced the same day, and was continued the two following days. The grain was so forward that the stalks were very easily cut by the sword and sabre without the least fear that any could sprout again. Not a single head remained. The fields stretched from a league and a half to two leagues from the fort: The destruction was complete. A lame girl was found concealed under a tree, and her life was spared.
>
> An old man, also captured, did not experience the same fate. M. le Comte's intention, after he had interrogated him, was to spare his life on account of his great age, but the savages who had taken him and to whom he was given were so excited that it was not deemed prudent to dissuade them from the desire they felt to burn him. He had, no doubt, prepared himself during his long life to die with firmness, however cruel the tortures he should have to endure. Not the slightest complaint escaped his lips. On the contrary he exhorted those who tormented him to remember his death, so as to display the same courage when those of his nation would take vengeance on them; and when a savage, weary of his harangues, gave him some

cuts of a knife, "I thank thee," he cried, "but thou oughtst to complete my death by fire. Learn, French dogs! and ye, savages! their
allies — that ye are the dogs of dogs. Remember what ye ought to
do, when you will be in the same position as I am." Similar sentiments
will be found perhaps to flow rather from ferociousness than true
valour; but there are heroes among barbarians as well as among the
most polished nations, and what would be brutality in us may pass
for valour with an Iroquois.

When my wife and I bought our farmhouse, in 1962, we
could afford only thirty-eight acres of the surrounding fields
and woods. Though that might seem more than adequate for a
family with no intention of farming who had previously lived in
a series of apartments and houses on city lots, I wanted propri-
etorship of the entire one hundred and seventy-three acres that
had belonged to the farm almost from the time it had become
private property. During the American Revolution, the Iroquois
remained loyal to their British allies, and as a consequence the
Continental Congress sent a punitive force under the command
of General John Sullivan into our region, its swath of Indian
villages and fields so thorough that the Iroquois were routed
forever. After the War of 1812, the federal government divided
the region into parcels as payments for the service of soldiers in
that second struggle against the British (a conflict initiated by
our young nation chiefly from the desire to gain more land from
them as well as from Indians in the Northwest). Most of the
veterans sold their tracts to land speculators who sold them in
turn to farmers like Thomas Kelsey, the one who had built the
house that now was ours.

Through luck, a small equity, and a good lawyer, we managed, within a few years, to gain back everything that had belonged to Thomas Kelsey and those who had followed him. But
I was surprised to find that the rewritten mortgage didn't give
me the satisfaction I had been counting on. Maybe if I had
worked that land, as generations before me had, I would have
felt myself a valid inheritor of the soil; as it was, though, sim~~
ownership wasn't enough. Thinking that knowledge ~~
might give me rightful possession, I became a r~
archaeologist, searching for signs of earlier hum~
on our own and nearby land. Not much more than~

our front door, an Indian village once prospered; another, an additional mile down a little-used gravel road, is still commemorated by a deteriorating state historical marker (a relic itself, from the days in which families took leisurely weekend drives in their new Fords or Studebakers) as an "Immense Early Iroquois Site." The marker goes on to say that remnants of a circular palisade enclose a pond — neither of which I have ever been able to discern. The Indians found the clay here suitable for pottery; possibly this site was in use before the establishment of the Iroquois Confederacy. The one closer to our home is of later origin, and surely would have been a village like those destroyed by Frontenac and Sullivan. According to various books I have read, it would have contained a "long house" serving both as communal dwelling and metaphor for the family of nations, as well as a sacred oak whose roots were held to knit together the cosmos within which that larger family dwelt. Unlike one of my sons, who found not only arrowheads but a stone knife with its edge still sharp, I came across no Indian artifacts, but I did discover many signs of my white predecessors on our own and adjacent property.

The earliest map of my county that I have seen indicates that a sawmill once stood by the creek a half mile down the dirt road from our house, which also is located on the map; here the logs would have been taken to be transformed into the planks and joists and siding from which the house was constructed in 1831, as the fields were being cleared. At first, I thought the sawmill could have operated only intermittently, for, though the creek it depended upon for power never dries up, it is a silver serpent between rocky pools in the dry months, and only after a two-day spring or autumnal downpour can I hear it from our porch roaring like a distant freight train. While engaged in an early exploration, I was delighted to find, on the little hill above the creek, the eroded remnants of a previous road that curved away from the present one, and the rounded embankments of an earthen dam (the center of which has long since washed away) upon which the earlier road had been built. From the contours of the terrain, I could tell that the dam would have backed up enough water to make a millpond covering the quarter mile to the woods, part of which now belonged to my family.

Deep within those woods, the creek divides; up one of those branches I discovered the twin embankments of what must have been a much earlier dam — one less difficult to build, the ravine here being deep but narrow. The cart trail to it is a pair of mossy channels, discernible only on the slope; on the forested ground above the ravine, the trail has been erased by what appear to be shallow bomb craters in the loam. Actually, as I came to realize, these depressions are a consequence of the ripping out of huge tree-root systems, in a wholly natural process. The topsoil in this area of the woods is a thin covering over an almost impervious clay, causing the roots of the hard maples, oaks, pines, and beeches to spread out just beneath the surface; were there boulders for the roots to fasten around or into, as there are on the slopes of the ravine, the trees would still have managed to withstand high winds. Given the geological conditions, though, the trees most successful in outdistancing the others in the race to the sky are the ones to topple in the winter gales.

That portion of the ravine containing the old dam is almost at the center of a square mile whose borders are the country roads, and hence is as secluded a place as my neighborhood provides. Just downstream from the dam the ravine widens into a glen, with a little swamp at one end. Though not even a puckered hole remains to indicate a fruit cellar, a line of decaying stumps and a haphazard assortment of withered apple and cherry trees in that glen, no doubt volunteers from an original orchard, indicate that a settler had a cabin nearby. The spongy cart channels, the remains of the dam, the stumps and gnarled volunteers, seem part of the fading impress of memory upon the wrinkled surface of the mind of the *Terra Mater* worshiped by Indians; indeed, on the hill on the other side of the creek — that boundary of my family's domain — two long and curving mounds or banks of earth long ago were built for a purpose obscure enough to me that I decided at once those banks to be sacred Iroquoian earthworks.

It was within the glen itself that, on a spring afternoon twenty years ago, I experienced, with my wife, Jean, and our five-year-old son, Jimmy, a moment of such extraordinary happiness that it should have ended forever my search for whatever was required to give my mortgage its necessary spiritual seal. We had been marking, with strips of red cloth knotted around the still bare saplings and tree limbs, the best route for the trail we were planning to make through the woods that summer. Jean and I had left a note on the front door for our two older sons upon their return home by school bus, telling them that if they wished to find us they should follow those red strips into the woods. I sat with Jean and Jimmy, the three of us hidden in a bed of weeds in the glen, listening to the ever-closer cries of the older boys as they came across each new token of our whereabouts. As we heard not only their shouts but the nearby crackling of underbrush, Jimmy's eyes began to glow with the anticipation that Jean and I also felt; and, at the instant before they found us, I knew the kind of love for family that resonates against love for place, with family imposing value on land even as land, the Earth itself, grants value to the intertwining human lives.

To commemorate this moment, as well as to establish an observation post over the secret heart of a territory that now seemed to belong more firmly to me, I built (once Jimmy was old enough to be my assistant) a tree house with a porch overlooking the creek and its glen. We constructed this cozy home between two tall beeches — survivors of storm because their roots are anchored in boulders, survivors of saws and axes because beech (until the scarcity of other kinds of lumber raised its value) was considered a worthless wood. Though the Indians who might have built the mounds on the opposing slope would have considered *my* cosmos pretty small, they would have understood that a playhouse in the trees might serve as a metaphor for it.

That was what I thought while enjoying the work with my son high in the leafy beeches. One holds on to a poignant spiritual experience by commemorating it with a structure, but what happens when the fun of hammering is over? Jimmy wanted to build a second tree house in a neighboring maple, connecting the two with a suspension bridge, while I thought of dredging the swamp to make a forest pool for bathing. No, I wasn't quite satisfied with what I had, not yet. In later months and years, while sitting in a folding lawn chair on the porch of that tree house and looking toward the creek and the opposite slope, I thought that what I still lacked was the ownership of the property containing the mounds, significant with mystery as they were. The bearded proprietor of that and much other land lived a couple of miles away on the state highway, where he ran a junkyard. Maybe the desire he saw in my eyes when I inquired about the purchase of a strip of real estate adjoining my own raised its worth to him. Like me, he wasn't about to sell off a section of his property to anybody. No doubt he would have bought part or all of mine, had he been able to. I guess that, in our separate ways, both of us were land speculators, hoping for an eventual increase in the value of what we already had or hoped to gain.

On three or four occasions in my life, I have been strongly drawn to strangers, probably because they seem to me projections of the self I would like to be. Marcos (I never learned his last name) is one of this number. I met him only once, and for less than a couple of hours. The encounter took place nine years ago, while I was vacationing in Greece with Jean and Jimmy in the summer preceding that youngest son's entrance into college.

As part of our month-long exploration of Greece, we spent a week on Crete; it was here that we came across Marcos, the guard and caretaker at Gournia, whose partially excavated ruins (he told us) are the most "real," being the least tampered with, of all the Minoan sites on that island. We had rented a car at Heraklion to travel about Crete, and with it visited such major Minoan ruins as the palaces at Knossos, Phaistos, and Zakro, as well as the legendary birthplace of Zeus at the bottom of a cave that went like a mineshaft deep into a mountain. ("Baby Zeus here," our guide into the cave said, pointing to a damp ledge and cradling his arms to suggest a sleeping infant.) Perhaps because no attempts at reconstruction have been made, Gournia is not a popular tourist site; we came upon it by chance about 8 P.M. while on our return to our hotel at Agios Nikolaos after a day's swimming and sunbathing at the beach at Vai — Jean happened to glance at the stones rising up a hill a short distance from the highway, and, because it was too early for any Greek restaurateur to be serving dinner, we stopped.

Except for Marcos, wearing his guard's cap and sitting on a wall at the very top of the hill, the site was deserted. We wandered around, not knowing what to look for, until he approached us; he resembled, I thought, the white-bearded, older Hemingway.

"How do you like our little town?" he asked, as serious as he was polite; and then, without waiting for an answer, took us on an extended tour, showing us the altar — with its groove for the ax, the drain for the blood of sacrificed animals, and the stone for grain offerings to the gods — and the other ruins, explaining, as we walked, the function of each building, and how all of them had been constructed to withstand minor earth tremors. He had been guard and caretaker here for years, he said; he and his wife lived in a house hidden behind the hill, where they had raised their son and three daughters. One of the daughters now worked at the excavations at Zakro. In giving us the history of the digging at Gournia, Marcos used "we" and "our" whenever he spoke of the decisions and findings of the archaeologists, even those whose research preceded his arrival; until I recognized the degree of his interest and involvement, I thought his use of pronouns the consequence of an uncertain command of English. (A travel agent in Agios Nikolaos told us the next day we were lucky to have been shown the site by Marcos, for he knew far more about it than did any of the licensed guides: "Marcos not only knows, he cares," she said.)

He knew, certainly, and with a scope far greater than any study of my woods had provided me, of nature's ability to destroy both her own works and those of man: he spoke not only of the shiftings of the land that over the millennia had sent parts of Gournia under the sea, but of the 1956 quake he had lived through. At eleven o'clock one May morning, he heard the earth make a sound — "It went 'mmmm,' " he said — and that murmur was followed by intense tremors and a tidal wave. The fresh-water pool connected to the harbor at Agios Nikolaos turned yellow and then black, and all the fish died; for that deep pool, according to Marcos, was a window of the volcano on Santorini which, about 1500 b.c., exploded in the cataclysm that destroyed the Minoan civilization.

And then he spoke of the Eteo-Cretans, small people with

oval eyes (one happened to pass by on a bicycle as we talked), who originally came to Crete from Anatolia, the Asian part of modern Turkey, and who claim to be descendants of the Minoans. To most Greeks we had met, any mention of Turkey would have been followed by a reference to Turks as historic plunderers of Greece, savage aggressors upon another's soil, the conflict over Cyprus being the contemporary instance; but Marcos ignored the opportunity. "The Eteo-Cretans tell the rest of us on Crete, 'We brought you the Light,' because their ancestors came from the East," he said.

As he was answering our questions — and we had many, for no guide had so stimulated our desire for knowledge — a line of tiny flames, which for some time had been gradually moving up a distant hillside like a row of red-coated soldiers, burst at midpoint into a pillar of fire. "It is very dry," Marcos said. "It is sad that so many olive and almond trees will burn." But then a bell began to ring from his hidden house, and he smiled. "That is my wife calling me to dinner. We eat early, an American custom: all the archaeologists here have been Americans."

Not wanting him to leave quite yet, I asked him how many languages he spoke. "Seven altogether," he said. "In my house, I speak Greek, of course. Here on the site I speak mainly English, German, French, or Italian, and know them best. But I can speak Swedish and, less well, Japanese. I learn my languages from the people who visit Gournia; they don't know they are teaching me while I am teaching them." He paused to watch the conflagration. "Look, the flames are dying. The firefighters from Agios Nikolaos have arrived . . . Gournia is my home, but it is not mine more than it is another's. It belongs to all who have come to it, which is why I try so hard to learn their languages. It belongs to the Eteo-Cretans, though they don't come. It belongs to the past, which I also try to know, as best I can." He took off his cap to rub the sweat from his forehead, and then looked, for the longest moment, at that cap. "Sometimes," he said, "I wonder where I will go."

"You're near retirement?" I asked. "You must leave Gournia?"

"Oh, no, no, no," he said, vigorously shaking his head. "What I mean is, where will my soul go, when I die? But it is a foolish worry, for I don't think there is a heaven — certainly one divided into areas according to the different languages." The bell clanged sharply. "I am not a considerate husband," he said. "Even the bell becomes angry. Goodbye," and he shook hands with each of us.

I took out my wallet, to pay for our guided tour here as I had elsewhere, but Marcos backed away. "Our little Gournia has no proper tourist facilities, no kiosk for cigarettes and postcards and souvenirs," he said, with an ironic sweep of his hand that suggested his pleasure in the fact. "I want no gratuity," and, turning, he bounded up the hill like a man half his age, waved his cap to us from the crest, and vanished.

Like "hero," their epithet for the quasi-divine dead, "barbarian" is a word that comes from the ancient Greeks, who used it to differentiate others from themselves, all those others who didn't speak in the civilized and rational measures of the native tongue and whose words sounded in Athenian ears like the unintelligible "bar-bar." As word and political concept for freedom, "democracy" also comes from the Greeks, and they were thus the first to invoke its name in justification of questionable territorial claims or of simple domination ("hegemony" is yet another word we owe to them) over not only the barbarians but some who shared their own language.

During a recent rainsquall, a dead limb dropped upon the tree house I had built so many years ago, putting a hole in its Fiberglas roof. While walking the half mile through the woods to the tree house, carrying a roll of duct tape and a bucket of roof patch for the repairs, I found myself thinking about those etymologies in connection with the Iran-Contra affair, still very much in the news, the revelations of activities both legal and illegal frequently being justified, even glorified, by our highest officials through the use of such Greek terms; and with a PBS documentary I had watched some weeks earlier that dealt with the way the populace of any given nation will praise its own warriors while turning its enemies — its ideological opponents, its rivals for territory — into abstractions, the better to kill them.

A decade ago, I would not have thought of etymologies or sociopolitical matters while engaged in such a seemingly nos-

talgic task as repairing a tree house I had built with a young
son. I've heard it said that all of us, as we age, tend in our
thinking to replace the concrete or the real (the world of human
relationships) with intellectual or moral abstractions — not, of
course, to murder what has mattered most to us in the past, but
probably as part of our attempt to get a handle on life during
the period of our gradual disengagement from our identities as
parents and workers. In any event, while balancing on my toes
on the tree house's porch railing as I tried to reach a gouge in
the roof I couldn't see, my mind was less on my task or my
personal experiences or even on the twenty-foot drop to the
glen than it was on notions of possession and hegemony. Initially, my thoughts were on the Iroquois (whose Confederacy
became one of the models for our Constitution) and their view
of a natural cosmos too sacred to be owned by any nation or
mortal. Then I found myself comparing the long-ago destruction, in my neighborhood, of Iroquois villages and their inhabitants in conflicts for possession by larger, rival powers, with the
current ravaging of Nicaraguan villages by our Contras and
whatever "good" Indians could be coerced into the democratic
cause, the pillagers now being praised as freedom fighters or
the moral equivalent of our Founding Fathers for their efforts
to topple a legitimate, if Marxist-oriented, government in defense of our hegemony in Central America. Against all that, I
put what I could: a remembered account of the bravery of an
old Iroquois undergoing torture as well as my personal memory
of a caretaker on Crete, and his view of the ownership of some
ruins he loved.

As for me, I understood only then how fully I had lost —
along with certain other passions with which it no doubt was
connected, as it is throughout our animal kingdom — the territorial desire, which in mankind alone is typically justified as
spiritual or ideological in nature; and, as a corollary loss, the
belief in any possible relationship between owning and loving
or even knowing. But how I had yearned, at one time, to possess
more land, and then just a bit more — the latter so that I could
own a pair of nondescript mounds of unknown origin that my
imagination had made sacred!

These are the sort of abstract things a man of sixty-five is apt to think about or remember while in the process of acknowledging to himself that he is presently engaged in a pretty foolish and irresponsible activity — in my case, the going out without a partner into the woods to teeter upon a slippery railing in order to patch the roof of an observation post over territory I no longer would or even could claim as mine alone, except in a dry and legal sense.

Afterwards, though, sitting on the cot in the snug little room and looking upward at my patch, I was glad to see that I had successfully sealed the hole. Our children are grown and either away from home or too occupied with the business of life to spend a night in the tree house, but Jean and I still on occasion do; it is a good feeling to sit here before a candle in the forest dark, drinking wine until we get drowsy and a bit tipsy, and then to wake in the morning in the tree limbs, hearing the twitter of birds and the murmur of water over stones, and — if we are lucky — seeing a deer or two walk the trail they have made that goes between the pair of beeches (and so the deer pass directly beneath our feet!) before wending down the hill to the creek. The "No Trespassing" signs we once posted at the edge of the woods have long since disappeared, some of them torn down by hunters. Even if the tree house no longer marks the heart of a private cosmos, it still overlooks a spot that for personal reasons is as holy to us as any refuge can be, for adherents of no particular faith in these final decades of a century that still can't find the answer to history's persistent and ever-more-desperate question.

GEORGE GARRETT

My Two One-Eyed Coaches

FROM THE VIRGINIA QUARTERLY REVIEW

I CAME TO reading and writing more or less naturally. As, for example, you might come to swimming early and easily. Which, matter of fact, I did; learning to swim at about the same time I learned to walk. I can very well remember the name of the man (he was the swimming coach at Rollins College near Orlando, where I grew up during the Depression years) who took me as a toddler and threw me off the end of a dock into a deep lake where I had the existential choice of sinking or swimming. And chose to swim, thank you very much. His name was, I swear, Fleetwood Peoples. Could I forget a name like that? More to the point, could I invent that name? For reading we had all the riches of my father's one great extravagance — an overflowing library of some thousands of books. Books of all kinds in book-cases and piles and on tables everywhere in the house. Everybody read and read. And so did I. I remember reading Kipling and Stevenson and Dickens and Scott sooner than I was able to. And you could earn a quarter anytime for reading any one of any number of hard books that my father thought anybody and everybody ought to read.

A few words here about my father. For there were many things, more than the love of reading and writing and the gift of the ways and means to enjoy both, which he taught me by example and which at least precluded the possibility that most teachers could ever be as influential as he was. But athletic teaching was the one great thing that he could not do for me, and this, now that I am forced to think of it, must have led me to seek out coaches as teachers. He had been an athlete and, I am told on good authority, a very good one, playing ice hockey and rowing in school and college. And he had led, for a time, a rugged physical life, dropping out of M.I.T. to work in Utah as a copper miner. He wanted to be a mining engineer some day, but midway his money ran out; so he went to work in the mines out west; and he hoped to save enough to go back to school. He had a slightly mangled left hand, missing two full fingers, and bulked, powerful shoulder muscles and a sinewy eighteen-inch collar size to show for his hard years as a miner. He had his charter membership in the United Mine Workers framed and on the wall; and in the attic there was a dusty old metal suitcase full of one kind and another of ore samples he had dug out himself. But he was crippled, which was what he called it, not being ever an advocate of euphemisms. Lame was more like it, though; for he had a bad left leg and a limp left arm. Neither of which greatly impeded his apparent vigor and energy and, indeed, were scarcely noticeable unless he tried to hurry, to run, or to leap out of a chair. His lameness came in part from an injury and in part from a severe case of polio which had almost killed him. Now he could still swim — an awkward, but powerful sidestroke; and he learned to play a pretty good game of tennis, hobbling it is true, but overpowering many good players with a hard backhand and a truly devastating and deadly forehand. He also had a quality possessed by one of his tennis heroes, Bitsy Grant. Somehow or other, in spite of all awkwardness and all disability, he would manage to return almost anything hit at him. He was hard to ace and you couldn't often get by him. When I was a boy, he was a ranked player, fairly high on the ladder of the local tennis club.

By the time I was born, he was a prominent, controversial, daring, and, in fact, feared lawyer, Fearless himself. Together with his partner, he ran the Ku Klux Klan, then a real political power, completely out of Kissimmee, Florida. And lived to enjoy the victory. Took on the big railroads — the Atlantic Coast Line, the Florida East Coast, the Seaboard, and the Southern — and beat them again and again. Tried not one, but a number of cases before the U.S. Supreme Court. Yet, at the same time and always, gave hours and hours of time, without stint, to those who were once called downtrodden. Especially to Negroes who were more downtrodden than most anyone else. When black people came to see him at home, they came in by the front door and sat in the living room like anybody else. And nobody said a word about that or any of his other social eccentricities. Because most of them, white and black, respected him and depended on him. Those who did not respect him were afraid of him. With good reason. Once in my presence (for, by his practice, all the family were included in anything that happened at our house) a deputation of lawyers from the various railroads offered him a retainer, much more money than he earned, in effect *not* to try any more cases against them. He didn't wait or consider his reply, though he surprised all of us by being polite. He thanked them for their flattering interest. He allowed as how it was a generous and tempting proposition.

"I would be almost a rich man," he said. "But what would I do for *fun?*"

And, laughing, he more shooed them than showed them out the door.

Naturally the thing I thought I needed and wanted most of all was someone who could teach me hopping and skipping and jumping. Someone who could teach me how to run and how to throw a ball without the least hint of awkwardness. That was, I suppose, my kind of rebellion.

Besides all that, there were writers, real ones, on both sides of our family. On my mother's side was my grandfather's cousin. Harry Stillwell Edwards. Whom I never met or even saw, but about whom I heard all kinds of family stories. One that stuck like a stickaburr, and I liked a lot, was how Edwards, who was then postmaster of Macon, Georgia, won a $10,000 *Chicago Tribune* prize for his novel *Sons and Fathers*. Now that was a plenty of money, big money, even then when I heard about it. Child or not, I knew that much. But it was, as I would later learn, a huge sum, in the last years of the nineteenth century, to fall into the hands of a Southerner of most modest means. One who my grandfather always claimed owed him some modest sum of money. Didn't choose to repay it. Chose instead to rent a whole

Pullman car, fill it with family and friends, and take them all to New York City. Where the money was all spent in a week or ten days. Then back to Macon and life at the P.O.

Nobody ever had to teach me anything about the potential joys and pleasures of the writer's life.

On the other side was an aunt, Helen Garrett, who wrote some truly wonderful children's books and even won some national prizes for them, too. But she always wanted to be a novelist for adults, also; and somehow she never managed that.

Then there was Oliver H. P. Garrett, my father's surviving younger brother. (Another brother had been a mountain climber and a professional guide who vanished in a blizzard.) Oliver Garrett was a much decorated soldier from the Great War; newspaper reporter for the old *New York Sun* who had interviewed Al Capone and, yes, Adolf Hitler, too, twice. First time on the occasion of the 1923 *Putsch,* from which Oliver Garrett predicted Hitler would recover and most likely come to some kind of dangerous power and influence. Finally in the early 1930s, with the advent of sound movies, Oliver went out, at the same time as a number of other good newspaper reporters, to Hollywood to be a screenwriter. And was, I learned much later, a very good one. Wrote dozens of good and bad and indifferent films. I have in front of me a copy of *Time* for Aug. 4, 1930, which has a review of his movie *For the Defense* and a picture of him (p. 25) and describes him as "said to be Manhattan's best-informed reporter on police and criminal matters." Adding this little personal touch: "When Paramount began its policy of trying out newspapermen as scenario writers, he was one of the first reporters to become definitely successful in Hollywood. He is fond of driving a car fast, takes tennis lessons without noticeable improvement to his game, lives simply in a Beverly Hills bungalow with his son Peter, his wife Louise. Recently finding that he was going bald, he had all his hair cut off." He was one of the uncles, and a godfather, who sent extravagant and memorable presents at birthdays and Christmas; and once in a great while he would, suddenly and without any warning, appear for a visit. I recall a large man with a beret (first beret I had ever seen) and a long, yellow, open car, with shiny spoked wheels and chrome superchargers. And colorful short-sleeved shirts. And, usually, a beautiful wife or companion — there were several, of course. I remember that he could sing and play the guitar by a campfire on the beach. And most of what I know about World War I, I learned from him, from his stories of it.

Well, then. No lack of "role models" in those days. And early on, after I had announced that I intended to grow up and be a writer, I even managed to win a crucial approval. My grandfather on my mother's side, Colonel William Morrison Toomer, thoughtfully allowed that it would probably be all right for me to be a writer because: "It is as good a way to be poor as any other." He added that I should not expect him to lend me any money, not after what cousin Harry did with all that prize money without bothering to pay Papa (as we called him) back whatever he owed him. Anyway, what could he say to me with sincerity and conviction when one of his own five sons, my uncles, was a professional golfer and another was a dancer? He was a little worried about what I would find to write about, concerned about my sheltered life and lack of experience. I must have been at most twelve years old when we talked. Well, when the captain and only other person on board was knocked cold and unconscious by the boom, my grandfather, at six years of age, had managed to sail a large schooner with a full load of cut timber successfully into Charleston harbor. What he didn't stop to consider was that I already planned to use him and a lot of his experience, whenever possible, to make up for the absence of my own.

II

In school there were teachers, some very good ones as I remember, who were kind and were interested and who, I'm sure, tried to help me along at one time and another. But I was always what was politely known then as an "indifferent student," all the way through kindergarten, grammar school, junior high, and through most of my high school years. Those high school years were spent at the Sewanee Military Academy in Sewanee, Tennessee, that lonesome, isolated, beautiful, and changeless mountain village. The Academy, or S.M.A. as it was known then, is no longer with us. In those days it was part of the complex that formed the University of the South. Within the context of the South, military schools have always been considered more conventional than elsewhere and therefore they have not been wholly designed for and dominated by juvenile delinquents. True, we had our share of them, brutes sent off to be as far away from home as possible, to be, if possible, tamed and reformed without the stigma of reform school. And, as if to give these predators some function and sense of purpose, there was also a modest number of others, sissies in the persistent American term (remember Harry Truman calling Adlai Stevenson a "sissy"?); these latter sent off to be toughened, turned into "men." There were some of both types at Sewanee, but the majority were made of more ordinary stuff; though normalcy was tested to the quick by a schedule which began promptly, rain or shine, at 5:00 A.M. and ended with the bugling of Taps, and lights out at Quintard Barracks, at 10:00 P.M., and all the time between (it seemed) spent in the daze of a dead run, running, marching, gulping meals — formations, classes, inspections, military science and tactics, all of it controlled by constant bugle calls. At one point, really until recently, I knew, by heart and by hard knocks, every single American military bugle call — from First Call to Taps and including such things as Tattoo, Call to Quarters, Guard Mount, Mail Call, Church Call — the whole Battalion of Cadets marched, armed, flags flying and the band playing "Onward Christian Soldiers" to the chapel of the University of the South every Sunday morning regardless of creed or country of national origin. (There were no black students in white schools in the South in those days.) The handful of Catholics, Jews, and, in British terminology, Other Denominations were officially Episcopalians for the duration of their time at S.M.A. A rigorous schedule, then. And rigorous regulations, too. Only seniors, and then only as a special earned privilege, were allowed to possess radios, one per room. No point in it, anyway. There were about thirty minutes a day when the radio could be legally turned on. Everything you owned, folded in a precise manner and to the precise measured inch, had to fit neatly in a tin wall locker. No pennants, pictures, or decorations of any kind whatsoever. I remember that each cadet

was allowed to possess one snapshot. Which was to be taped in
its specific place and displayed on the wall locker. Some cadets
put up a photo of a parent or parents. Some put up a (fully and
decently clad; no bathing suits allowed) picture of a girlfriend.
There was quite a flap one year, as I recall, when a cadet, who
grew up and lived on a large Central Florida cattle ranch, taped
up a picture of his favorite cow. This caused a great deal of
controversy until it was finally decided, in favor of the cadet and
the cow, by the superintendent who was a brigadier general of
the United States Army, in fact on active duty at the time. As
were a fairly large percentage of the faculty. For these were the
years at the beginning of World War II. Military training was
very serious in any event and especially at a few places in the
country like Sewanee which still, in those days, could confer a
direct commission on their outstanding graduates. Others went
to West Point, V.M.I., the Citadel and, I swear to you, reported
back that they found these places relaxed and pleasant and
easygoing in comparison with S.M.A.

So there we were in the cool, fog-haunted, heavily timbered
mountains of East Tennessee. We were lean and if not thriving,
then enduring on skimpy institutional food, for which we had
to furnish our ration cards and tickets like everybody else.
There were moments in those days when most of us would have
cheerfully fought to the death, or mighty close to it, for the sake
of a hamburger or a piece of beefsteak. Still, the University had
a first-class dairy herd (as did so many Southern schools and
colleges in the Depression and wartime); and, in the absence of
any other students except ourselves, a small V-12 Navy detach-
ment, and a few 4F's and discharged casualties, we had all the
milk and butter and cheese we could manage. Treats — a Coca-
Cola, an ice cream cone — were available at the University
Store, the "Soupy Store," about half a mile or so from our barracks and which we were allowed to visit, providing you were
not restricted to barracks for demerits or any other disciplinary
or academic reason, on Sunday afternoons, following noon dinner and prior to Parade formation, roughly from 1:30 to 3:30
P.M. Most of that time would be spent in line at the counter,
listening to Jo Stafford records (over and over again, "Long Ago
and Far Away," tunes like that on the handsome and primitive

Seberg machine, or was it an early Wurlitzer?), hoping against hope to get served in time to drink or eat whatever it was that was available and which you could afford before the sound of the bugle blowing First Call for Parade sent everyone at a frantic, stomach-sloshing, breathless run back to barracks, to grab our rifles, our beautiful 1903–A3 Springfield rifles, and fall in for Parade . . .

Girls? Odd you should ask. There were a few on the Mountain, as I recall, altogether untouchable and, of course, utterably desirable. Otherwise there were formal dances once or twice a year. Some nice girls from some nice schools in Chattanooga and Nashville might be brought in by bus. Spic and span, barbered, scrubbed and brushed, shined and polished, we timidly met them at the gym and tried to fill out our dance cards (yes!) before the music began to play. I remember half-lights and the scattered reflections of a rotating ceiling globe. How the whole gym seemed to seethe with the exotic odors of powder and perfumes. I think the little band must have played "Body and Soul" over and over again. I remember a lot of standing and watching from the sidelines. There were some wise cadets, old timers, who, given the choice, chose not to attend the dance. Went to the library instead. Or enjoyed the odd peace and quiet of an almost empty barracks. Without temptation and maybe without regret.

III

Athletics were everything. A way to escape the drudgery (and sometimes, for new cadets and younger ones, the danger) of the afternoons in the barracks or study hall. To be on a team meant an excused absence from some mundane and onerous chores. Best of all, it allowed for occasional forays off the Mountain. A trip to play another school. Where there might be a chance to get a candy bar and a Coke, a Grapette and a Moonpie, at a bus stop or country store. A chance to see girls, maybe even, with luck, to speak to one. A chance in the "contact" sports to move beyond simple competition and to heap some measure of fury and frustration upon some stranger who was, most likely, seeking to do exactly the same thing to you.

Whom did we play against? It was, of course, the same set of schools and places in all sports. But when I try to summon it up, I think of team sports. Of football most of all. It seems to me we played all the time, almost as much as we practiced. I suspect now that some of the games didn't really count. Were merely game scrimmages. Who knows? I do know that it was a long season, beginning in late summer and ending in boredom and bone weariness sometime after Thanksgiving. We sometimes played a couple of games in the same week. On the one hand we played against East Tennessee high schools — Tullahoma, Murfreesboro, Lynchberg, etc., together with tiny country schools whose names I've long since forgotten. On the other we played against the other military schools: Baylor and McCallie in Chattanooga, both of which were bigger and generally better than we were, but for whom we had sneering contempt because their military lifestyle was casual (in our view), easygoing; Columbia Military Academy, which was, we believed, *all* athletics with no academics worth mentioning to interfere with sports, and where the players were bigger and more numerous than anywhere else; Tennessee Military Institute, which appeared to be *really* a reform school of some kind, wire fence around it, catwalks and search lights and shabby khaki uniforms. And always our Episcopal nieghbor, St. Andrews, with its monks and its poor boys who grew their own food. When we played them, we had to play barefooted because they had no football shoes. They had a considerable advantage, tougher feet from playing barefoot all the time.

If this was Real Life, if this was all the world that mattered and we were in it, then coaches were urgently important to us all. Trouble was that most of them didn't *teach* anything. They exhorted and denounced, praised and blamed, honored and ridiculed, but they seldom had any practical advice or real instruction for us. Those who (somehow) already knew what to do were all right. And there were always a few athletes with great natural ability at this or that who figured out what to do by trial and error, intuition and inspiration. The rest of us ran about in shrill gangs, packs, and herds, desperately trying to make the elaborate diagrams of the coaches in our playbooks come to represent something real on the ground. The chaos of circles and X's on paper bore very little resemblance to anything happening in fact and particular. Nobody on either team ever seemed to be where he was supposed to be. But only the most cynical and worldly-wise among us concluded that the fault wasn't ours. There was a great deal of dust and confusion on the playing field. Missed assignments, on both sides, were almost the rule rather than the exception. Luck, pure dumb luck, became a much more crucial factor in every game. So did tricks and trickery. Fake substitution plays were common. Fake punts and field goals were frequent. The old Statue of Liberty Play was always worth a try. I seem to recall rehearsing an elaborate fake fumble play. All this only added to the general confusion and to the unpredictability of the games. Upsets were so commonplace they could hardly be called upsets. With so many variable and changing factors, even a state-of-the-art computer would be hard pressed to come up with any good clear patterns of probability.

. . . Well, now, you are surely thinking. All of that must have been wonderful training for a life in the American literary world: hard knocks, massive confusion, fake punts, fake passes and fake field goals, ceaseless trickery and treachery; and all of it depending on luck, on pure dumb luck . . .

And, once in a while, on coaching.

The coach who first reached me, taught me anything above and beyond the most basic fundamentals of the game, was Lieutenant Towles. I think. That is the name I remember. And the nickname, used by everyone except in front of himself — "Lou-Two." Let us call him that, since that is what he was called.

Lou-Two was young and tall and lean, a splendid physical specimen. Except that he had somewhere lost an eye. Had one glass eye. And it was that which kept him out of the war. I picture him now not in uniform but in a neat sweat suit, long-legged and moving about the playing field in a sort of a lope, which was either imitated from or maybe borrowed by his two loping boxers, who always seemed to be at his heels. He was quick and just a little bit awkward, this latter I think because of being one-eyed. Some of the guys thought he was funny.

It was from Lou-Two that I began to learn some of the things which made a big difference in my life. I do not know if it was his intention to teach the things I learned. We sometimes learn what we want to quite beyond the intentions of pedagogy. (As Theodore Roethke put it — we learn by going where we have to go.) His concern and interest at that time was teaching athletic skill. And that coincided with my interests. I had not the faintest notion that I might be learning things which would be transferable and could later be transformed into something altogether different — the art of writing. Athletic skill would grow, then fade later on with injuries, age, and change of interests. But attitudes and habits, together with something deeper than either, *rituals* really, would become so ingrained as to be part of my being.

At any rate I followed him into whatever sports he coached, season by season. He was one of several football coaches, an assistant; but he was head coach of boxing in winter and track in springtime. I had no particular natural ability at either of these sports. Swimming, which came easily, was my best sport. But I gave it up. To be coached by Lou-Two. I suppose I followed him because he had taken an interest in me and had encouraged me at a time when I was very eager but very easily discouraged.

His interest in and encouragement of myself and others, scrubs in life as well as athletics, now astonish me more than they did then. By and large coaches have their hands full just teaching and encouraging the few pupils who are already demonstrably talented and essential to the success of any given team. Which is why the great art or craft of contemporary coaching is more a matter of careful and clever *recruiting* than anything else. They assemble teams of the gifted and experienced, and they teach refinements only. Of course, this is one reason why, when you watch many college football games today, you will see that the main and often crucial mistakes are made in matters of fundamentals — missed blocks and tackles, dropped passes and fumbles.

But in a little school like S.M.A., where teams were so often overmatched, it was probably good sense to try to make something out of the scrubs. They could, after all, make a difference as, inevitably, the basic team and its best backup players were worn down by attrition during the long season.

I am still speaking of football. Which was my chief goal. Like every other red-blooded Southern boy. It never occurred to me, then, to doubt that playing football was the most important thing a young man could ever do with himself. Except, maybe, to get laid or to go to the war. From track I learned to run and then to run faster and faster. From boxing's hard school I learned to cultivate a certain kind of aggressiveness, out of self-defense if nothing else. And I experienced a sharper, keener sense of contact. It soon dawned on me that for the most part and most of the time football was neither as tiring nor as dangerous as boxing. From boxing I began to learn to take punishment better; to know that it was coming; to bear it. But at the same time I was learning, with the pleasure of instant and palpable results, to dish out punishment. Learned by doing, by giving and taking, that other, even better athletes did not enjoy receiving punishment any more than I did. I learned then that there was at least this much equality and that if I went after my opponents, quickly, there were times when I could take command.

Shall I, may I, say a word or two about pride and skill? Please understand that I am now, for better or worse, possessed by precious few illusions. I had even fewer at the age of fifteen or sixteen. I was never a very good athlete. But, on the other hand, I have been there and I have known the ups and downs, the feel of it all from head to toe. Which is (I do believe) mostly much the same for all who have been there — regardless of their share of good luck or their degree of skill. I have won and lost races on hot cinder tracks and in cool swimming pools. In the ring I have won and lost decisions, knocked out other young men and, myself, have been beaten to the dazed, vague, bloody, and bruised edges of consciousness. Never knocked out (yet) I'm here to tell you, though. I have known those times when my mouth and jaws were too swollen to open up for a teaspoon and when my bruised hands and sprained thumbs failed me at the simple chores of buttons and shoelaces. In football, in high school and college, I have experienced a few moments I can honorably remember. I have run the ball and passed the ball. I have caught passes and punts. Once upon a time, and once only, I ran back a kickoff for a grand total of twelve yards. And one wonderful afternoon I managed somehow to block and generally manhandle an All-American tackle. Who must have been just as astonished as I was when he kept on finding himself sitting firmly on his altogether ample ass. Oh sure, there are booboos and stupidities which will still wake me up in the middle of the night wincing with shame.

But I guess now I am grateful for all of it, if only because it taught me early and forever that most *literary* accounts of athletic events and adventures, from Hemingway to Mailer and through McGuane, are bullshit.

But from Lou-Two I was also learning other things which would prove useful. From him, first of all, I learned conditioning. Conditioning, then as now, only more so then, was more a mystery, more a matter of craft and secrets, than any kind of science. Faith and hope, I venture, had as much to do with being in shape as anything else. The same thing was true of the repair and healing of injuries in those days before there was anything called "Sports Medicine." Except for broken bones, the care of injuries was in the hands of trainers. Ours was the celebrated trainer of the University of the South, who, for the duration, had no teams to care for. He was an ancient black man named Willie Six. It, too, was a mostly nonverbal experience. You went to his den at the University gym. He did things with heat and cold, with strong-scented and mysterious ointments and salves of his own making and with deft massage. It, too, was a vaguely religious experience. Sometimes, made whole as much by faith as treatment, I imagine, those who had hobbled in left cured and ready to play again.

Conditioning was mysterious like that. What you learned was that if you did certain things (and did without certain things) and performed certain rituals, your body would answer you by tiring more slowly and by recovering much more quickly from weariness, wear and tear. You learned to know and to listen to your body. Since all this was aimed toward the performance of a particular sport, its focus was less narcissistic than conditioning for its own sake or to improve appearance or health. The practical results of being in good shape showed up in performance. That, in itself, was a lesson which would carry over — that you could establish a relationship with the self of the body and could train it and teach it to work for you. And that you need not, indeed should not be crazy or tyrannical in this matter. If you overtrained or mistreated your body, you lost ground.

What was happening, even during this period of concentration upon the body, was a kind of self-transcendence. In which, gradually and inexorably, the body, one's own, became in part something separate and distinct, an apparatus, a sensory instrument designed to do things and to feel things and to accomplish certain chores. It need not be a thing of beauty. It need only be able to perform, to the extent of its own learned limits, specific tasks. Inevitably one was, ideally, observing the body-self in action from a different angle and vantage point. An early lesson in point of view.

The larger value of this learning experience, however, was more complex. It was a matter of learning one kind of concentration, of a kind which would be very useful to an artist. Concentrating on preparation, one could not afford to waste either time or energy worrying about anything beyond that. You were too busy preparing to worry about the game (or match or meet) until its moment arrived. And when that happened, it was pointless to worry about anything else, past or future, except the present experience. You learned to concentrate wholly on the moment at hand and to abandon yourself completely to it.

And *that* made some sense out of all the chaos and confusion. Wholly given over to the present, you likewise limited focus to your own small space. To what you had to do. You became, for yourself, a single lamp burning in a dark house. You learned to live in that light and space with only the most minimal regard for or awareness of all the rest of it, going on all around you. You learned to play your part, early or late the same, and without regard for the score. Winning or losing didn't matter much.

The athletic advantages of this knowledge and concentration, particularly for an athlete who was making up for the absence of great natural skill, were considerable. Concentration gave you an edge and advantage over many of your opponents, even your betters, who could not isolate themselves to that degree. For example, in football if they were ahead (or behind) by several touchdowns, if the game itself seemed to have been settled, they tended to slack off, to ease off a little, certainly to relax their own concentration. It was then that your own unwavering concentration and your own indifference to the larger point of view paid off. At the very least you could deal out surprise and discomfort to your opponents.

But it was more than that. Do you see? The ritual of physical concentration, of acute engagement in a small space while disregarding all the clamor and demands of the larger world, was the best possible lesson in precisely the kind of selfish intensity needed to create and to finish a poem, a story, or a novel. This alone mattered while all the world going on, with and without you, did not.

I was learning first in muscle, blood, and bone, not from literature and not from teachers of literature or the arts or the natural sciences, but from coaches, in particular this one coach who paid me enough attention to influence me to teach some things to myself. I was learning about art and life through the abstraction of athletics in much the same way that a soldier is, to an extent, prepared for war by endless parade ground drill. His body must learn to be a soldier before heart, mind, and spirit can.

Lou-Two, perhaps without realizing or intending it, initiated me. But it would be another man, a better athlete and a better coach, who would teach me most and point me toward the art and craft I have given my grown-up life to. I could not have gained or learned anything from the second man, the next coach and teacher, if I had not just come under the benign if shadowy influence of the first man.

A final track season, graduation; and I went my way, having so much by then absorbed what he had to teach that I took it all for granted without any special gratitude toward Lieutenant Towles or any special memory of him until now. I remember the two boxer dogs first. I fill in the man loping between them.

IV

The next man had a certain fame. He was Joseph Brown at Princeton University.

With Joe Brown I now encountered an artist, a sculptor, and

a coach who had once been a great athlete. Never defeated as a professional fighter. And *just* missed being a world champion. Missed because he lost an eye in an accident while training for a championship fight. As a coach, he had much to teach me. Or, better, there was so much to learn from him. For one thing, he was able to show me that there were things, particularly habits derived not from poor coaching but from experience, which it was already too late to unlearn. Things I would have to live with. There were things, beginning with my basic stance as a fighter, which were "wrong" and less than wholly efficient and effective. I fought out of a kind of sideways stance which allowed for a good sharp left jab and even a left hook and was an effective defensive stance, but limited the use of my right hand except in very close. He taught me how to analyze that stance (and my other habits) and how, rather than discarding it and disregarding all the experience which had gone into forming it, to modify it slightly so as to take best advantage of its strengths and at the same time to compensate for its more obvious weaknesses. Compensation, that's what he showed me first. How to compensate for inherent physical defect or bad habits.

What was happening, then, was the introduction of mind, of *thinking,* into a process which had been, until then, all intuition and inspiration, all ritual and mystery. He did not seek to eliminate these things, but he added another dimension to them.

From Joe Brown, both by teaching and example (he was still, close up, the best fighter I had ever seen), I began to learn the habits of professionalism, the kind of professionalism which would be demanded of me as an artist. Never mind "good" artist or "bad" artist. I even learned, through the habits of this kind of professionalism and the experience of trying and testing myself and my habits against others who also knew what they were doing, that nobody else, except maybe a critic-coach like Joe Brown who knew that was happening at all levels of his being, could honestly judge and evaluate your performance. I learned to recognize that the audience, even the more or less knowledgeable audience, never really knew what was going on. Nor should they be expected to.

I learned that in the end you alone can know and judge your own performance, that finally even the one wonderful coach-critic is expendable. He can solve a practical problem for you, problems of craft; but he cannot and should not meddle with the mystery of it.

I learned something, then, about brotherhood, the brotherhood of fighters. People went into this brutal and often self-destructive activity for a rich variety of motivations, most of them bitterly antisocial and some verging on the psychotic. Most of the fighters I knew of were wounded people who felt a deep, powerful urge to wound others at real risk to themselves. In the beginning . . . What happened was that in almost every case, there was so much self-discipline required and craft involved, so much else besides one's original motivations to concentrate on, that these motivations became at least cloudy and vague and were often finally forgotten. Many good and experienced fighters become gentle and kind people. Maybe not "good" people. But they do have the habit of leaving all their fight in the ring. And even there, in the ring, it is dangerous to invoke too much anger. It can be a stimulant but is very expensive of energy. It is impractical to get mad most of the time.

In a sense this was not good training for the literary world. For the good camaraderie of good athletes is not an adequate preparation for the small-minded, mean-spirited, selfish, and ruthless competitiveness of most of the writers and literary types (not all, thank God) I have enountered. They do things which any self-respecting jock would be ashamed of. They treat each other as no fighter would ever dare to.

And all the time they talk about . . . *Art*. With a capital A. With a kind of public and mindless piety and genuflection.

Ever since my youth, since the days of first the shadowy Lieutenant Towles and then the unforgettable Joe Brown, I have been deeply suspicious of pious amateurs.

From Joe Brown I also learned something of the permissible vanity of the professional. Joe had long since outgrown any of the false and foolish pride of the athlete. But he knew himself well enough to know that some pride was earned and all right. Once in a great while he would go to the fights in New York at Madison Square Garden or St. Nick's. If he went, he would be recognized, starting in the lobby with the old guys walking on their heels who sold programs. And the ushers. Before the main fight he would be introduced from the ring. He liked that moment even when it embarrassed him. It was a homecoming. He wrote a fine short story about it called "And You Hear Your Name."

Joe Brown was an artist, and he was as articulate about his art as he was about his sport. He could talk about it, though always simply and plainly. For those who were tuned in to his kind of talk it was valuable. R. P. Blackmur, for example, used to discuss literary matters and matters of aesthetics with Joe. It was from Joe, Blackmur said, that he got one of his best known titles — *Language As Gesture.* Which was a reversal of something I, myself, had heard Joe say: in sculpture gesture was his language. Many of his athletes also went, one night a week, to his sculpture class. It was, in those days before coeducation came to Princeton, the only place you could be sure to see a naked woman on the campus. A powerful inducement. We managed to learn a little about modeling clay and about the craft of hand and eye. For most of us what we learned was that we could never ever be sculptors even if we wanted to. But, hand and eye, we learned some things that would carry over, despite a lack of natural talent.

Some of the intellectual lessons Joe Brown taught were brutally simple. In boxing, for example, he was fond of reminding his guys that to win in boxing you had to hit the other guy. To hit the other guy you had to move in close enough for him to hit you. No other way. One of the immutable lessons of boxing was that there was no free lunch. To succeed you had to be at risk. You had to choose to be at risk. That choice was the chief act of will and courage. After that you might win or lose, on the basis of luck or skill, but the choice itself was all that mattered.

Or a matter of sculpture. Teaching something of the same sort of lesson. At one stage Joe was making a lot of interesting pieces for children's playgrounds. This in response to some Swedish things which were being put up in New Jersey and which, in Joe's view, while aesthetically interesting, had nothing special to do with *play.* He said a piece for a playground should be something you could play on and with. One of his pieces, I remember, was a kind of an abstract whale shape. High "tail" in the air and a slide from the "tail," through the inside of the

"body" and out of the "mouth." It was tricky to get to the top of
the "tail." There was no one and easy way to climb there. Many
different ways as possibilities. Some of them a *little* bit risky. You
could fall down. So? You can fall out of a tree, too, or off a
fence. Once at the top of the "tail" there was the wonderful,
steep S-shaped slide waiting. Only right in the middle it leveled
off. The experience of the slide was briefly interrupted.

Why?

"I want these kids to learn the truth," he said. "You can have
a great slide, a great experience. But to do it all the way you've
got to get up off your ass and contribute at least one or two
steps of your own."

My first lesson in . . . *meaning in Art.*

As I am thinking about these things so much has changed.
My father has been dead for many years. Lieutenant Towles has
disappeared from my life. I have no idea where he may be, even
if he is alive or dead. And as I write this, I have news that Joe
Brown died recently in Princeton. Thirty-five years and more
have passed since he was my coach and teacher. And likewise
the half-child, myself, who came to him to try to learn and to
improve his boxing skills, is long gone also, even though, by
being alive, I can still carry the memory of him and thus, also,
of Joe Brown. I can summon up the sweat and stink of that
gym. Pure joy of it when things went well. Pain when they did
not.

Ironically, I tend to dismiss most comparisons of athletics to
art and to "the creative process." But only because, I think, so
much that is claimed for both is untrue. But I have come to
believe—indeed I have to believe it insofar as I believe in the
validity and efficacy of art—that what comes to us first and
foremost through the body, as a sensuous affective experience,
is taken and transformed by mind and self into a thing of the
spirit. Which is only to say that what the body learns and is
taught is of enormous significance — at least until the last light
of the body fails.

BERNARD COOPER

Beacons Burning Down

FROM THE GEORGIA REVIEW

By Any Other Name

"Is this Mr. Felix Ott?"

"Yes, this is Felix."

"Greetings! This is the (mumble, mumble) radio program calling. If you can answer today's quiz question correctly, you will be the winner of a two-hundred-dollar cash prize!"

"How many hundred?"

"Now listen closely: If Elvis Presley's nickname is Elvis the Pelvis, Mr. Ott, what — for the cash — is the nickname of his brother, Enis?"

A long pause in which our hearts were pounding and our breath held back, and then we would start to sputter and laugh, three kids with flushed faces crowded around the earpiece of the phone. Not one of our intended victims was fool enough to venture a guess. Not Birdie Turley, Gilliam Ong, Venus Deitz, Lafayette Lipshitz, Panos Injijikian, Porntip Yang, or Buster Hummer — names we picked from the phonebook after great deliberation, after gales of hysteria which left us limp on the sea-green carpet. We'd base our choices on assonance, or on the alliteration some parents had bestowed, a mellifluous gift to their offspring which made us roll our eyes. More poets than pranksters, we thrilled to language in its abstract conditions, were amazed by the ways a name could bluster and make us as giddy as the pop tunes of the time: *My boy lollipop, he makes my heart go giddy-up* and *Da do ron ron ron, da do ron ron.*

But our most significant discoveries, extracted from alphabetical columns, were the names in which a sentence was encoded: Iva Wright, Hugo First, Pat A. Head, R. U. Standing. To find them took hours of textual analysis, and often, after much vetoing and page turning, we were so embroiled in the nonsense of sound (our minds balked, our eyes blurred) that it was hard to tell if those flukes of unintended syntax were the genuine article or the product of imagination. Were we trying to will meaning into being? Jeffrey, the youngest among us, would become nearly delirious from our endeavor. Entranced by any old ordinary word, he'd begin to say it over and over. Mary, his sister, once let out an ear-splitting scream because, after a flurry of our crank calls, Jeffrey sat in a corner incessantly chanting "cheese."

It would be five years before I heard Shakespeare's comment on the name for a rose, but had I heard it then, I'm afraid I'd have disagreed. For example, wasn't the smell of Limburger somehow linked to its foul sound? Weren't the forget-me-nots blooming on Mary's blouse made softer and bluer by their designation? Weren't names designed to enhance the matter to which they referred?

My own name was problematic. While Jeff and Mary could go to the five-and-dime and find cups and wallets bearing their names — evidence that they belonged to a vast and accepted subset of humanity — Bernard was always out of the question, however much I'd spin the squeaking racks and dig in the bins with hope: Andy, Art, Bill, Bobby, Charles. Even my mother had trouble with my name; calling me home at dusk, she'd stand in the doorway and shout the names of my older brothers — Richard, Robert, Ronald! — before she remembered mine. A recurring dream I have involves just this childhood scene, but in the dream my mother continues bellowing names, and soon her friends and relatives, the postman and the grocer, her hairdresser and podiatrist — *everyone* — converges on the house, her voice drawing life from the dream's dark corners.

In an attempt to make up for her habitual oversight, my mother once showed me the page in *What to Name the Baby* that explained the derivation of Bernard. Far from the bearish obstinance and earthiness the name was said to imply, it held for

me the connotations of myopia, introversion, and bookishness
that my destiny has borne out. But more important, I was astonished that the mothers of America were so unmoved by their
own sense of cadence that they had to rely on a book. In those
days I had little inclination toward being a parent, yet I imagined playing with my progeny and wondered what I'd call them.
Soon I came up with Praline for a girl (this came to me one
night during dessert) and Conch for a boy (a visit to Marine
Land). Perhaps it was the common ring of my brothers' names
that led them to dub their daughters Dalisa, Cambria, and Jor-
dana, names as strange as orchids at the florist's — throats on
fire with purple and pink as though they're about to announce
what they are: Cymbidium, Miltonia, Catalaya.

Running the gamut from airplane pilot to zoologist, the ambitions of my playmates were subject to daily fluctuations. For
almost a year, I wanted to be the man who got to name the paint
chips at Bromley's Hardware. I'd cram them in my pockets,
sneak them home, fan them open, contemplate. Fiesta Magenta,
Magma Red, Sunstroke, Topaz, Obsidian, Smoke. Surely the
advent of metallic and fluorescent paint would increase the demand for persons with my calling. I pictured myself with a huge
palette, mixing new additions to the language of chromatics.
Before me loomed a long good life — Carrot Orange, Eden
Green — of indulgence in the spectrum.

Unfortunately, my schoolwork suffered as a result of my passion for nomenclature. In biology, for instance, instead of concentrating on the position and function of the bones in the
skeletal system, I imagined Ulna, Tibia, and Fibula as visitors
from outer space; during lengthy fantasies, I'd try to teach them
English. Astronomy, on the other hand, with its vocabulary of
umbra, penumbra, corona, and nova, was inspiration for the
names of colors but shed little light on my place among the
planets. Reading was the only subject at which I excelled —
especially poetry, a treasure-trove of rhyme from which one
melodramatic teacher, her arms akimbo, her glasses awry,
would unearth a jewel like "Gitche Gumee."

One trick I learned in the sixth grade (and which tempts me
to this day) was to yell out the names of passengers while traveling through a tunnel. There was something elegiac in hearing

the names of friends I loved — Mary *ary ary*, Jeff *eff eff* — re-
bounding against the underground walls, buffeted by oncoming
traffic, fading with every echo. And then we'd be restored to the
light and the road, and the sky was robin's-egg blue, and a
cringing parent behind the wheel would admonish me by name,
two syllables rippling out on the surface of time.

The Heralds

Religion meant people with shrouded heads mumbling in
vaulted chambers. I sank when I saw a deacon's censer wafting
incense into the world like the tailpipe of a hot rod. Or rabbis
who davened like wind-up toys. Or meditating Buddhist monks
as still as my rock collection. Once, *Life* magazine featured "The
Great Cathedrals of Europe," and what I saw, or tasted rather,
after turning the pages and licking my index finger, was the
bitterness of ink, a flavor that matched the photographs of
expressionless death masks, prostrate statues, and apothecary
jars (more ornate than our pharmacist's) in which slept slivers
of the saints.

You don't really expect me to believe that Joseph Smith translated the Book of Mormon by picking up a Roman soldier's gold
breastplate he found in the forest and peering through the
holes where the nipples would have been, do you? Think about
it. Either Mr. Smith's eyes would have to be very far apart, or
the soldier who fortuitously left his armor had a chest cavity the
size of the average cranium. I mean, I wish it were true. I wish
I could find it and spend the afternoon reading translations of
the *Inferno* and the *Kama Sutra* through a beautiful amber mask.
But I was exempted from miracles way back in kindergarten
when I watched *Romper Room* on television and the hostess, Miss
Mary, with her high, sibylline voice, would give a long look into
the camera and claim to see right through the cathode tube to
her flock of amazed and devoted children. "There's Judy," she'd
intone, or "I spy David and Suzy and Frank." But it never occurred to her that there was a child out there with a name as
strange as "Bernard," so I knew she was a charlatan.

Look, I like cherubim as much as the next guy. They've got
good intentions and tiny genitalia. They must smell and feel like

lilac sachets. My life, however, is busy and baroque without their intervention. Sure, I've got work enough for a legion of angels: insurmountable personal fears, a vendetta against international evil, friends to raise from the dead. Why, just yesterday I was lamenting all these things when I saw a stream of black birds soaring over the city. Endless they were, like winged pieces of letters, like a moving sign in Times Square, heraldic and quick and colossal. Except that a message never appeared. Their transmigration riddled the sky.

The Miracle Chicken (Glimpses into My Father's Scrapbook)

On 30 March 1940, the day he was notified that he had passed the California State Bar examination, my father began a scrapbook with two items: a letter requesting a seven-dollar fee that entitled him to become a legitimate attorney, and a solicitation from a wholesaler of leatherbound law books. After that come a hundred buckled newspaper clippings that betray his taste for handling unorthodox cases.

One article is emblazoned with the headline "CASE OF THE BAKING NEWLYWED," about Mrs. Beverly Cleveland, a woman who claimed her husband, Jake, kept her cooking from dawn to dusk during the first ten days of marriage — waffles, casseroles, pies from scratch — so that no time was left for affection. But my father subpoenaed witnesses who testified under oath that Jake Cleveland's appetite was notoriously meager. "Never ate what *I* slaved to make," whispered his first wife under her breath. "Just look at the guy — he's built like a broom," said Mr. Luft of the Chow Now lunch truck. In his final argument, my father spoke of his "kissless client" whose "connubial crisis" was exacerbated during a ten-day "hellmoon." Not only was there an annulment, but my father convinced the court to fine the former Mrs. Cleveland fifty dollars in punitive damages for wasting groceries in a ploy to avoid her wifely obligation.

Profiting from the frequency of tumultuous marriages, my father moved his office into wood-paneled quarters on the fifth floor of the elegant Biscott Building. On his door was stenciled "Edward S. Cooper" in large gold letters. "Attorney at Law" was relegated to a smaller, less illustrious print. On the sill behind his desk, he placed a brass statuette of justice: her toga cleaved her figure as though she were walking against the wind; her scales, loaded with candy, bobbed in the slightest breeze.

The office windows overlooked a small park frequented at noon by secretaries — Caucasian, Asian, Hispanic, Black — wearing cat-eye glasses held in place by chains. Some of them met my father for assignations over the years in a dark downtown hotel. His lust for the opposite sex (in all their ethnic variety), his clandestine romances, his cultivation of a subterfuge my mother didn't suspect until she was in her sixties — these made him all the more adept at drumming up the deceits that made his divorce trials so bathetic they became genuinely sad, reminding everyone who followed them in the papers that, when love sought justice, both were blind.

And yet my father's most publicized trial had nothing to do with the vicissitudes of human love, though the case of The Miracle Chicken would outstrip his previous arbitrations with its sheer theatricality, media appeal, and metaphysical intimations. Filed in Superior Court on 20 April 1950, Mrs. Martha Green's suit against the Society for the Prevention of Cruelty to Animals describes how she purchased a three-and-one-half-pound rooster, with its head cut off, at a San Bernardino market. She placed it in the bottom of her grocery bag and covered it with at least ten pounds of "victuals." Six hours later she lifted oranges, potatoes, and eggs from the bag, and up fluttered the headless rooster. For four days Mrs. Green reverently nurtured her miracle, naming him Lazarus and feeding him a solution of raw egg and warm milk through an eyedropper. Hundreds of people ventured to her home to glimpse the creature. It was even rumored that a famous actress asked to feed the bird personally, squeezing the vital drops with bejeweled fingers as her chauffeur held its wings. Many people prayed at the sight of Lazarus, some claiming to be instantaneously cured of lifelong afflictions, including one woman who flung away her crutches with the remark, "If that bird can get along without a head, I can get along without these crutches."

Then two men from the city humane department intruded with an order that Mrs. Green either put the rooster out of its misery within twelve hours or face imprisonment. Instead, early that night, under cover of darkness, Mrs. Green smuggled Lazarus to a local veterinarian, Dr. Allan Rice, rather than kill him a second time. But Dr. Rice hardly had time to make Lazarus comfortable (in a cage lined with newspapers full of reports about Mrs. Green) before two SPCA men came and forcibly took the bird — deaf and blind to this onslaught of intrigue — to an undisclosed location.

At midnight, in a frenzy of apprehension, Mrs. Green had a vision in which a benevolent, faceless figure in a feathered cloak walked into her bedroom through the southeast wall and implored her to consider chapter nine, verse eight in the Gospel of Matthew: "When the multitude saw it they marveled and glorified God which had given power unto men." That's when she phoned my father.

Photographed beside the brooding Mrs. Green, my father tried to address the issue from a perspective both secular and devout, telling the reporter from *Life* magazine that Lazarus had come to Mrs. Green as an act of Providence for the interest and benefit of science and mankind — adding that she wanted him back, or five thousand bucks. Meanwhile, Father hired a filmmaker to document the incident for posterity, and the scrapbook contains an itemization of the man's expenditures, including pancake makeup for Mrs. Green, extra eggs for Lazarus, gas to San Bernardino and back. But perhaps the most worthwhile expenditure was for the poster that advertised the film. This was inset with snapshots of a lump with wings, a question mark hovering over its head, the layout rampant with boldface captions: **The Miracle Chicken. Not a Hollywood Make-believe Movie. Headless Rooster Hope of Millions. Bird Cures Blind, Lame, and Sick. Humble Home of Mystic Bird a Shrine.**

The public sentiment in favor of Mrs. Green prompted the SPCA to forgo a court battle and return Lazarus only one week after his abduction, with a decorous apology broadcast on radio. Accompanied by the two henchmen, the miracle was wrapped in a blue flannel blanket. After being examined by Dr. Rice, Lazarus was handed over to the beaming Mrs. Green, her eye-dropper at the ready.

Little was said when Lazarus died quietly a few months later.

Only my father came to pay condolences, as sure as Mrs. Green that the hoopla had killed it, that no one on earth can cope with divinity. While Mrs. Green lowered the large coffee can containing Lazarus into his grave, my father doffed his fedora and shielded his eyes against the sun.

For years after, he collected every reference to the precedent of The Miracle Chicken. The last page of his scrapbook is covered by a column entitled, "Blames Bubble in Mercy Case," in which a physician was accused of injecting an air bubble into the comatose Mrs. Abbie C. Borroto, thus causing a fatal embolism. During his cross-examination, Dr. Robert Biron, an expert witness, was grilled by the attorney for the prosecution regarding the clinical definition of death:

"Dr. Biron, have you ever seen a chicken with its head cut off?"

"Yes."

"If a chicken's head is cut off, and the body is still moving, is the chicken dead or alive?"

"There is life in the tissue."

"Just tell me, Dr. Biron, is that chicken still living?"

"I can't answer that. There is life in the tissue."

"I repeat, Doctor, is a chicken with his head cut off still living? Just answer yes or no."

"I can't answer that. That is impossible to answer."

Eighty-one years old, retired, my father is just out of the hospital after an operation to drain a pool of water that had formed around his heart. Gaining weight again, he eats lunch with gusto, telling me about echocardiograms as he looks into the mirrored walls of the Crystal Room, his haunt, and catches a glimpse of himself, alive and almost infinite. Then he shifts his gaze to the silver-haired waitress who, all busy reflection, seems to scatter in different directions like a drop of mercury. Assuming that I too find her alluring, he looks at me and cocks an eyebrow.

All afternoon, conversation fluctuates between his brush with death — cold kiss of the stethoscope, bitter breathfuls of ether — and a running commentary on the waitress, responding now to his winks and piling our empty plates on her arm, with her freckled cleavage seeming to stir in him an impulse as strong as the will to survive. His eyes grow moist at the advent of arousal, each brown iris blazing with highlights. When he pivots to track that aproned anatomy, I can see from across the table that his head of white hair, redolent of tonic, is faintly yellow like old pages.

I hand him back his scrapbook before I hug him goodbye, and I hug him goodbye with a fierceness that startles even me. His iridescent suit, within my embrace, displays its shades of dark and light. I tell him I'm just trying to wring the last of the water out of him. It's a miracle, I tell him, that the heart can float.

Chapter After Chapter

When the Symbolist poets spoke of "Le Livre," the voluminous book into which all experience settles as beautiful language, it is improbable, but not impossible, that they had someone like my mother in mind. Weekly, she'd announce another anecdote, wrenched from her past, that she planned to immortalize in the book of her life, the tome she absolutely without fail was going to write just as soon as she was less busy and had some extra cash. But the longer the book was postponed, and the further away she was from the original events, the less truthful these stories became. Preposterously exaggerated, they were told with eerie, quivering conviction.

My favorite was about how she swam to America from Russia. She was two, she said. The dark, salty ocean was quite an adversary, but her parents were of strong stock and excellent swimmers.

How could I have believed her? Why did I carry with me, all through my childhood, an image of Mother, Grandma, and Grandpa arising fully clothed like phantoms from the breakers, stopping for a moment to pant on the sand, and then proceeding, hands linked, hems wet and limp, into a new society?

On the other hand, were my mother alive today, she would probably doubt the importance of the anecdotes I reserve for paper.

For example, yesterday, driving to a play, I sat in my car,

stalled in traffic, and watched a slow cavalcade of honking cars. It was a wedding of the type I'd forgotten — streamer-laden American cars, perfectly polished, their antennas crowned with balloons and bouquets. Bride and groom led the procession, blushing and beaming with hope. Brimming carloads of friends followed, their faces charged with vicarious bliss. Then the parents, their smiles weary, their car like an ominous cloud. After that, a few cars of total strangers honked sarcastically just for the fun of it. Finally the onrushing rest of the world, late for their lives, their wives and routines. Horns cried and foreheads sweated. I seemed to feel their awful impatience as I cautiously turned and edged in among them. It was five thirty-five, late in August. Sun filled the windshield.

I was late for the play. It was very bad. The protagonist, a fallen man, drank and confessed, drank and confessed, stumbling toward an epiphany. The set was dim and he stared into air, screaming to his departed mother, "Your eyes are like beacons burning down!" As the lights came up, I blushed with embarrassment, believing both art and life were hopeless.

Yet hours later that line began to haunt me, to move me by virtue of its obvious corniness. And by midnight I grew to love that line, the way you come to love an intimate's obvious weakness. I tossed and turned in a kind of wild rapture, trying to find a way to write my mother's book for her, and I'm sorry to say I can't — I'd like to, but I'm just too busy writing my own book, or trying to, and it's really difficult. But if I could, the dust jacket would be beautiful, and in between would be long, eloquent, haunting passages about the big tumultuous ocean, and the sun in August, and life in the city, and the dedication would make you cry, and I'd title it *Beacons Burning Down*.

PAUL HORGAN

L'Après-midi de Mary Garden

FROM THE YALE REVIEW

ON TUESDAY MORNING, 29 January 1935, in New York, I awoke to a state of alarm mixed with elation. It was the publication day of *No Quarter Given,* my second novel, and Harper and Brothers were giving an all-out cocktail party for the occasion. In those days, the literary cocktail party was more of an event than it is now. All of New York's literary *gratin* turned out. Faces famous in caricature, minds tautly competitive, common charity disdained, the guests came to be seen and reported. The guest of honor was often said to be the least of the attractions. I had read all this in New Mexico, where I lived. Now about to be thrown in the thick of it, I thought how comfortable it would be simply to bolt. The dreadful day yawned ahead of me. How to get through it until five o'clock, when I must appear? Whenever the thought of the coming ordeal struck me, I felt the classic symptoms of stage fright — a tightening of the scalp, a thump at the solar plexus.

At breakfast, a sudden refuge in distraction faced me in the *New York Times.* There I found an item announcing that Mary Garden, the lustrous opera singer and actress, would present a lecture-recital in the Plaza Hotel ballroom at three o'clock that day. Her subject was Claude Debussy. Tickets could be had at a box office in the hotel. All my life — I was thirty-two — I had wanted to see and hear this amazing artist.

To mention Caruso, Melba, Farrar, Chaliapin, or, for today, Maria Callas, is to suggest the like position of Mary Garden in the international operatic world of her time. Much of her lore

was known to me. I knew her voice through recordings. While
still a vocal student in Paris she had won instant fame by bril-
liantly taking over the lead role in Charpentier's *Louise* when
the artist singing the part became ill. On that night, Garden was
established for life. She was twenty-three. Two years later Debussy chose her to create the role of Mélisande. Another
triumph. As Massenet's Thaïs she inflamed her artistic success
with her erotic enactment of the courtesan — a performance
which gave the public its stubborn opinion, however mistaken,
about how "daring" her private life must be. For one year she
was general manager of the great Chicago Opera, grandly bank-
rupting the company by the beauty and extravagance of her
productions. James Gibbons Huneker and Carl Van Vechten
had written paeans to her which I had read. Here was my
chance to attend this great artist, and also take my mind off my
trouble for a good part of the afternoon.

But it would help to be with friends. One came happily to
mind — Natalie Hall, the operatic soprano. She and her mezzo-
soprano sister Bettina were known for starring in a long-run-
ning Broadway operetta. I telephoned Natalie. To hear, to see
Garden? Wildly grateful. Could she bring Bettina, whom I'd
never met? We would meet, all three, at two forty-five in the
Plaza Palm Court. I telephoned for reservations and was asked
to take up the tickets by half past two — the ballroom was selling
out. My day began to look up.

In good time I arrived at the Plaza, already somewhat insulated against my nervous state — but not for long. In the lobby
was a portentous reminder — a large-lettered display announcing the day's events in the hotel:

> MISS MARY GARDEN, LECTURE-RECITAL
> 3 P.M., Grand Ballroom
> Second Floor South

And below that, ominously:

> RECEPTION FOR MR. PAUL HORGAN
> Harper & Brothers
> 5 to 7, White and Gold Suite
> Second Floor North

There seemed to be no escape. At the box office I asked for my
tickets. The young woman clerk shuffled them out and I was
about to pay for them when behind her a tall, glossy, young-
ish man wearing a gardenia in his buttonhole snapped up the
tickets, palmed my money aside, and said, "No, n'no, Mr.
Horgan: with our compliments," and handed the three tickets
to me.

"But why? Thank you, but I don't understand."

"I am Mr. Piza, Madame's manager. I have seen notice of
your reception. My congratulations." Swarthy and elegant, he
bowed like a South American. "We are delighted. Allow me."

Confused but elevated, I thanked him again and went to the
Palm Court. There they were, the two beauties, one for each
arm. Embraces. We made our way to the elevator.

"Garden: how exciting," said Natalie, the classic brunette, and
Bettina, the glowing blonde, said, "Fabulous."

The ballroom was filling fast. We found our spindly gold
chairs in a box on the right side of the room with a fine view of
the small formal stage where a concert grand piano waited.

Suddenly the stage bloomed with light. There was a bated
pause, and with a sudden step, Mary Garden appeared from
stage right, halted, raised her arm to rest her hand on the pro-
scenium, and held her pose. (A fleeting reminder of Toulouse-
Lautrec's Yvette Guilbert.) Everyone stood. She let them, and
then, with all standing, she made a wide gesture, showing the
insides of her wrists, and leaned forward slowly in a bow that
was not at all the grateful player's humble thanks, but a grant
of permission to attend. She then went to the bend of the piano,
poised in command, as the house settled. Already there was a
sense of great occasion — how great, we did not then know, for
it was her final appearance in public as a singer.

Small and delicate as she was, she had an affinity of counte-
nance with the great cats, here refined exquisitely to retain the
tiger's high cheeks above the fixed, meaningless smile; intent
gaze; alert focus on all environs; thoughtless confidence of
power; all supported by the gift of seeming beautiful at will. So,
too, her movement, lithe, exact, gracile, was of the feline order.
She was fifty-eight years old, she had abandoned the opera, and

she was not any age. She was robed in who she was, which was enough to give the world.

Otherwise, her costume suggested both theater and salon, as best I can recall this — and all that follows.

She wore a close-fitting hat of black silk with a mesh of veil that came down just past her eyes — her eyes gleamed with a tigerish light in a little blue cave of shadow that put the years at a distance, and yet conveyed the vivid present. Her hair was a tawny gold. A floor-length fall of pale yellow satin, her gown was so tight over her straight hips that you wondered how she could step. A short-sleeved torero jacket in black sparkling stuff met long white gloves and reached above the elbows. A necklace of big pearls was looped once about her throat, with the rest of it swaying almost to her knees. How tall was she? A few inches over five feet, it was recorded somewhere; but she was a figure so commanding that illusion created height. By her valiant posture she seemed to tell us not to be nervous — all would be well, indeed brilliant.

And it was.

She went right to work, saying something like, "Claude Debussy. The most fascinating yet mysterious public person I have ever met."

She then went on to speak for perhaps thirty minutes, in an international accent. Her tone was conversational, emphatic when proper, beguiling when memory was tender; always correct as to the language, though when she needed French, the pronunciation made no pretense to sound native.

In particles, then: Debussy was "a very strange man," as she wrote fifteen years later in her autobiography. (Much that she wrote and much that she said in her lecture are merged in my memory.) She said he was not tall, rather stocky. Quite extraordinarily, he had *two* foreheads — yes, two, one bulging on top over which he brushed his dark hair, the other showing in the clear above his black brows. His eyes, dark, sometimes quite expressionless, were fascinating. You never quite knew what he was thinking. Things he said were original, quite. He was mad about women, though one didn't know if he ever loved anyone, really. People always wondered, of course, some even asked, if he and she had ever been lovers. The idea was preposterous — not that he did not make the attempt one day on a railroad platform in Versailles, but no, there was nothing to it. A perfect artistic understanding, that was all, and it was enough. They rehearsed *Pélleas et Mélisande* for four months. Debussy attended, Messager conducted, they had forty orchestra rehearsals, unheard of. But when the opening came, Debussy was not there, and in fact he never attended a public performance. Some were offended. Not she. She understood when he said that for ten years the opera had been his life, and as he knew it best in that way, no other way was as real to him. When the role of Mélisande became hers at his desire, the author of the play, Maeterlinck, made a scandal, tried to have her removed in favor of his mistress, Mme. Georgette Leblanc, but no, Debussy held fast, he never gave in, Mélisande remained hers, then, and for as long as she, and *she herself,* chose, in whatever opera company she was singing. Debussy had a devoted first wife, Lily, who adored him, she overlooked much, but never expected what happened, when he left her quite abruptly for a rich woman. Lily tried to kill herself, and at that he seemed concerned, but in the hospital when she assured him that she would now live, he shrugged and simply went away, and that was all of that. A very strange man, but yes, fascinating, a great pianist, though a poor singer when he sang the part to everyone in a first reading — his voice was small and husky. He adored Mélisande's voice (he always used that name instead of "Mary Garden") and he loved her voice so much that he composed and dedicated to her a whole group of songs, the *Ariettes. . . .*

And I remembered this when years afterward I read in his letters that Debussy wrote of her: "Le succès de 'notre Garden' ne m'étonne pas; il faudrait autrement, avoir des oreilles boucher a l'émeri pour résister au charme de sa voix. Pour ma part, je ne puis concevoir un timbre plus doucement insinuant. Cela ressemble même à de la tyrannie, tant il est impossible de l'oublier." (I am not amazed at the success of "our Garden"; you'd have to have your ears plugged by a ground-glass stopper to resist the spell of her voice. I can't imagine a timbre more softly persuasive. It's like a tyranny, impossible to put out of mind.)

And she remembered what he said of her to Carré, the director of the Opéra Comique at a rehearsal of *Pélleas et Mélisande*
while she was creating the character: *Je n'ai rien à lui dire* — he
could suggest nothing to enhance her realization of the role.
But that was how it always was with her work — she never *studied* how to do a part — she always simply *knew,* it came from
nowhere, and it was always the truth. At the end of that particular rehearsal she heard him say to Carré, "What a strange
person, this child." Then in his baffling, remote way, he picked
up his hat and walked off — he was always doing that, suddenly
walking out. . . .

In the Plaza Hotel Grand Ballroom, she was up to her old
tricks — casting a spell, as she had done in countless opera per-
formances. With her random notes on Claude Debussy, she
brought him before us and we believed. When she finished
speaking, she allowed a long, thoughtful pause; and then, with
peremptory grace, she turned toward the wings, extending her
hand to bring forth her accompanist, Jean Dansereau, and a
self-effacing youth who would turn pages. Now they would give
us songs by Debussy, fourteen of them, including, according to
the next day's *Times,* the air of *Lia* from *L'Enfant prodigue,* the
third of the *Ariettes, Je tremble en voyant ton image, Green, La Che-
velure,* and *Mandoline.* M. Dansereau, a small, wiry Frenchman,
played the piano texts with a tonal intelligence equal to hers —
by turns scintillant, brooding, declamatory.

How to be exact in describing a performance made of sound,
that medium as fugitive as time? Her voice was without luster
— she was past the age of brilliant tone. Perfect in pitch, it had
at moments almost a *parlando* quality, in a timbre reminiscent of
dried leaves stirred by air. But what expression, now smoky with
passion, again rueful for life's shadows! What musicality; and
what sense of meaning — the texts of Guignand, Bourget,
Pierre Louÿs, Verlaine, Baudelaire, came forth in all the beauty
and power of Debussy's description: "the spell of her voice . . .
so softly persuasive." We were persuaded. Did any artist more
fully know who, and what, she was? Was this the first attribute
of the interpretive genius?

For two hours I forgot my coming trial, and when the concert
ended, my companions and I were in lingering thrall. I said we

must try to go backstage to pay our respects, and as singers, the Misses Hall agreed with stars in their eyes.

At the hidden entrance to the stage, then, I presented us to Mr. Piza, who was on guard there. Could we say one word to Miss Garden of our perfect fulfillment?

"Ah, thank you, I'm afraid not. You see, Madame never receives after a performance. But I will tell her. Thank you."

"No, it is our thanks," I said. And then, in a leap beyond the bounds of the plausible, I added, "But you so kindly invited me to your occasion, perhaps you would let me invite Madame and yourself to my own party," and I mentioned the reception for my new book, already under way at well after five.

"Yes, I know, of course. But again — " Mr. Piza was extremely polite in excusing Madame from unscheduled and, in fact, unexamined events.

We sighed and turned away. I began to feel the familiar stress under my necktie again. Natalie looked at me and said, "You'll be all right."

By her concern she drove home my dread. I nodded. Compelled to a brave show, I took the sisters to the lobby where I bought flowers for us all — violets for them to hold, a dark red carnation for my buttonhole.

"Let's go up, then," I said, viewing the elevator with its brass lace as a tumbril. But the Hall sisters had to leave me: they must have an early supper to be ready for their evening show. With a gaunt smile I embraced them and saw them go; and then I ascended to the White and Gold Suite on the second floor, to be discharged upon a waste of polished parquet. Three lofty rooms facing the park were thrown into one, which at first glance seemed almost empty.

Where was the party, that clamorous huddle of people at cocktails, shouting each other down with a high decibel count thermally stimulated by their massed body heat? But as I looked about I saw that there were guests present — perhaps sixty or so — who were ranged tightly on little gold chairs lining the walls. A few were talking to others beside them, others sat silent, holding drinks. In the center of the floor was a Harper group of three persons, waiting for me impassively. I advanced upon Mr. Cass Canfield, the publisher, Mr. Eugene Saxton, my first

great editor, and Miss Ramona Herdman, the charming publicity chief.

"You're late," said Mr. Canfield dryly.

"Not fatally," said Mr. Saxton with his perpetually amused
smile.

The wallside chairs became aware and glanced in my direction, but no moves were made. The party seemed enclosed in
ice. A waiter came our way and I acquired a martini.

Finally, "Shouldn't you meet people?" asked Miss Herdman.

She took me to the wall and walked me along to shake hands
as we went. The guests looked briefly at me and returned to
their self-absorptions. I had a sense that every known Van
Doren was present, and I recognized other glittering names, for
none of which, of course, was mine a match. The gathering,
meant to be festive, was lost to the lifeless inane. Something had
to be done if Harper and Brothers were not to endure a total
waste. The case was so poor — a young writer from the far
provinces facing his first New York public event — that nothing
was at risk, even to my making a fool of myself. If nobody would
talk to me, I would invade them in another persona. To play
the host, I became a waiter. I took a tray of canapés and began
to go down the rows of gilt chairs offering a bite here, another
there, which were accepted as intrusions or declined as inter-
ruptions.

And then: there should have been a fanfare for tympani and
cymbals. Glancing along the wall in my duty I had a sudden
shock of peripheral vision which made me turn sharply for a
direct view.

There in the central doorway of the party rooms stood Mary
Garden, in her pose of permitting herself to the public. As there
was no one to announce her, she was waiting to be received.
Behind her were the members of her *cuadrilla*, extending the
symbol of her torero jacket: Mr. Piza; M. Jean Dansereau; the
female secretary, Miss Croucher (or some such name) in tweeds;
a maid holding two fur coats and three large handbags; and,
hugging his music briefcase, the remote young man who turned
pages. The great world was there for me.

I managed to set my tray down on a vacant chair and go to
the doorway. Euphoria gave me character. Reaching the pres-

ence, I bowed like a Renaissance courtier and declared, I think
ringingly, "Madame! You pay us an enchanting honor!"

With a piercing gleam out of her veiled cave, Mary Garden
raised her right hand in a torchlike gesture and briskly demanded of her manager behind her shoulder, "Piza-who-is-
this?"

"It is your host, madame, Mr. Paul Horgan, for whom the
reception is held."

"So it is. *Allons.*"

And so it was that I led her procession into the room, while
all around us the murmur arose, *Look, look, it's Mary Garden!*
which she acknowledged only by a slight lift of her shoulders. I
heard Mr. Canfield inquire flatly, "Was she invited?" and Miss
Herdman reply, "No, I made the list," and I, feeling like someone else, said, "*I* invited her" and escorted Madame to the precise middle of the room, where in her habit of center stage she
elected to take up her position. The *cuadrilla* ranged itself behind her. The gilt chairs were emptying fast as guests came
about us to form a dense circle, though instinctively at a respect-
ful distance. I was aloft in the translation of character which
came to my rescue. As Harper and Brothers loomed a little
nearer, politeness required that I say:

"Madame, may I introduce — "

"No-no," she interrupted in an elevated voice, "I will speak
only to you," adding a smile worthy of Thaïs. An audience-hush
fell over the company. There I was, trapped with glory and
fame. What could I, must I say, further?

"May I offer you a drink, Madame?"

She excused the banality with a crosswise wave of her forefin-
ger.

"A cigarette?"

"*Jamais — ma voix.*"

With the genius of desperation I knew I must play above my
form. I said, "This has been an historic afternoon for the centuries, Miss Garden!"

"You attended my *séance musicale*?"

"Yes, Madame, the event of a lifetime of musical events."

"Lifetime?" She made a smile of devastating wistfulness. "A
lifetime: how old are you?"

"Thirty-two. But — "

"How perfect — neither an ending nor a beginning! But my afternoon — "

"Yes, the superb lecture. You hardly seemed to speak, Madame. You created pictures in the air."

"Pictures in the air. How lovely."

"Your text was astonishing. You spoke, not in phrases, not in sentences, but in paragraphs!"

"I did?" She commanded the *cuadrilla*. "Piza? Did you hear? Miss Croucher, write that down, make a note, so valuable, we must keep this."

She knew I was talking nonsense, but she felt the extremity that compelled it, and together we wrote our scene out of thin air in the ping-pong of drawing-room comedy.

"Yes," I said, "and the songs: never such musical line, never such penetration beyond what the poet meant!"

"Yes," she said, "poetry alone has never touched me, except to make me restless and nervous."

"Yes, good poetry is all nerves. When poetry is bracing, it is all bad."

"But then Debussy's music was always the right music for the words. Think of it: until we parted, but not as friends, he always said he was going to write an opera of Romeo and Juliet for me."

She spoke fast and imperiously, her voice a little edgy; and she made little steps in place, a miniature dance, to animate the scene and hold attention. Juliet invoked hazy romance. She measured me down and up with her veiled rays. I was only an underweight specimen at best, but . . .

"Piza, look at him!" she declaimed. "Did you ever see a figure more *soigné*?" She danced a little near me and reached out her white-gloved hands and molded my flanks, waist, and hips, and cried, "Don't, you must promise me, don't you ever gain a single pound!"

From the always-growing throng of onlookers came a wordless murmur that meant, *Really!*

"Tell me," she said, "what do you write? I hope novels. I adore novels. When I want the truth I go to fiction."

"Yes, a novel, *No Quarter Given*."

"No quarter: I never gave quarter. What is it about?"

"It's enormous. It's about — "

"What a novel I could write! Perhaps one day I shall. Though perhaps I have already lived my novel. One should never repeat. I shall never forget what someone said to me — was it Paul Bourget or Jacques-Emile Blanche? I forget — one should never repeat except in love. You will write many more books. I must have them all, I am an excellent critic."

And so on, and so on, as the minutes flew. Questions like sparks that died away, with hardly a pause for an answer; and *le tout New York* craned and stared for every word and gesture. I did what I could to keep the ball in the air, and I broke the law only twice — once when my sister Rosemary (to whom my novel was dedicated) arrived, and I introduced her to Madame. Again, when I saw an old friend appear despite a state of mourning for her husband's recent death — Mrs. Isabel Ames of New Mexico. I was touched that under the circumstances she came to my party and I broke ranks to go to greet her. In the piercing voice of an elderly lady used to coping with deafness in the family, Mrs. Ames said:

"They tell me that you are talking to someone named Mary Garden. Is she anything to the real one?"

"It *is* the real one," I murmured, trying to hush my friend.

"My God," cried Mrs. Ames, a lifetime of laughter in her endearing old face, "I thought she was dead years ago!"

Madame's management of this cheerful affront was masterly. Everyone had heard it. All leaned to see what she would do about it. She simply grew tall, raised her gaze well above everyone present, and defied comment. The effect of vitality was immense. In an instant I was back in her service. Finger on lip, she brooded a moment, and then:

"I want to ask you something — you *will* do it, won't you: I want you to do it: you are the one to do it: I can tell, I can *always* tell, you are the one to do it."

"But anything, Miss Garden, of course."

"Then I want you to write a play for me — a delicious three-act comedy of manners, very high style, *gaie comme les hirondelles*, witty, blazing with epigrams, don't you know, yet with an under-

tone of sadness — not *sad,* don't you know, but *triste,* like a lovely
day in autumn and full of love — *amusing* love, don't you know,
nobody throwing themselves about, but so touching. And
please: Mr. Horgan: give me just one little song to sing? the
second act? perhaps, yes, I think, just before the curtain, so
the *meaning* of the song will come to us in the *last* act! Do you
think?"

With becoming extravagance I agreed to write the play. A
book news reporter or two made notes. Mr. Canfield loomed
open-mouthed. Mr. Saxton beamed indulgently. The comedy
was running down. Mr. Piza leaned across Madame's shoulder
and showed her his watch, made murmur about waiting obliga-
tions; and, facing me — "Ah!" — the white-gloved hand rose to
the brow deploring the second-rate demands made upon the
numinous.

"I must go. Send me your novel, Hotel Pierre. I will read it. I
will write you instantly about it. You have been gallant. We must
meet soon again. Do not neglect my play."

She made a sweeping turn toward the exit, creating a parabola of knee-length pearls, and I escorted her away with the
cuadrilla in tow. As I bent to kiss her hand, I caught a glimpse
of the smile with which she made an open secret of the farce in
our scene; and then she dutifully held a farewell pose in the
elevator gates. The gates clanged shut. Behind me, the crowd
had shifted to observe insatiably, someone started to clap, the
ovation grew, and to farewell applause, Mary Garden's car de-
scended with the effect of a great sigh of release.

I returned to the party. It was exploding in a clamor of talk.
Everyone had the same thing to talk about. The ice was not only
broken, it was shattered. I was besieged with questions — what
else had she said; did she mean it all; had I known her before;
where; would I really write her a play; tell about your novel; do
you often come East from New Mexico. Suddenly, in the New
York way, I had many ten-minute friends. Briefly I was a hero.
Nobody left before nine o'clock.

On the following morning I went to Brentano's where I inscribed a copy of *No Quarter Given* to Mary Garden and asked
that it be sent to her at the Pierre Hotel. In hopes of a rapturous

reply, I included my hotel address. Nothing came from her, either about the novel or our future collaboration. After some days of growing realism, I telephoned the Pierre Hotel. Miss Garden had checked out days ago.

Any forwarding address?

"Of course not," replied the Pierre Hotel coldly, in defense of the vanishing point of celebrity.

ELIZABETH HARDWICK

The Heart of the Seasons

FROM HOUSE & GARDEN

SUMMER — a high, candid, definite time. It may slither out of
the ambiguity, hesitance, or too early ripeness of spring and
edge toward the soothing peculiarities of autumn, but summer
is downright, a true companion of winter. It is an extreme, a
returning, a vivid comparative. It does not signify that some are
cool and some are dry and sweltering; summer is a kind of
entity, poetic, but not a poetic mystery. The sun is at its zenith
in the tropic of Cancer, a culmination.

Our frantic, crowded summers are not now as they once were.
There was a time when girls did not lie about the beach in pieces
of string, offering an intimidating revelation. Think of those
yellow afternoons of the last century, lazy moments one can
imagine by turning the pages of a collection of paintings in the
new Terra Museum of American Art in Chicago. Then, we
believe, it was another world — quiet, perhaps not so much reflective as drowsy and wondering. Summer was a luxurious
pause, an inattention except for the concentration on pleasure.
A caesura to honor the sun, the warm waters, the breezes of the
mountains, and the hope of some dreamlike diversion of destiny in the pause.

There is a languorous game of croquet painted by Winslow
Homer. It appears that this game may be one too many, too
much like yesterday, a routine, and nothing to surprise. And
Charles Curran's bursting, voluptuous water lilies. The sun has
ravished the flowers, full force, and how ferocious they are amid
the passive, sheltered glances of the young women in the boat.

What a lot of clothes the women are dragging about in these rich-toned landscapes. Hats, sleeves, petticoats, ties at the neck, parasols — a shroud of protection, giving a somewhat fatigued femininity to these lost summer days. Sargent's summer painter must be putting the bush and the field and the reflection of the stream on canvas. He looks much as a man would today: white suit, coquettish red belt, and what appears to be a handkerchief on his head.

But she, the companion, is reading in a hat like a haystack, a dark skirt, and holding the inevitable lacy umbrella, a thing of no apparent utility unless it be a weapon against a change of his mood there in the erotic sleepiness of a full summer afternoon, and the ground dry and not even a dog in sight.

I like to remember the summer season coming to those who just stay at home the year round, that is, most of the world. The plain patterns of simple domestic life meet each year with a routine. Nothing is unexpected. An almanac of memories disputes claims of the hottest day in decades or the level of the rainfall.

The furnace is shut down and the fireplace, if there should be one, is emptied and the tiles relieved of grit and polished to an oily sienna sheen. Windows washed, everything aired; moths seeking the bedroom light bulb; grass and weeds pushing up out of the hard winter soil; leaves on the maples and elms — nothing special; doors latched back and covered by a flapping screen — with a hole in it and rusty hinges; voices calling out of the windows; perennials determined to exhibit their workhorse nature, if most a little disgruntled and with more stem than flower; insects strong as poison; the smell of chlorine in a child's hair — from the community pool across town.

The congratulation of summer is that it can make the homely and the humble if not exactly beautiful, beautifully acceptable. Such brightness at midday and then the benign pastels, blues and pinks and lavenders of the summer sky. Much may wither and exhaust, but so great is the glow and greater the freedom of the season that every extreme will be accommodated. There are great gardens filled with jewels as precious as those dug out of the earth and then the hand that planted the sparse petunias and impatiens in the window box — there's that, too.

I remember days from the summers in the upper South and sights from certain towns in the Middle West, in Ohio and Indiana, places just passed through long ago. There's something touching about the summer streets of middle-size towns: everything a bit worn down in July, all slow and somnolent except for the supersonic hummingbird in the browning hydrangea bush at the edge of the porch. The disaster of the repetitive but solid architecture of the 1920s — once perceived as quite an accomplishment of ownership, and suitable — comfortable according to what was possible.

The front porches. That unalterable, dominating, front-face mistake left over from the time before the absolute, unconditional surrender to the automobile and to traffic. There was a time when not everyone had a car, and to children then the traffic was interesting. The brand names, the out-of-state license plates — a primitive pleasure to take note of them, like stamping your palm at the sight of a white horse. And the family on the front porch, watching the life of the street.

This porch in front and so unsightly and useless and awful in the winter with the gray of the splintered planks and the soggy sag of the furniture often left out to hibernate in public view. The old eyesores, defining the houses, many of them spacious, with gables, and bits of colored glass from a catalogue over the door, in a fan shape. If nothing else, summer redeems the dismal overhang of the porch, for a few months, and even the darkened halls and parlors within might be glad of an escape from the heat.

Somewhere there is water. Not too far away there will be an abandoned quarry, difficult to climb into and cold as a lake in Nova Scotia. There will be a stream or a river, not very deep and muddy at the banks — Middle Western water.

If there are no neighbors to be seen on the streets, they can be seen and heard at the back, there on the patio where tubs standing on tripods and filled with charcoal lumps are ready to receive marinated bits of flesh. There is pleasure in all this, in the smoke, in the luscious brown of the chicken leg — on your own little plot where you fed the chickadee last winter.

These scenes, local as the unearned wildflower, the goldenrod with its harsh cinnamon scent, are not splendid. Little of the charm of the ocean view and the table set with blue linen, and the delectable salmon, so well designed for painterly display, laid out on a platter among scattered stems of watercress. Still the American town streets — those angling off the main drag seen on the way to the airport — are a landscape of the American summer. And why should we groan with pain at the sight of the plastic flamingo on the lawn or the dead whiteness of the large inflated duck coming into its decorative own nowadays? There's not much else to buy downtown, for one thing.

These things remind me of those elders who used to go abroad every summer to the same pension, to dusty interiors and dining rooms where the wine bottle with your name on it returned every night to the table until it was empty. Perhaps in Florence or outside Siena or in the north, to the band concert in the park by a German lake.

In Russian fiction people go off to the Crimea and sigh, how dull it is here. But since there is to be a plot, the scene is not to be so dull after all. In the salon, with the violin whining and the fish overcooked, the same faces take up their posts for the same complaints and posturings. Then someone new appears to the defensive snubs of the old-timers or to the guarded curiosity of the bored. It might be a sulky young girl with a chaperone or her mother; or a woman, not a girl, to be seated on the same side of the room as the tall man from Moscow, away from his family for two weeks and subject to dreaming. And it begins to begin . . .

Summer romance — when the two words are brought together, each takes on a swift linguistic undercurrent. As a phrase, it is something akin to "summer soldier" — the romance carries away and the summer soldier runs away from duty or from the reality of things. Heaven is something with a girl in summer: a line of Robert Lowell's. The summer romance will have the sharpness and sweetness and the indescribable wonder of the native strawberry, raspberry, blueberry, and toward the end the somewhat gritty cling of the late blackberry.

The sun-filled romance is the dramatic background of much fiction. There is the accident of the meeting and the unreasonable heightening of the season. And classically there is often an imbalance in the lovers, an imbalance of class or situation, hard, chilly truths swept away by the soft clouds, the fields and the urgency of the burst-open water lilies.

Edith Wharton wrote a short novel called *Summer*. In it you will find a love affair between a pretty and poor young girl from the New England hills and a clever young man from the city who likes to study the old houses of the region. As always, he is alone, happily solitary, idling about in the sunshine, and she is there, as she has always been. In the way of these sudden romances everything before and ahead seems to fade. Of course, it is not to last, at least not to last for the young man who, as it turns out, is engaged to someone of his own sort . . . and so on.

Tess of the D'Urbervilles: "Rays from the sunrise drew forth the buds and stretched them in long stalks, lifted up sap in noiseless streams, opened petals, and sucked out scents in invisible jets and breathings." This is the summer landscape that engulfs Tess and Angel Clare and finally leads to a despair of such magnitude only the genius of Thomas Hardy could imagine it and embody it in the changing seasons and the changing structure of the English countryside.

In Chekhov's story "The Lady with the Dog," the lady and the man are both married. They meet in Yalta in the summer and the romance flows along on a pitiless tide, without any possible ending except misery. When they believe the love will at last end or the devastation will have a solution, the final line says no, "it was only just beginning."

So in spite of the meadows and the picnic under the shade of the copper beech tree, the days will grow longer and there will again be buying and selling and coming and going elsewhere. The romantic ritual of the season fades, even if it will be staged again next summer with other lovers in other places. The freedom of the summer remains in the memory.

In the mountains, there you feel free . . . Yes. Under Mount Monadnock in New Hampshire — a storm of stars in the heavens, a pattern of gorgeous gleaming dots on the dark blue silk of the sky, all spreading down like a huge soft cloak to the edge of the field.

The mountains are perhaps not quite in such demand as they once were in summer. Too lonely and overwhelming, the pleasures offered no longer quite suitable to the extraordinary energies of those who rush to the long, long expressways on a Friday afternoon — flat roads ahead, and yet they mean getting there. The weekend, commuting distance, breads and cheeses and bottles of wine, Vivaldi on the cassette, and a lot of work to be done and gladly.

Impatience with the division of city and country, or what is more or less "country," has changed the heart of the seasons. Many face a February weekend as if it were July. There is a need for an eternal summer, some mutant need created by the demand for nature, for weekend nature, even as nature disappears along the route.

Eternal summer, kind only as a metaphor. Night is the winter of the tropics, as the saying has it. On the equator the days are twelve hours long. Withering rivers and unrelenting lassitude in the never-ending summertime. In Bombay in January, blissful for the citizens, but to those accustomed to the temperate sections of the United States, the heat of January in India spreads around like an infamous August swelter.

The gardens, the terraces, the flowers in vases. The first peas, the lettuce out of the ground, the always too greatly abundant zucchini — and at last a genuine tomato. No doubt the taste for these has grown sharper from the fact that we have them all year round in an inauthentic condition of preservation. Where the memory is never allowed to subside, according to each thing in its time, the true taste is more astonishing. One of summer's intensifications. Very much like actually swimming or sailing after the presence of the sea or lake known only as a view.

Summer, the season of crops. The concreteness of it. Not as perfumed and delicate and sudden as spring and not as *triste* as autumn. Yet for the enjoyment of summer's pleasures, for the beach, the crowded airplane to Venice, most of us consent to work all year long.

SUSAN MITCHELL

Dreaming in Public:
A Provincetown Memoir

FROM PROVINCETOWN ARTS

THE WINTER OF 1979, I lived in a condominium down by the
tennis courts at the east end of Provincetown. The apartment
was large enough to span the land world and the sea world,
each with its own flora and fauna, sounds and smells. When I
stood under the skylight on the land side and looked out on
Commercial Street, men slim as their ten-speed bicycles shad-
owed past, and pink-jeaned girls with enormous eyes whizzed
by on roller skates faster than my IBM Selectric could type
"anorexia" or "cocaine." Under the skylight was a waterbed, and
drifting out on it, I stared up into sky. "I have done a good deal
of skying," Constable wrote in 1822, the year he painted most
of his cloud studies. I did a good deal of skying, too — into the
green and black foliage of cumulonimbus, into that gaseous,
chloroformed light that precedes sudden and violent storms.
Sometimes a strong wind tossed and lowered a tree branch
against the skylight. In fine weather, that tree pulsed with small
golden birds, finches that must have eaten food touched by
Midas — even their excrement was liquid gold. I loved skying
into weather just developing: clouds rapidly changing to mist,
swirling apart until suddenly the skylight framed shades of
blue; blurs and blots of clouds, a vast calligraphy that kept eras-
ing, then rewriting itself in an excess, an exuberance of alpha-
bets, or into a patois of bruises, a jargon of violet streakings,

thick squid ink that seemed the very opacity of language and
desire.

The bedroom, with its white chest of drawers, white chair,
blue rug, and white curtains was on the bay side. The low bed
seemed a part of that bay: propped on one elbow, I could look
out at 4 A.M. — the fishing boats returning to Provincetown harbor, all thirteen of them, their lights a rope pulling toward
shore. Their return was a clock chiming, a parent's key turning
in the lock of childhood. At high tide, waves would break against
the foundation of the building, so that even in the dark, even
with eyes closed, I knew, as if something had shifted in my own
blood and marrow, the bay was at flood. During hurricanes and
gales, the Atlantic was shaken into me, a vibration so deep —
that boom, boom of fist against body bag when Marvin Hagler
worked out at the Provincetown Inn the following fall — its
percussions became part of my sleep, a disturbance of the flesh.
Even after I left that apartment and Provincetown, even in
Charlottesville and in those breathtaking absences of the
Midwest, I could have sworn I felt it — the tide changing,
the Atlantic heaving itself on Truro, Wellfleet, Race Point, the
waist-high grass of Indiana prairie bending westward.

I grew up in N.Y.C., where I learned to drift with crowds, to be
one shining particle in those streaming currents of phosphores-
cense that merge and intersect around Fifth and Fifty-seventh,
especially on late winter afternoons. As one sparkling corpuscle,
I delighted in the speed, the thrust, even the bumps and jolts of
all those other glittering corpuscles. Black, white, Hispanic,
Asian, Native American, we made up one Amazonian blood-
stream. In those crowds, I savored my anonymity, that deli-
ciously sensuous private space where I could dream in public,
sensing the outermost edges of other people's dreams: that
woman striding past me in a green suede coat, lighting up a
Mary J — the burned eggplant smell drifted back to me, spreading, smudging the purely olfactory calligraphy of her dream.
Long after she disappeared into the crowded distance, her
dream flowed from her nostrils, enigmatic, persistent.

In Provincetown, everyone seems to dream in public. The
summer I lived in a studio at the west end, Georgie would stand

in front of me as I sunbathed in the garden and dream out
loud. We had moved into the cottage on the same day, Georgie
in the studio below mine. "Hi," he said, "I'm Georgie the
Whore," the only name I ever knew him by. Midmorning, as I
stirred silty coffee with a twig and watched black islands break
loose from the sun, Georgie would read to me from the dream
diaries clients had left with him, clients he usually met at Tuesday afternoon tea dances at one of the restaurants on Commercial Street. Georgie was a perfectionist who found ways to con-
cretize down to the last detail his clients' amorphous yearnings
for mingled pain and pleasure. But what Georgie loved to
dream most was the male body. If he could have found a way,
he would have entered through the anus and exited from the
mouth, having traveled every tortuous channel of mazy entrails,
as if lovemaking, to be any good, had to re-enact our births, the
cry of orgasm recalling the glistening moment when we scream
out our arrival on earth. How many times that summer I heard
his clients arrive, four maybe five arrivals each night, the cars
racing up, then falling back down the gravel driveway, as the
men replaced one another, their cries always sounding somehow the same. As Georgie talked, the male body turned inside
out or rolled into a gleaming ball, arms grasping ankles, or
became a wheel, legs reaching back toward the head — all those
intricate combinations of cat's cradle I played as a child, Georgie
never tiring of the game, the knots never slipping through his
fingers, but only through his heart: they were all "teddy bears"
whose small bodies nestled against his chest. Georgie's lovers
were contortionists, sexual acrobats, so that finally, for me, the
image that represented them all was Picasso's *Femme Couche,*
with its simultaneous, all-embracing view of breasts, buttocks,
and vaginal face. What Georgie dreamed out loud each morning was sex as collage: every possible way of taking a man, fantasy superimposed on fantasy, maps and ground plans for
fantastic cities of desire, the cities lapping and overlapping one
another, each city with its own lymphatic network pumping,
pulsating, spilling from fountain to baroque fountain.

Sometimes when a morning listening to Georgie made me feel
too lethargic to write, I'd devote the afternoon to a small shop
on Commercial Street that sold magic tricks and costumes. The

magic tricks — hats that promised disappearance, rubber spiders quivering on black legs, glasses with false bottoms — were not what interested me: it was the masks, those rubber faces that fit over my own like a second, or a first, skin. There were animal masks — cat, gorilla, bear, and an odd one-of-a-kind fanged face that reminded me of Cocteau's dream animal for *Beauty and the Beast*. The fanged face even came with a costume that swathed and engulfed the body in velvet. Masks are not to be put on frivolously. All through the filming of *Beauty and the Beast* Cocteau was so disfigured by eczema that he wore "a veil made of black paper, fastened to the brim of his hat with clothespins, with holes for his eyes and mouth." What I never tired of were masks that opened to reveal still another mask: a dream inside a dream — or a dream with its own false bottom, the shock of mistaken identity. There was, for example, the Beautiful Lady mask from Italy, with her straight nose, thick mascaraed lashes, porcelain skin blushing at the cheeks — and a black chiffon scarf draped across the mouth. Unfasten the scarf: the mouth bloomed up a crimson gash, a gaping blood-smeared wound. The Beautiful Lady was so versatile, an alluring woman who, at the drop of a veil, could transform herself into something hideous — or, depending on the viewer's taste, perhaps something more alluring. Beautiful Lady reminded me of the mask worn by the Echo Dancer in Kwakiutl winter ceremonies. When the Echo Dancer appears, he wears a mask bearing humanlike features. Moving around the fire, he covers his face with the corner of his blanket, then suddenly lets the covering drop to reveal a different mouthpiece on the mask. As the dance progresses, the performer displays a series of mouthpieces — animal, bird, sea creature. But the Beautiful Lady also brought to mind those Ovidian myths where the hunter is transformed into the victim — Actaeon changed into a stag, then torn to pieces by his own dogs, which mistake him for the animal he was pursuing. But unlike Actaeon, the Beautiful Lady had the ability to heal herself: only cover her mouth, and what was bloody and torn is made whole; cover her mouth, and whatever story she inspires can start over from its innocent beginning.

I approached the Beautiful Lady mask gingerly, with respect, but never tried it on. It was the King Kong hands that I loved to slip over my own like burglar's gloves, that leathery black skin exchanging cells with mine: the gorilla hands were somewhat humanized by my gestures while some animal trace revived my body, electrifying each hair on my head. I have seen every one of the King Kong films, each refilming a reflection of some subtle change in our idea of the erotic. In the version that stars Jessica Lange, the essence of the heroine's sexuality is amnesia, her ability to forget each narrow escape as soon as it's over. As a result, she starts each adventure anew, fearless. When the geological team arrives on Kong's island, Jessica rushes ahead on the stony beach, despite the foreboding chill created by the ominously swirling mists. It's not a beach I would care to walk alone. But Jessica, ignorant of the cues that immediately alert the aficionado of the fantasy genre, senses no danger. Like the Beautiful Lady, she is self-healing, a perpetual virgin in the garden of fantasy sex.

During the winter of 1979, as I read in front of a window over-looking Provincetown Bay, I often thought of Keats the reader: "I should like the window to open onto the Lake of Geneva," he wrote Fanny, "and there I'd sit and read all day, like the picture of somebody reading." Perhaps like those women looking out of windows in paintings by Caspar David Friedrich and M. V. Schwind that had such a vogue in the early and mid 1800s. Backs turned on the dark interiors that make up most of the pictorial space, these women seem to drift out of the paintings — not toward, but away from us, out over the horizon where our own thoughts are traveling. Painters of this period frequently portrayed themselves before windows, and there is even a painting, attributed to M. Drolling the elder, of a Paris interior (Wadsworth Atheneum, Hartford) where the view through the open window is depicted on a canvas on the easel. Like these artists, like Keats looking out on Lake Geneva, I was simultaneously inside and outside, snug and far away, contained and dispersed as I sat by my window. The natural world with its gulls, sandpipers, boats, and winding windrows of kelp and sea-grape intermingled with the poems and novels I read, such as in Spenser's Bower of Bliss living vines and tendrils entwine themselves around artificial plants. That strange long-drawn cry that Emma Bovary hears after making love with Rudolphe, the cry that hangs on the air of Steegmuller's superb translation before it mingles with Emma's own jangled nerves seemed to come from out over the bay, the cry of a gull suddenly rising from the silence. The natural world flowed into, washed over, and nurtured whatever I read, dreamed, and wrote. I was a creature in a tidal pool, sometimes drinking the incoming waves at flood, other times breathing air and that extraordinary Provincetown light that always comes from several directions at once — bouncing off the bay, raining down through the skylight, crackling out of the wood stove. I was a straddler, inhabiting a world of art prolonged by dream and a natural world guided by some deeper dream. On sunny, surprisingly warm December afternoons, I sipped margaritas at the Red Inn, and as the sun set, licked salt from the rim of the ocean. This was my third year in Provincetown. No longer a fellow at the Fine Arts Work Center, I stayed on with a grant from the Artists Foundation, sometimes sharing the sunset with two other former fellows, a sculptor and a painter. What I remember now were our long, impassioned talks about Nancy Holt, whose *Sun Tunnels,* constructed during the seventies in Utah's Great Basin Desert, invited us to meditate on inside and outside, sensations from within the body and perceptions sucked in through openings in the tunnels and pipes. Late at night, when the moon loomed, an enormous floating city that illuminated whatever I was reading, I thought of the moon penetrating Holt's tunnels, the different shapes that light takes as it encroaches on darkness. Even when I read in the bath, glass of scotch beside the soap, I could sense the lunar tug, the pull the moon exerted on the bay, on the syrupy undulations of the waterbed, on the water I bathed in. On the stereo, John Anderson slurred "Going Down Hill," the moon dragging at his vocal cords, thickening the sound.

Late at night, I drifted through all the apartments I had ever lived in: the little apartment on the rue du Cherche Midi that looked down on a cobblestone courtyard that gleamed on chill, wet October nights; the hotel room in Paris, its windows opening onto a garden of blossoming pear trees — my home for a year, it also looked into another room where each night a man and woman made love without bothering to draw the curtains;

the pink stucco apartment that looked out on Porto Cervo where a harbor vendor sold bright orange roe of sea urchins, the sticky tickertape of history I gulped down with lemon and the rough burn of Sardinian Vernaccia, future urchin beds swallowed whole; the balcony in N.Y.C. that looked down on swaying barges of light, hanging bridges, neon gardens floating miraculously thirty stories above the street; the dark blue tiles of the apartment overlooking Positano, cool under bare feet, the *persiani* half closed on hot afternoons, the ocean boiling at the cliff bottom, sizzling, breeze of garlic and onion. Through the window at Provincetown I looked out through all those other windows, the window in Paris opening to reveal the window in Porto Cervo, which opened wide to reveal the balcony in N.Y.C. — as if I were pulling a spy glass to its furthest extension. Or as if the windows opened onto each other like those stories in the *Arabian Nights* that do not really end but, instead, spill into one another, story overflowing into story, until I am standing in the garden at Positano where Danish's cat has just given birth to the rhythm of "Sergeant Pepper's Lonely Hearts Club Band." The rooster crows and dawn arrives with the smell of lemon and mimosa. The rooster knows the exact moment. All roosters everywhere know the moment. In Provincetown, it's conch pink, slippery, the thin line that separates night from day, the exact moment when morning appears like a sail on the horizon. Such thresholds have always seemed magical to me, those fine threads of the world that have the power to renew us if we can only grab hold of them: the flicker of light that appears between bands of color in Rothko's paintings, that marginal world, the dividing line, the moment of change when everything still seems possible. Once, walking near Pilgrim Heights, I tried to follow the shrill of peepers to its source, that spring where the sound wells up and spills into rivulets of water. Louder and louder the shrilling grew — and then, just when I had almost found its source, the shrilling stopped, all the peepers holding their breath at once. So the source is secret, magical, withholding itself, retreating into what Mallarmé called the "last spiritual casket."

It was at Pilgrim Heights that William Bradford and an exploring party from the *Mayflower* had their first drink of American water. Before going on to Plymouth and founding our nation on rock, the Pilgrims first tried to found it on water in Provincetown Harbor. It was in Provincetown Bay that the women of the *Mayflower* washed their clothes after the long crossing. And it was in Provincetown Bay that Bradford's wife, Anne, in a state of despair, drowned herself. You will not find her mentioned in the *Encyclopaedia Britannica,* though William's career is summarized there. You will not find her suicide mentioned in Bradford's chronicle, *The History of Plimoth Plantation:* not a ripple of her passing disturbs his account of the Pilgrim venture. Within the fullness of the first Thanksgiving there is this absence, Anne's: within the desire to build, to construct, to found, to create something new, this tug in the opposite direction, this desire not to begin, not to, not to — the secret absence out of which all great things start up.

I have visited the spring where supposedly Bradford and his exploring expedition had their first taste of "sweet water." The first time alone, the second time with Otukwei Okai, a poet from Ghana in residence at the Fine Arts Work Center. This was my second year as a fellow, the spring of 1979. The car I had bought the previous year still smelled new, and its shiny black exterior had not yet lost its sex appeal. Every afternoon, Otukwei passed the car, patted the hood, and said something complimentary, until finally it dawned on me: he wanted us to go for a drive and fulfill his version of the American dream — fast car, loud rock, hamburgers, shakes and fries, and all the windows open. It seemed so clichéd to me, this dream, but well, why not do it? — especially since my own myth of Africa was probably just as hackneyed: tawny lions, as marvelously unreal as Rousseau's, creeping up on villagers. My pleas for lion stories invariably reduced Otukwei to frowning silence. The day I satisfied his dream down to the last greasy fried potato, Otukwei, his wife Beatrice, and their infant daughter, swaddled in pink, drove with me to Pilgrim Heights for our own taste of the famous spring. Along the way, Otukwei and I spilled out ideas for poems, our creative juices keeping pace with the rock music, the membranes of our fetal poems so thin that images swam back and forth between us. It was one enormous poem we were writing as we got out of the car and walked the spongy forest trail covered with amber needles to a high place that looks down on the water, which barely seems to move between banks of yellow-brown reeds. An egret shuddered up, its flight hardly faster than the river's. The air was redolent of pine. It was here, supposedly, that the Pilgrims saw footprints made by local Native Americans. I spared Otukwei my skepticism about the role of this particular spring in American history and simply knelt with him: it tasted as before — warm, sandy. On the drive back to Provincetown, suddenly out of the flow of conversation, it erupted — Otukwei's lion story. A very large lion. The men carrying it on a pole back to the village, its tail so long it dragged in the dust.

Recently, on a flight to West Palm Beach, as a south wind carried wave after wave of rain against the windows, I felt it again, the deep boom of Provincetown Bay slapping at foundations, sucking its breath in, holding it, holding it, then heaving it out. We were threading our way between storm systems in an eerie yellow-green light, the wake of a passing tornado. Bouldery clouds, stacked precariously on one another, trembled, stretching, towering higher and higher above the plane, then suddenly toppled, the plane falling with them as if through a trap door. I had entered the realm of process, where skying was all that mattered. To the left, racing us, was a thick black cloud, flat as a mattress, a flying carpet with three dark threads tentacling down. As we banked, cloud after cloud tumbled toward us, breakers, whitecapped, foaming, spewing spray — and then it was the ocean, all its teeth bared.

Sometimes the ocean returns to me in surprising ways — as this past Christmas in the powder room of a N.Y.C. department store. It was my favorite hour. Outside, the lights had just come on, snow was beginning to fall, each flake a momentary jewel in the hair of passersby. As I yawned into the mirror, a stall door opened behind me: the woman enthroned on the toilet puckered her glossy red lips, sweeping her hands up her shiny black hair caught in a chignon. Still sitting, she wiggled out of black lace pantyhose and into crotchless panties. The woman who had just left her stall resembled the woman I had chatted with the night before at a dinner party: same blond bangs, same thick hair squared at the jaw, same sad eyes and drained face. Now I watched them both in the mirror. The prostitute was radiant, glowing, as she removed the crotchless panties, lowering them slowly to the floor, a gesture that suddenly seemed the essence of her appeal. Nothing can dirty me, that gesture said. Not the dirt on the floor. Not the water oozing out of the toilets. Not the urine spotting the toilet seats. Not the faded blonde whose sadness leaves a sour taste only in her own mouth. The prostitute waved a leg in my direction and smiled: "Boy, oh boy, oh boy," she said, her voice entirely different from what I had expected; it seemed to come from another body, from a delivery boy's or a cab driver's. Still looking in the mirror, I smiled back, thinking of the ocean licking itself clean all those nights in Provincetown as I listened in the dark. The ocean that heals instantly around whatever penetrates it. The ocean lubed to a shine. In a mirror, the ocean looks at itself and sees that it is wearing a rose. And sees that it has no hats. This ocean that goes on talking in my sleep, that keeps kneading itself like dough, like prayer.

ELEANOR MUNRO

On the Pilgrim's Path to Lourdes

FROM THE SAN FRANCISCO EXAMINER AND CHRONICLE

AMONG SACRED PILGRIMAGE sites of the world — far-off snowy peaks on which gods are thought to dance, thronged temples by the Ganges, gold-domed cathedrals or humble country altars — the French shrine of Lourdes in its gloomy mountain setting may be one of the most instructive.

That is to say, if you look beyond the blatant commercialism of the new town and steep yourself instead in the geography, architecture and massed population of the sacred precinct, you may gain an inkling of the meaning of this ancient and universal human practice. For pilgrimage is an enterprise of deep antiquity and powerful psychological appeal, and its associated rites are much the same across all religions, and the same today as in the past.

When a pilgrim arrives at his destination (it can as well be a natural feature, rock, tree or riverbank as a man-made church or temple), he invariably can be seen walking a circular path around or in it, often following the clockwise course of the sun. If by night, he will carry a candle or torch, which, multiplied many times in many hands, becomes a galaxy of stars turning slowly in darkness. The metaphor holds. In these circumambulations, the pilgrim imitates the flight of the stars and planets, which orbit the celestial pole, disappearing and reappearing in a harmonic order we on earth find both beautiful and eternal. So the pilgrim enacts the answer to his longing for immortality.

Indeed, the folklore that has grown up around Lourdes describes its location at "the confluence of seven valleys" — seven being one of those immemorial mystical numbers in scripture and myth referring to the visible planets, the outermost travelers of the solar system. Mystical Lourdes thus is identified as its axis.

Legend in this case enhances geography. Actual Lourdes lies betwixt gorges and bare cliffs, where icy torrents off the high slopes collide in a perpetual tumult of white water, ethereal rainbows and ghostly low-hanging clouds.

A hundred years ago, when its modern history began, Lourdes was no more than a scatter of wretched stone huts wedged along a couple of crooked climbing streets. Perched on an overhanging rock stood the town jail. In one of those freezing dwellings lived a poor miller, sometimes resident in the jail, and his wife and children, all of them suffering from hunger and ill health.

It was a bitter February day in 1858 when Bernadette, the eldest child, went with her sister to the riverbank to gather kindling. And there, as she later recalled with the help of her confessor and other priests of the region, "I heard a noise like a gust of wind. I saw the trees were not swaying. I heard the same noise again. As I lifted my head and looked at the grotto, I saw a lady in white. Fear took hold of me. My hand shook."

What she reported seeing in an "aureole of sunlight" was a woman who much resembled a statue of the Madonna in a church nearby, save that instead of treading on a snake as the plaster woman did, the Beautiful Lady wore on each foot a yellow rose.

Not till her third visit did the Lady explain who she was, adding, "I cannot promise to make you happy in this world, but in *the other*." A skeptic may suppose Bernadette's life history shaped her visions, for she had twice been sent as a boarder to another village, once in infancy and later as a hired shepherdess, where she enjoyed milk and bread in abundance offered by a warm-hearted foster mother. In any case, at her ninth appearance, the Lady spoke words both motherly and rural: "Go drink and wash at the fountain. Eat the grass you will find there."

So strange a suggestion led Bernadette to tear hungrily at the grass by the cliff and so to widen the opening over an underground spring which today, some 125 years later, is the most famous water source in the Western world. Over four million pilgrims visit it each summer, and it has become the nexus of a vast ecclesiastical, touristic and economic bureaucracy.

For the Beautiful Lady, who in the end identified herself in terms Bernadette said she had never heard before — "I am the Immaculate Conception" — asked that a chapel be built by the spring and pilgrims attend it "in procession." And so it was done, and so they do, but not by miracle alone.

Four years before the visions, in 1854, the Pope, against stiff opposition from within the church but in response to a centuries-long groundswell of popular faith, had announced the dogma of the Immaculate Conception of the Virgin. Bernadette's visions, tailored and broadcast by her confessors, brought that arcane dogma down to earth and gave it sentimental color.

She herself died at thirty-six, a reclusive nun, leaving only a modest disclaimer: "The Blessed Lady used me. I am nothing without her." In 1925, she was beatified and, eight years later, on the Feast Day of the Immaculate Conception, canonized. The Vatican still maintains a stiffish attitude toward the occasional reported cures at the place, but pastors from all over Europe shepherd their charges there, often in special railroad cars fitted out as hospitals. Even if the cures are dubious or short-lasting, the patients return home, sometimes to institutions that are their lifelong homes, lifted in mind and heart by the experience.

The modern commercial town of Lourdes offers hotels and boarding houses great and small — some four hundred of them — wax museums, audio-visual instructional parlors and shops where you can pick up a cuckoo clock, pine candy, a skein of Pyrenees wool, a set of cowbells, color prints of the Angelus and all sizes of plastic Virgin-shaped water bottles.

Near the sacred precinct stands the Hospice of Our Lady of Seven Sorrows, where bedridden pilgrims are tenderly housed and fed before and after their ritual visit to the shrine. The order was started four years after the visions were officially accepted, by Marie St. Frai, a mountain woman with a mission toward the terminally ill. Her nuns still wear black in bereavement. But the rule of the order is *allegresse,* lightness of heart, and so these sisters' spirit seems to be.

I asked one of them, Sister Stanislaw, a dainty young person with dancing eyes, how she came to the order. She grew up in a secular, bourgeois home, in which she danced and partied and wore pretty clothes. But, she said, "I loved the poor and I followed the thread to the end. When I came into the order, I shut the door behind me. And ever since, it's as if I were in heaven."

The mystical center or axis of heavenly Lourdes is the place by the riverbank where Bernadette knelt to tear at the grass. There bubbles the famous spring, its open mouth protected by plate glass. Its waters are piped off into twice-seven tubs in as many little cold bathrooms where volunteer attendants convey the suffering hopeful. Alternately, in the open air is a row of bright copper taps, through which water is constantly drawn off into gallon tanks, thermoses and bottles to be carried to Christian homes around the world.

Behind that place of holy power, the ground rises sharply toward the cliff top, where great trees fill with mountain wind, bending half-over under the scudding clouds. At the axial summit stands the basilica, a neo-Gothic concoction like a Disneyland castle. In the sanctuary's mosaic-adorned dome, a smiling teenage Bernadette in a golden crown holds out thin arms to her petitioners.

At four each afternoon and again at eight in the evening, a procession takes place in Lourdes. The pilgrims form rows, six abreast, some walking but most wheeled by attendants in chairs or litters.

The lines, also guided by ecclesiastics in full regalia, move gravely, in perfect order, along the base of the cliff beside the spring and the water taps, then out along a wide, tree-shaded alley leading toward the commercial town, where they turn as if in orbit to return toward the basilica and begin again.

I stood there one afternoon watching and asking myself what the meaning was of what I saw.

I was standing as if on a shore while toward me flowed faces by the six, by the twelve, by the hundred — peasant faces and faces suggestive of high station, such a host of sufferers I couldn't have imagined without being there. I even wished for the power of a Homer to help me describe that tremendous host — thick fingers twisted in blankets or splayed upon them, wasted flesh gray as cement, cheeks and noses sharp as cut stone, black brows bristling over sunken eyes; polio-afflicted children in their mothers' arms; a handsome woman whose well-combed hair framed frantic, maniacal eyes; men with barrel chests and legs like rolled towels, stretching anguished faces back toward the spring even after their litters had been wheeled on past.

Look, these shapes on their beds seemed to be saying to the clouds — Look on us: *your handiwork.*

There were still more painful cases to come, reaching with hands flailing like flags run off their pulleys, crossing themselves with the heels of those flapping hands. There were beings without legs or arms at all, with swollen heads too heavy to lift, or shaped like turnips.

The procession moved to amplified music, minor-keyed folk songs, plaintive chants, wistful children's choirs, until at last, inevitably, came the cry from loudspeakers all along the way: *Lord . . . heal us.*

That evening I stood on the balcony of my hotel looking down on thousands of little lights turning in rainy darkness, asking myself whether it was morbidity that had kept me fixed to the sight of so many individuals there in extremes of deformity and fear. But I thought it was not.

I was transfixed at Lourdes because through those imprisoning bodies, some entangled yet separate *will* to continue living had glinted out with shocking immediacy — the same I had witnessed elsewhere in travels to other pilgrimage sites.

In India, you see human suffering in the open, unapologetically displayed, considered an inevitable feature of the material world. Hindu religious practice helps you overlook immediate pain and dwell instead on vast metaphysical abstractions. Western religious thought focuses on the narrower, more piercing mystery of human consciousness in an inhuman world. And every single person who walked or was rolled before my eyes at

Lourdes was like a plumb-weight pulling the cords of a whole belief system into alignment.

I went down to the shrine where the lights were still turning among the trees and took a flame from a taper in the hand of a country woman with averted eyes and heavy facial hair who, when I thanked her, replied in the deep stoic timbre of a hermaphrodite.

There came into my mind then the well-known words *Eppur si muove:* And still it moves. That there exists some natural law or force that binds such pilgrims into their passionate faith and labor seems to me as unarguable — yet still as mysterious — as was, to Galileo, the turning of the earth around the sun.

RICHARD SELZER

A Mask on the Face of Death

FROM LIFE

IT IS TEN O'CLOCK at night as we drive up to the Copacabana, a dilapidated brothel on the rue Dessalines in the red-light district of Port-au-Prince. My guide is a young Haitian, Jean-Bernard. Ten years before, J-B tells me, at the age of fourteen, "like every good Haitian boy" he had been brought here by his older cousins for his *rite de passage*. From the car to the entrance, we are accosted by a half dozen men and women for sex. We enter, go down a long hall that breaks upon a cavernous room with a stone floor. The cubicles of the prostitutes, I am told, are in an attached wing of the building. Save for a red-purple glow from small lights on the walls, the place is unlit. Dark shapes float by, each with a blindingly white stripe of teeth. Latin music is blaring. We take seats at the table farthest from the door. Just outside, there is the rhythmic lapping of the Caribbean Sea. About twenty men are seated at the tables or lean against the walls. Brightly dressed women, singly or in twos or threes, stroll about, now and then exchanging banter with the men. It is as though we have been deposited in act two of Bizet's *Carmen*. If this place isn't Lillas Pastia's tavern, what is it?

Within minutes, three light-skinned young women arrive at our table. They are very beautiful and young and lively. Let them be Carmen, Mercedes and Frasquita.

"I want the old one," says Frasquita, ruffling my hair. The women laugh uproariously.

"Don't bother looking any further," says Mercedes. "We are the prettiest ones."

"We only want to talk," I tell her.

"Aaah, aaah," she crows. "*Massissi.* You are *massissi.*" It is the contemptuous Creole term for homosexual. If we want only to talk, we must be gay. Mercedes and Carmen are slender, each weighing one hundred pounds or less. Frasquita is tall and hefty. They are dressed for work: red taffeta, purple chiffon and black sequins. Among them a thousand gold bracelets and earrings multiply every speck of light. Their bare shoulders are like animated lamps gleaming in the shadowy room. Since there is as yet no business, the women agree to sit with us. J-B orders beer and cigarettes. We pay each woman $10.

"Where are you from?" I begin.

"We are Dominican."

"Do you miss your country?"

"Oh, yes, we do." Six eyes go muzzy with longing. "Our country is the most beautiful in the world. No country is like the Dominican. And it doesn't stink like this one."

"Then why don't you work there? Why come to Haiti?"

"Santo Domingo has too many whores. All beautiful, like us. All light-skinned. The Haitian men like to sleep with light women."

"Why is that?"

"Because always, the whites have all the power and the money. The black men can imagine they do, too, when they have us in bed."

Eleven o'clock. I looked around the room that is still sparsely peopled with men.

"It isn't getting any busier," I say. Frasquita glances over her shoulder. Her eyes drill the darkness.

"It is still early," she says.

"Could it be that the men are afraid of getting sick?" Frasquita is offended.

"Sick! They do not get sick from us. We are healthy, strong. Every week we go for a checkup. Besides, we know how to tell if we are getting sick."

"I mean sick with AIDS." The word sets off a hurricane of taffeta, chiffon and gold jewelry. They are all gesticulation and fury. It is Carmen who speaks.

"AIDS!" Her lips curl about the syllable. "There is no such

thing. It is a false disease invented by the American government to take advantage of the poor countries. The American President hates poor people, so now he makes up AIDS to take away the little we have." The others nod vehemently.

"*Mira, mon cher.* Look, my dear," Carmen continues. "One day the police came here. Believe me, they are worse than the *tonton macoutes* with their submachine guns. They rounded up one hundred and five of us and they took our blood. That was a year ago. None of us have died, you see? We are all still here. *Mira,* we sleep with all the men and we are not sick."

"But aren't there some of you who have lost weight and have diarrhea?"

"One or two, maybe. But they don't eat. That is why they are weak."

"Only the men die," says Mercedes. "They stop eating, so they die. It is hard to kill a woman."

"Do you eat well?"

"Oh, yes, don't worry, we do. We eat like poor people, but we eat." There is a sudden scream from Frasquita. She points to a large rat that has emerged from beneath our table.

"My God!" she exclaims. "It is big like a pig." They burst into laughter. For a moment the women fall silent. There is only the restlessness of their many bracelets. I give them each another $10.

"Are many of the men here bisexual?"

"Too many. They do it for money. Afterward, they come to us." Carmen lights a cigarette and looks down at the small lace handkerchief she has been folding and unfolding with immense precision on the table. All at once she turns it over as though it were the ace of spades.

"*Mira, blanc* . . . look, white man," she says in a voice suddenly full of foreboding. Her skin too seems to darken to coincide with the tone of her voice.

"*Mira,* soon many Dominican women will die in Haiti!"

"Die of what?"

She shrugs. "It is what they do to us."

"Carmen," I say, "if you knew that you had AIDS, that your blood was bad, would you still sleep with men?" Abruptly, she throws back her head and laughs. It is the same laughter with which Frasquita had greeted the rat at our feet. She stands and the others follow.

"*Méchant!* You wicked man," she says. Then, with terrible solemnity, "You don't know anything."

"But you are killing the Haitian men," I say.

"As for that," she says, "everyone is killing everyone else." All at once, I want to know everything about these three — their childhood, their dreams, what they do in the afternoon, what they eat for lunch.

"Don't leave," I say. "Stay a little more." Again, I reach for my wallet. But they are gone, taking all the light in the room with them — Mercedes and Carmen to sit at another table where three men have been waiting. Frasquita is strolling about the room. Now and then, as if captured by the music, she breaks into a few dance steps, snapping her fingers, singing to herself.

Midnight. And the Copacabana is filling up. Now it is like any other seedy nightclub where men and women go hunting. We get up to leave. In the center a couple are dancing a *méringue*. He is the most graceful dancer I have ever watched; she, the most voluptuous. Together they seem to be riding the back of the music as it gallops to a precisely sexual beat. Closer up, I see that the man is short of breath, sweating. All at once, he collapses into a chair. The woman bends over him, coaxing, teasing, but he is through. A young man with a long polished stick blocks my way.

"I come with you?" he asks. "Very good time. You say yes? Ten dollars? Five?"

I have been invited by Dr. Jean William Pape to attend the AIDS clinic of which he is the director. Nothing from the outside of the low whitewashed structure would suggest it as a medical facility. Inside, it is divided into many small cubicles and a labyrinth of corridors. At nine A.M. the hallways are already full of emaciated silent men and women, some sitting on the few benches, the rest leaning against the walls. The only sounds are subdued moans of discomfort interspersed with coughs. How they eat us with their eyes as we pass.

The room where Pape and I work is perhaps ten feet by ten. It contains a desk, two chairs and a narrow wooden table that is

covered with a sheet that will not be changed during the day.
The patients are called in one at a time, asked how they feel and
whether there is any change in their symptoms, then examined
on the table. If the patient is new to the clinic, he or she is
questioned about sexual activities.

A twenty-seven-year-old man whose given name is Miracle
enters. He is wobbly, panting, like a groggy boxer who has let
down his arms and is waiting for the last punch. He is neatly
dressed and wears, despite the heat, a heavy woolen cap. When
he removes it, I see that his hair is thin, dull reddish and
straight. It is one of the signs of AIDS in Haiti, Pape tells me.
The man's skin is covered with a dry itchy rash. Throughout
the interview and examination he scratches himself slowly, ab-
sentmindedly. The rash is called prurigo. It is another symptom
of AIDS in Haiti. This man has had diarrhea for six months.
The laboratory reports that the diarrhea is due to an organism
called cryptosporidium, for which there is no treatment. The
telltale rattling of the tuberculous moisture in his chest is audi-
ble without a stethoscope. He is like a leaky cistern that bubbles
and froths. And, clearly, exhausted.

"Where do you live?" I ask.

"Kenscoff." A village in the hills above Port-au-Prince.

"How did you come here today?"

"I came on the *tap-tap.*" It is the name given to the small buses
that swarm the city, each one extravagantly decorated with religious slogans, icons, flowers, animals, all painted in psychedelic
colors. I have never seen a *tap-tap* that was not covered with
passengers as well, riding outside and hanging on. The vehicles
are little masterpieces of contagion, if not of AIDS then of the
multitude of germs which Haitian flesh is heir to. Miracle is
given a prescription for a supply of Sera, which is something
like Gatorade, and told to return in a month.

"*Mangé kou bêf,*" says the doctor in farewell. "Eat like an ox."
What can he mean? The man has no food or money to buy any.
Even had he food, he has not the appetite to eat or the ability to
retain it. To each departing patient the doctor will say the same
words — "*Mangé kou bêf.*" I see that it is his way of offering a
hopeful goodbye.

"Will he live until his next appointment?" I ask.

"No." Miracle leaves to catch the *tap-tap* for Kenscoff.

Next is a woman of twenty-six who enters holding her right hand to her forehead in a kind of permanent salute. In fact, she is shielding her eye from view. This is her third visit to the clinic. I see that she is still quite well nourished.

"Now, you'll see something beautiful, tremendous," the doctor says. Once seated upon the table, she is told to lower her hand. When she does, I see that her right eye and its eyelid are replaced by a huge fungating ulcerated tumor, a side product of her AIDS. As she turns her head, the cluster of lymph glands in her neck to which the tumor has spread is thrown into relief. Two years ago she received a blood transfusion at a time when the country's main blood bank was grossly contaminated with AIDS. It has since been closed down. The only blood available in Haiti is a small supply procured from the Red Cross.

"Can you give me medicine?" the woman wails.

"No."

"Can you cut it away?"

"No."

"Is there radiation therapy?" I ask.

"No."

"Chemotherapy?" The doctor looks at me in what some might call weary amusement. I see that there is nothing to do. She has come here because there is nowhere else to go.

"What will she do?"

"Tomorrow or the next day or the day after that she will climb up into the mountains to seek relief from the *houngan,* the voodoo priest, just as her slave ancestors did two hundred years ago."

Then comes a frail man in his thirties, with a strangely spiritualized face, like a child's. Pus runs from one ear onto his cheek, where it has dried and caked. He has trouble remembering, he tells us. In fact, he seems confused. It is from toxoplasmosis of the brain, an effect of his AIDS. This man is bisexual. Two years ago he engaged in oral sex with foreign men for money. As I palpate the swollen glands of his neck, a mosquito flies between our faces. I swat at it, miss. Just before coming to Haiti I had read that the AIDS virus had been isolated from a certain mosquito. The doctor senses my thought.

"Not to worry," he says. "So far as we know there has never been a case transmitted by insects."

"Yes," I say. "I see."

And so it goes until the last, the thirty-sixth AIDS patient has been seen. At the end of the day I am invited to wash my hands before leaving. I go down a long hall to a sink. I turn on the faucets but there is no water.

"But what about *you*?" I ask the doctor. "You are at great personal risk here — the tuberculosis, the other infections, no water to wash . . ." He shrugs, smiles faintly and lifts his hands palm upward.

We are driving up a serpiginous steep road into the barren mountains above Port-au-Prince. Even in the bright sunshine the countryside has the bloodless color of exhaustion and indifference. Our destination is the Baptist Mission Hospital, where many cases of AIDS have been reported. Along the road there are slow straggles of schoolchildren in blue uniforms who stretch out their hands as we pass and call out, "Give me something." Already a crowd of outpatients has gathered at the entrance to the mission compound. A tour of the premises reveals that in contrast to the aridity outside the gates, this is an enclave of productivity, lush with fruit trees and poinsettia.

The hospital is clean and smells of creosote. Of the forty beds, less than a third are occupied. In one male ward of twelve beds, there are two patients. The chief physician tells us that last year he saw ten cases of AIDS each week. Lately the number has decreased to four or five.

"Why is that?" we want to know.

"Because we do not admit them to the hospital, so they have learned not to come here."

"Why don't you admit them?"

"Because we would have nothing but AIDS here then. So we send them away."

"But I see that you have very few patients in bed."

"That is also true."

"Where do the AIDS patients go?"

"Some go to the clinic in Port-au-Prince or the general hospital in the city. Others go home to die or to the voodoo priest."

"Do the people with AIDS know what they have before they come here?"

"Oh, yes, they know very well, and they know there is nothing to be done for them."

Outside, the crowd of people is dispersing toward the gate. The clinic has been canceled for the day. No one knows why. We are conducted to the office of the reigning American pastor. He is a tall, handsome Midwesterner with an ecclesiastical smile.

"It is voodoo that is the devil here." He warms to his subject. "It is a demonic religion, a cancer on Haiti. Voodoo is worse than AIDS. And it is one of the reasons for the epidemic. Did you know that in order for a man to become a *houngan* he must perform anal sodomy on another man? No, of course you didn't. And it doesn't stop there. The *houngans* tell the men that in order to appease the spirits they too must do the same thing. So you have ritualized homosexuality. That's what is spreading the AIDS." The pastor tells us of a nun who witnessed two acts of sodomy in a provincial hospital where she came upon a man sexually assaulting a houseboy and another man mounting a male patient in his bed.

"Fornication," he says. "It is Sodom and Gomorrah all over again, so what can you expect from these people?" Outside his office we are shown a cage of terrified, cowering monkeys to whom he coos affectionately. It is clear that he loves them. At the car, we shake hands.

"By the way," the pastor says, "what is your religion? Perhaps I am a kinsman?"

"While I am in Haiti," I tell him, "it will be voodoo or it will be nothing at all."

Abruptly, the smile breaks. It is as though a crack had suddenly appeared in the face of an idol.

From the mission we go to the general hospital. In the heart of Port-au-Prince, it is the exact antithesis of the immaculate facility we have just left — filthy, crowded, hectic and staffed entirely by young interns and residents. Though it is associated with a medical school, I do not see any members of the faculty. We are shown around by Jocelyne, a young intern in a scrub suit. Each bed in three large wards is occupied. On the floor about the beds, hunkered in the posture of the innocent poor, are family members of the patients. In the corridor that constitutes the emergency room, someone lies on a stretcher receiving an intravenous infusion. She is hardly more than a cadaver.

"Where are the doctors in charge?" I ask Jocelyne. She looks at me questioningly.

"We are in charge."

"I mean your teachers, the faculty."

"They do not come here."

"What is wrong with that woman?"

"She has had diarrhea for three months. Now she is dehydrated." I ask the woman to open her mouth. Her throat is covered with the white plaques of thrush, a fungus infection associated with AIDS.

"How many AIDS patients do you see here?"

"Three or four a day. We send them home. Sometimes the families abandon them, then we must admit them to the hospital. Every day, then, a relative comes to see if the patient has died. They want to take the body. That is important to them. But they know very well that AIDS is contagious and they are afraid to keep them at home. Even so, once or twice a week the truck comes to take away the bodies. Many are children. They are buried in mass graves."

"Where do the wealthy patients go?"

"There is a private hospital called Canapé Vert. Or else they go to Miami. Most of them, rich and poor, do not go to the hospital. Most are never diagnosed."

"How do you know these people have AIDS?"

"We don't know sometimes. The blood test is inaccurate. There are many false positives and false negatives. Fifteen percent of those with the disease have negative blood tests. We go by their infections — tuberculosis, diarrhea, fungi, herpes, skin rashes. It is not hard to tell."

"Do they know what they have?"

"Yes. They understand at once and they are prepared to die."

"Do the patients know how AIDS is transmitted?"

"They know, but they do not like to talk about it. It is taboo.

Their memories do not seem to reach back to the true origins
of their disaster. It is understandable, is it not?"

"Whatever you write, don't hurt us any more than we have
already been hurt." It is a young Haitian journalist with whom
I am drinking a rum punch. He means that any further linkage
of AIDS and Haiti in the media would complete the economic
destruction of the country. The damage was done early in the
epidemic when the Centers for Disease Control in Atlanta
added Haitians to the three other high-risk groups — hemo-
philiacs, intravenous drug users and homosexual and bisexual
men. In fact, Haitians are no more susceptible to AIDS than
anyone else. Although the CDC removed Haitians from special
scrutiny in 1985, the lucrative tourism on which so much of the
country's economy was based was crippled. Along with tourism
went much of the foreign business investment. Worst of all was
the injury to the national pride. Suddenly Haiti was indicted as
the source of AIDS in the western hemisphere.

What caused the misunderstanding was the discovery of a
large number of Haitian men living in Miami with AIDS anti-
bodies in their blood. They denied absolutely they were homo-
sexuals. But the CDC investigators did not know that homosexuality is the strongest taboo in Haiti and that no man would
ever admit to it. Bisexuality, however, is not uncommon. Many
married men and heterosexually oriented males will occasionally seek out other men for sex. Further, many, if not most,
Haitian men visit female prostitutes from time to time. It is not
difficult to see that once the virus was set loose in Haiti, the
spread would be swift through both genders.

Exactly how the virus of AIDS arrived is not known. Could it
have been brought home by the Cuban soldiers stationed in
Angola and thence to Haiti, about fifty miles away? Could it
have been passed on by the thousands of Haitians living in exile
in Zaire, who later returned home or immigrated to the United
States? Could it have come from the American and Canadian
homosexual tourists, and, yes, even some U.S. diplomats who
have traveled to the island to have sex with impoverished Haitian men all too willing to sell themselves to feed their families?

Throughout the international gay community Haiti was known as a good place to go for sex.

On a private tip from an official at the Ministry of Tourism, J-B and I drive to a town some fifty miles from Port-au-Prince. The hotel is owned by two Frenchmen who are out of the country, one of the staff tells us. He is a man of about thirty and clearly he is desperately ill. Tottering, short of breath, he shows us about the empty hotel. The furnishings are opulent and extreme — tiger skins on the wall, a live leopard in the garden, a bedroom containing a giant bathtub with gold faucets. Is it the heat of the day or the heat of my imagination that makes these walls echo with the painful cries of pederasty?

The hotel where we are staying is in Pétionville, the fashionable suburb of Port-au-Prince. It is the height of the season but there are no tourists, only a dozen or so French and American businessmen. The swimming pool is used once or twice a day by a single person. Otherwise, the water remains undisturbed until dusk, when the fruit bats come down to drink in midswoop. The hotel keeper is an American. He is eager to set me straight on Haiti.

"What did and should attract foreign investment is a combination of reliable weather, an honest and friendly populace, low wages and multilingual managers."

"What spoiled it?"

"Political instability and a bad American press about AIDS." He pauses, then adds: "To which I hope you won't be contributing."

"What about just telling the truth?" I suggest.

"Look," he says, "there is no more danger of catching AIDS in Haiti than in New York or Santo Domingo. It is not where you are but what you do that counts." Agreeing, I ask if he had any idea that much of the tourism in Haiti during the past few decades was based on sex.

"No idea whatsoever. It was only recently that we discovered that that was the case."

"How is it that you hoteliers, restaurant owners and the Ministry of Tourism did not know what *tout* Haiti knew?"

"Look. All I know is that this is a middle-class, family-oriented hotel. We don't allow guests to bring women, or for that matter men, into their rooms. If they did, we'd ask them to leave immediately."

At five A.M. the next day the telephone rings in my room. A Creole-accented male voice.

"Is the lady still with you, sir?"

"There is no lady here."

"In your room, sir, the lady I allowed to go up with a package?"

"There is no lady here, I tell you."

At seven A.M. I stop at the front desk. The clerk is a young man.

"Was it you who called my room at five o'clock?"

"Sorry," he says with a smile. "It was a mistake, sir. I meant to ring the room next door to yours." Still smiling, he holds up his shushing finger.

Next to Dr. Pape, director of the AIDS clinic, Bernard Liautaud, a dermatologist, is the most knowledgeable Haitian physician on the subject of the epidemic. Together, the two men have published a dozen articles on AIDS in international medical journals. In our meeting they present me with statistics:

• There are more than one thousand documented cases of AIDS in Haiti, and as many as one hundred thousand carriers of the virus.

• Eighty-seven percent of AIDS is now transmitted heterosexually. While it is true that the virus was introduced via the bisexual community, that route has decreased to 10 percent or less.

• Sixty percent of the wives or husbands of AIDS patients tested positive for the antibody.

• Fifty percent of the prostitutes tested in the Port-au-Prince area are infected.

• Eighty percent of the men with AIDS have had contact with prostitutes.

• The projected number of active cases in four years is ten thousand. (Since my last visit, the Haitian Medical Association broke its silence on the epidemic by warning that one million of the country's six million people could be carriers by 1992.)

The two doctors have more to tell. "The crossing over of the plague from the homosexual to the heterosexual community will follow in the United States within two years. This, despite the hesitation to say so by those who fear to sow panic among your population. In Haiti, because bisexuality is more common, there was an early crossover into the general population. The trend, inevitably, is the same in the two countries."

"What is there to do, then?"

"Only education, just as in America. But here the Haitians reject the use of condoms. Only the men who are too sick to have sex are celibate."

"What is to be the end of it?"

"When enough heterosexuals of the middle and upper classes die, perhaps there will be the panic necessary for the people to change their sexual lifestyles."

This evening I leave Haiti. For two weeks I have fastened myself to this lovely fragile land like an ear pressed to the ground. It is a country to break a traveler's heart. It occurs to me that I have not seen a single jogger. Such a public expenditure of energy while everywhere else strength is ebbing—it would be obscene. In my final hours, I go to the Cathédral of Sainte Trinité, the inner walls of which are covered with murals by Haiti's most renowned artists. Here are all the familiar Bible stories depicted in naîveté and piety, and all in such an exuberance of color as to tax the capacity of the retina to receive it, as though all the vitality of Haiti had been turned to paint and brushed upon these walls. How to explain its efflorescence at a time when all else is lassitude and inertia? Perhaps one day the plague will be rendered in poetry, music, painting, but not now. Not now.

KENNETH A. McCLANE

Walls: A Journey to Auburn

FROM COMMUNITY REVIEW

> People are trapped in history and history is trapped in them.
> — James Baldwin

PAUL

The willows are gold again
and now the season seems past thinking
seems past remembrances, seems past
the long lean taking of your breath:

I remember you Paul, always, how you strutted
among the city — Lord of the manor: how you
fought with the drivers, how you never
let one person call you *nigger.* I remember how

you struggled with Dad — loving him in the stridency
of your ill-covered conquest: you wanted to love him
and he you: Yours is the story too often repeated:
the city boy driven to alcohol, death:

But the willow once green is golden:
and I remember you part in desire, part in fact:
You would have hated the lie I make of you; you
would have hated the fact:

Still the willow turns green to golden and still
you visit me in mid-morning, telling me of this awful
place, of the omnipresent *them,* who would not let you live
and I listen:

You who were too proud to equivocate: you who loved as freely
and deeply, as messily, as the world could imagine:

Paul, I miss you. I miss your hear-bearing, stern confidence,
your anger which made ghettos of all of us:

No one struggled more; no one asked more; no one
took the risk of presence more sacredly: in your loss
I understood not only the shores of grief,
but how its walls seem forever rising.

— Kenneth A. McClane

At first glance, Auburn Correctional Facility calls to mind a
feudal castle or a stone and brick edifice worthy of Humphrey
Bogart or Edward G. Robinson. One readily envisions prisoners
dragging their balls and chains, the late night prison break, or
the lights slowly flickering, presaging the imminent electrocu-
tion. This is the stuff of movies, or prison lore. Yet for most of
us, these images, dispatched out of Hollywood, are all we shall
ever know about the real life in our nation's prisons. Most of us
will certainly not be sentenced there; few of us will choose one
as a place to visit.

Yet in every stereotype, there is also a residuum of truth:
people employ generalizations to celebrate a certain verity about
the world; and no myth would have any currency if it did not,
to some unassailable extent, identify something in actual experience. Certainly these cinematic incarnations are not the prison's reality, but they contain a grain of truth, nonetheless. Undeniably, though we may not know what a prison is, our
imaginings, however incompletely, convey that the prison is a
hellish place. Indeed, nothing in our arsenal of national fictions
suggests that the prison is other than horrific. In this case, it is
not a matter of correctness but degree. The prisons — at least
the prisons I have encountered — are infinitely more hellish
than our Hollywood dream makers relate. Inmates in these
places are not planning breakouts or prison riots; they are not
planning anything. To dream of escape is to believe that one
has something worthy of salvaging; to believe, that is, in the
proposition of a self-orchestrated future. The prisons I have
visited are spirit killers: the inmates — no matter how smart,
capable, or engaging — have little sense of their own inextin-
guishable worth, their own human possibility. And this is not by
accident.

Auburn Prison is certainly not the worst reformatory in this country, nor is it the best. Like most, it probably sits in the thick middle range: no inmate would ask to be sentenced there; certainly some might wish to be transferred out; a few of the hardnosed might even like it, its attraction resting in its utter banality. Neither good (that is, experimental) nor bad (and the word here has almost no meaning, since Auburn, at least to my eyes — and no doubt to those of its inmates — is bad enough), Auburn just is.

At bottom, to cast out is not to cast off, and the long trek to Auburn Prison — through the mill town and over the proverbial railroad tracks — is our reminder that the great prison is a great industry: people earn their livings there; whole towns, including Auburn, are built on the day-to-day catering to our national pariah. And like anything which both haunts and fascinates us, we come to the prison's gates armed with rocks and wonder.

Inescapably, and with great trepidation, we know that the inhabitants of our man-made Siberias are our brethren: indeed, it is this weighty realization, this sense that the murderer we so ruthlessly banish may not eternally quiet the potential murderer within, which so frightens us. For it takes but a few precious seconds for the mind's knife to become the hand's weapon. And all of us, at some terrible time, have walked that narrow footpath between the imagined and the horrific.

At Auburn, the first thing one confronts is its massive guard tower, with its rifle-shouldering, no-nonsense officer. By the time you have noticed him, he has noticed you. For a minute or so, he looks down at you, looks around you and, always unsmiling, moves back to his elevation and privacy. What is so astonishing is that *you* feel condemned. You sense in that coldly dismissive gaze, in the backdrop of the great prison, that Gandhi was right: *to think of evil is to act evilly.* And you feel — and this is essential to the prison's apparatus — that the common denominator of your humanity had been discovered: that you are a writer, or a college professor, or a dutiful husband is of little significance. Here, as the guard corroborates, there is no room for romanticism: he's seen your kind before.

One enters Auburn Prison through two gigantic brass doors,

each heavily tooled with elaborate metalwork, at the center of which, like an uneasy coupling, sits the famous symbol of Justice, with its blindfolded woman supporting her two delicately balanced weights. The rest of the portraiture is oddly cherubic, even sexual, as it seems the neoclassical invariably is. It is a celebration of everything, or a reminder of how everything — be it lust or justice — fights in this great amphitheater of a world. I wonder how I might understand this, should I be a prisoner passing on my way to serve a life sentence. He, certainly, knows that life is a great chaos — though this, I hazard, was not the artist's intention. It is, however, a possible interpretation; and it certainly was mine.

The prison's receiving room is reminiscent of an airport security check area, with much the same ingenious technology. At Auburn, there are two guards who inspect both your clothing and carriables. Since I had come to read from my poetry, I had a canvas bag filled with books, and never have my works been so finely perused. Each page was rigorously examined; the bag was checked and rechecked.

After all of us had passed through the metal detector, the guard stamped our right hands with an invisible substance. Then we were counted. Indeed, at the next twelve checkpoints, we were counted and counted again. At each checkpoint there is a "lock in": a holding area where one must remain until a guard electronically dislodges the massive gates. The twelve of us, eleven teachers from Elmira Community College's Inmate Higher Education Program and myself, journeyed from checkpoint to checkpoint like wary salmon. The group was a strange conglomeration. All, with the exception of myself, were white; two of the twelve were women. Six had taught at Auburn for the last two years, and four had worked at the prison for more than a decade. One of the teachers, who wore a jaunty red hat, was the frailest young man I had ever seen: I wondered how he had negotiated his twenty-five years, not to mention the prison's exactings. Yet no one was particularly large or muscular. Sporting his Special Forces army jacket, one man nearly looked the part. But most were aging college and high school teachers, stomachs a notch wider, dreams a bit more remote, than all would like.

Finally we reached "the Yard," and began the long walk through the corridor by cell block D. I say long walk, but it was only a thousand yards. All of a sudden, as if a wall of sound, the prisoners began chanting "Baby, you're beautiful" to the two women with us. Loosened through the stone and Plexiglas, the sound recalled that haunting, terrifying Malabar Caves sojourn, in Forster's *A Passage to India,* where human inadequacy and racism are shown as helpmeets. I kept thinking, *This is not sound; it is an indictment.* And then I realized, undeniably, shamefully, as if for the first time, what it must *cost* to be a woman: to have your body become, day in and day out, the receptacle for so much need, so much ill-digested, inchoate, dangerously poised lust.

I watched as the two women bore it, the college-aged one as strong as a serf in a Breton painting. Quickly her thin face closed down; she walked with a studied, disciplined bearing. Then someone, everyone yelling: *I'll kill you white motherfuckers.* The sound booming and pounding, as if the prison were a giant tuning fork.

Auburn Prison, built in 1816, is one of the oldest maximum security institutions in the United States. A pioneer in penology, Auburn was constructed with individual cells for each inmate, although the original design for these cells, the so-called "Auburn System," was pernicious to say the least. During the early part of the nineteenth century, Auburn became the focus for a unique penal "experiment," in which the most incorrigible inmates were sentenced to absolute, uninterrupted solitary confinement. Permitted neither to leave their cells nor to read nor work, the one hundred "selected" inmates were forced to stand for eight hours a day in total silence. Moreover, in the disturbingly convoluted thinking of the time, this practice was considered "a humane gesture," since it was assumed that an eternity of forced motionlessness might lead to muscle atrophy. No one, of course, questioned whether solitary confinement was in itself inhumane. No, in the rigidly Calvinistic teaching of the day, a prisoner's lot was to be cruel. One burned in hell for one's sins; and prison, most certainly, was this earth's hell.

As might be surmised, in the first year of this heinous experiment, of the hundred prisoners involved, nearly a half went mad, while the others succumbed to tuberculosis and pneumonia. Yet, as is so often the case with prisons, the public was of two minds: on the one hand, it wanted its "custodial houses" to keep the dangerous miscreants away from the community and expected the prison to salve the commonwealth of a serious problem; on the other, it was only willing to permit the prison such "corrective leeway" as might preserve the community's conscience. Clearly, although the public had wanted these Auburn convicts to be severely punished, it did not wish to see them die in plaguelike numbers, at least not within *its* institution. And so, after its first barbarous year, the experiment was ended.

Yet ideas die slowly, and the Auburn penologists — zealots that they were — still believed that solitary confinement was the only way to discipline the abject criminal. Indeed, just two years after their first ill-fated attempt, they began a new, yet no less severe, improvisation on the same theme. Realizing that absolute, forced human isolation encouraged death and psychosis, the Auburn authorities proposed a modified system, where inmates would work in a closely monitored common area, while always returning to their individual cells to sleep. Although the prisoners might come in contact with one another at work and at meals, at no time would they be permitted to talk, exchange letters, or communicate. In 1822, this rigidly proscribed denial of human intercourse — which is still the rubric in many of the world's penal systems — found its most eloquent spokesperson in Auburn's Warden Gersham Powers:

> The demands of nature must indeed be complied with; their [the prisoners] bodies must be fed and clothed . . . but they ought to be deprived of every enjoyment arising from social or kindred feelings and affections; of all knowledge of each other, the world, and their connections with it. Force them to reflection, and let self-tormenting guilt harrow up the tortures of accusing conscience, keener than scorpion stings; until the intensity of their sufferings subdues their stubborn spirits, and humbles them to a realizing sense of the enormity of their crimes and their obligation to reform.

Thankfully, the Auburn Prison of 1822 is not the institution that one confronts today. In 1986, as a case in point, even the term "prison" is anachronistic: Auburn is a "correctional facility." Yet even though Warden Powers is long buried, his philosophy, I surmise, still informs these halls. For Auburn, like any architecturally planned, functional structure, was constructed to facilitate a certain notion of reality. When these long tiers of individual cells were created — small, dark, and cramped — certain expectations were being fulfilled; certain others, suggested. Hopefully, the prisoner in 1986 will not die from long hours of standing in his cell, as fifty of his brethren once did; but he still will find his room terribly constrictive; he still will notice how the walls of his cell jut out into the corridor, a further hindrance to "unwanted talk"; and he still will discover — and this he will relish, albeit silently — that this is *his* cell: however cramped, squalid, and dark.

This, of course, is no insignificant development. However small his quarters, the inmate possesses something which is *his:* he can hang something on the wall (provided he has something to hang) and can, as much as is humanly possible, leave his mark on his space. For a time, he does not have to worry about someone else's belongings, feelings, or privacy — at least while *they* are in *their* cells. And if you are a prisoner, this is essential and important rest. Certainly, one may murder oneself in one's own cell; but amongst the prison community, there are literally hundreds of people who might potentially murder you, and all for some supposed slight, and one not even necessarily directed at them, but at their friend, lover, or even, God knows, at someone who is just a resident of their cell block. In one's cell — for a few precious hours then — one can safely "watch one's back." Of course, there might be a fire and one might perish; but there might be a nuclear disaster in New York, and all New York might evaporate in the conflagration. A prisoner, like most New Yorkers, is willing to live with that possibility. But he does not relish placing his life in harm's way, amongst people who know all too much about harm. And thus his cell is, in this darkest of places, "heaven sent."

Yet none of this enlightened humanitarianism — that social architects might applaud and Anton Chekhov, weary of Sahalin, might, understandably, envy — has much effect on the visitor.

He is far too much a victim of his own life, and the perilous nature of it. If he has not valued his freedom before coming to Auburn, if he has not thought about whom he is (and therefore what he must protect), he does so now. For whatever else a prison does, it demands that one confront it. If you are a prisoner, it might take you a dozen years to realize that the life you *hope* to create requires, above all else, that it be lived *within* these walls, for these *walls do not go away*. Here, of all the world's places, there is everything to accept.

For those of us who are *visiting* — and this, indeed, is the greatest privilege — our status is in our faces, our movements, our bowels. We know, and we cling to this as we might to our children, that *we shall walk out of here, tonight, at a certain hour*.

And it is just this privilege which both the prisoners and, to a lesser degree, the guards wish to cost us dear. When we walked through the corridors, the catcalls, the *Baby, you look beautiful,* and *I'll kill you white motherfuckers,* were an expression of lust, anger, and bitterness; but they were also an expression of our envious ability to put off that which the inmates could not elude. In our quick, stuttering movements, in our downturned faces, in our trying to look courageous we possessed a vulnerability — and how powerfully, in a different way, we sensed it — that they could ill afford. Indeed, it was this flabby indulgence, this possibility for openly embracing fear (swimming in it, as one might a fur coat), for which they despised us. Fear would set them to the barbells late at night; fear would turn them taciturn; fear would cause them to stuff the fork into another's ribs before he jabbed it into theirs; fear was *not* that mad dash between buildings, that shrinking, scared, trying-to-look-not-so movement which so claimed us.

I had been invited to Auburn Correctional Facility to read and talk about my poetry for an incredible two-and-a-half-hour class. I remember how my stomach tightened when I first learned that I had to perform for that length of time. By nature I am a one-hour person. Indeed, whenever I attend a lecture that swells on beyond that point, I find myself imaginatively melding with the audience, thinking how I must meet someone in three minutes, catch the late bus, or do the laundry. But more accurately, I clung to the question of time, because it was the easiest thing on which to cling. Although it would be difficult to fill one hundred and fifty minutes, my great confrontation was not with the clock, but with those time would place before me.

The forty inmates who made up my class were participants in Elmira Community College's Inmate Higher Education Program. Most of the students were black and in their early twenties; one man had gray hair. Conspicuously, the three white prisoners clustered together, in much the same way blacks often huddle together in the outer world. At Cornell, where I teach, this behavior is often looked upon as unfriendly at best, and racist at worst. Few whites would concede that blacks, like themselves, are merely desirous of fraternizing with people with whom they share a common interest and experience. Whites, because this is America, have never had to justify their actions; they sit with and entertain whomever they wish. Yet when blacks exercise the same human prerogative, it is considered an act of dismissal, subterfuge, or war.

At Auburn I couldn't help but wonder what those white inmates felt with the tables turned. Was their isolation that of the lonely island, or the citadel beyond assault? Clearly they were in the minority in the prison population, but they were also white; and I sensed, even in this last outcrop of civilization, that their color still had some sting. And even if it didn't call the heavens down, it did testify that they were, in prison parlance, some "bad muthafuckas." For the few whites who found themselves sent up to Auburn had been convicted of repeated, unusually brutal offenses. Indeed, the viciousness of whites' crimes seemed in inverse proportion to their numbers. As one of the black inmates described them, and not without a touch of envy, "If evil walked, them cats be Jesse Owens."

At Auburn one thing was immediately apparent: the inmates were delighted that I had come. In the first instance, I was someone they didn't know who took them away from the tedium of the ordinary; but, more importantly, I was the first black teacher they had encountered in twelve months. Once I read two poems, the questions began: Where had I been raised? What was my background? How had I managed to evade prison? I breathlessly explained that I had grown up in Harlem, amongst two good parents "who rode my ass"; but offered little else.

This, of course, was an oversimplification, if not a direct lie. I had been raised in Harlem, but in the most unusual of circumstances. My father was a physician, my mother was a brilliant artist and writer, and I had attended one of the finest — and personally, most ruinous — independent schools in the city. I lived in Harlem, which is to say that I saw much, but I certainly hadn't lived the lives these inmates had: indeed, I had spent my entire life keeping myself at a safe remove from anything which might bring me to Harlem's reality. Yes, I had done a little of this and a bit of that, but I was always at the sidelines. I knew where the deep water was — everyone knew that. But I remained a shore bird.

My brother, however, paid for my escape. A talented drummer who shared the same exact IQ as myself (something which my mother was always wont to remind me), he lived in those streets, and it, and the difficult contradictions he faced, broke him. My brother, Paul, would ultimately drink himself to death at twenty-nine. He was tough, independent, and full of bitterness. He was, as I read that evening, "hungry for the end of the world."

The inmates particularly liked my "brother" poems: they too had brothers they missed and loved, brothers whose ultimate lives might be even more menaced than their own. This I found oddly comforting: in our desire to transcend the horror of crime, we hasten to view the criminal as someone without any notion of family or community. Certainly, this is our clumsy way of insulating ourselves from *their* human truth: for it is far too frightening to imagine ourselves as potential criminals, and far more convenient, and comforting, to see the criminal as truly subhuman. Indeed, had they been born with twelve heads or twenty spikes, we might finally, irrevocably, divorce ourselves from them. But as they come with two arms, two legs, a pumping heart, and a wondrous mind, their profanation suggests our own ratty flesh; their banishment, our own ever possible exile.

In truth, the lies we fabricate to distance ourselves from others invariably rise to haunt us. We may lie *to* ourselves, but others are under no obligation to lie *for* us. Whatever these inmates were — and all of them were sentenced to Auburn for corporal crimes — they would not permit me to view them merely as maniacs, psychopaths, or what have you. They were people, cussed and joy-filled: people capable of tenderness and murder: people like me and yet unlike me, because I haven't yet, thank goodness, killed anyone.

I learned a great deal in those two hours and thirty minutes; much more, I trust, than those inmates learned from me. At one point, one of the students asked me to describe how it felt to enter the prison. I shall never forget how dangerous that question seemed to me, dangerous because it gave voice to all my inner disquiet. Quickly I found myself looking about the room, noticing that there were no guards within immediate reach. To this day I don't know what made me sense my immediate vulnerability: certainly it had to do with the poignancy of the question, for in some profound way, the inmate was asking me to unburden myself, to tell him how I had found a means to live with fear; yet just as centrally — and this was as palpable as air — he wanted to know if I thought he was a beast, if I had cast him beyond the shores of humanity (and if I had, he might make my suspicions *real*); but most fundamentally, most crucially, I realized that he, Lord knows how, had given language to my own questioning, my own inadequate "sew-work." I hadn't made peace with the prison, with him, or with myself. And he knew it.

After some time — it seemed like hours, it was merely seconds — I told him the truth. I stated that the prison was the most frightening, scary place I had ever seen. He was quiet for a moment, and then he smiled. He agreed with me. *Agreed with me. Yes,* this place was as hellish as he imagined. In my own terror, I had thought that he had been holding me to my life; in truth, I had been holding him to his. He, like all of us, needed to affirm that his own powers of discrimination were accurate, that his experience might be mirrored by others. Although Auburn was brutal and spirit-crushing, it had not yet destroyed his ability to perceive and differentiate shades of horror; it had not yet destroyed him. Of this, at least, I could bear witness.

There were two questions which were asked again and again of me. Inmate after inmate wanted to know if I thought I would continue to write and to teach. At first, I was not at all surprised at this question: it is a common one, asked eternally of writers. Yet on this particular occasion, whenever I attempted to answer the question, the audience would neither hear nor accept my response. Again and again I would state that Yes, I thought I would continue to teach, and again and again I would be presented with the same question. It was maddening.

Finally I realized what was happening. To these inmates, my tacit belief in the probability of an *assured* future, my notion that I could reasonably expect to find myself in a *certain* circumstance, at a *certain* time, was as mind-boggling as if I had just sprouted wings. For them, there had never been *one* veritable day of certainty: when they were in the streets, they had to live on mother wit; now, in prison, every minute brought new perils. Indeed, if there was one inexpugnable axiom for them, it was the present tense, the resounding *I am*. Of nothing else could they be certain.

Ultimately, their questions were, if you will, *pre*-questions: they were the first, tentative vocalizations of wonder. The inmates wanted me to repeat myself, because they could not understand the specifics of my answer until they understood the astonishing grammar from which it sprang. Miraculously, although we shared the ability to make sounds, we had yet to forge a common language. And it was just this which made us tongue-tied at revelation: having so much to say, and no means, no suitable lexicon for conveying it, we were exiles in a country more hideous, terrible, and unreachable than any Kafka had ever imagined.

If Auburn cut the prisoner off from the world, it, more horribly, sealed them into their *futureless* self. Usually, thankfully, human beings — because of imagination, spirit, and plain cantankerousness — evolve the means to transcend most anything, even the grim ghetto of self. Yet at Auburn, and I trust at most prisons, this could not be tolerated (*jails, we must remember, are to keep people in*). As any jailer knows, the walls of the present are always dismantled in the future; but there is *no* future, if there is no ability to set aside and reconstitute, to interdict and reposition, then the present becomes the almighty, and the walls become unconquerable. Although I did not interview the jailors, I did see the jailed. For most of them, the walls without had become the walls within; and such walls never, no matter what Joshua does, *come a-tumbling down.*

After I had finished reading, one student, who had heretofore been silent, spoke up, reminding me that although "we prisoners might seem like nice guys, we're here because we killed people," the last statement clearly intended to elicit a reaction from me, the naïve college professor. Now, after two long hours, I found myself getting angry: I wondered why he so wanted to frighten me, especially since it seemed that my easy fright was all he desired. But then I realized that he might be attempting something far more humanly essential and generous. As I had told him of my brother, had offered that intimate bond of personal experience and blood, so too would he share his only sacred gift — his experience — with me. Difficult and tentative as his motions were (and confession, by nature, is always stony), this man wanted to speak to me as man to man, witness to witness.

What first I had taken as a vitriolic assault was merely this man's life: he had offered it up, in the ready language at his disposal. I might not like the life he had, or the brutal language by which he expressed it, but I certainly should permit him his truth. It might sting; I might refuse to listen; but this is the privilege of the listener. The teller, sadly, can only recount his tale: he can lie, but that, in itself, is just another corner of revelation.

At bottom, this man was trying to claim his humanity as he tested mine. If I had my naïveté to lose, he had something far more essential to win, his personhood; and he would struggle for that at all costs. Indeed, it was the lopsidedness of this battle, the vast inequality of our two involvements, which so charged the moment. I, since I had not yet truly become pariah, had the privilege of arguing over the nature of my privilege (or even tossing it away if I so desired); while he, on the other hand, had no choice but to plead for his essential humanity. He, certainly, would not choose to walk into this prison — not with what he knew. Indeed, if there was light at the end of the proverbial tunnel for him, he had not only to create the light, but the instrument by which it might be seen. And since our predicaments were far from being reciprocal, the wolves loomed at every corner.

And yet remembering my childhood joy when I "acted the nigger" on the New York City bus, negotiating that delicious nether world that only the marginalized are allowed, I understood what that inmate felt. When those "high-class" whites saw me, the chocolate-faced boy, they knew that I was the flesh and blood repository of their assumptions — the authentic ghetto type; and I, even though I attended the crème-de-la-crème private school in the city, gave them a show worthy of their concern. Although I didn't have any real power, I could certainly fool those people. I'd talk jive, look evil, and "badmouth" the toughest looking white boy I could find. And then, laughing all the way, I'd romp over to the Collegiate School, the place where ninety percent of *their* children failed to gain entrance.

Yet notwithstanding my minor triumph, I bitterly decried the subterra in which it was purchased. Certainly one can, in extreme cases, extricate some pleasure out of hell; but hell is nonetheless hell; it is certainly never heaven. And thus the inmate, though he needed me to facilitate his journey to self-announcement, could excuse neither the brashness of my declaration — I was asking him to justify himself — nor the insubstantiality of my presence. Whatever else I was, to him and the rest of the prison population, my credentials were dubious at best. A Cornell professorship might mean something in the outer world; but here, it was as valuable as an expired driver's license, or an old football ticket. Power, we must remember, is negotiable only where it has validity: in the prison, had I been physically strong or good at cards, I might expect a measure of admiration, respect, and fellowship; but *sans* these talents, my degrees and professional standing, understandably, met with little interest. Indeed, the value system which had so honored me had exiled them. For those who had been ritually cast out, certainly, it would be an inhumanly bitter pill to swallow to be expected to salute the son as they suffered under his father. Blake to the contrary, the cut worm does *not* forgive the plow.

Ultimately the human voice is a very wondrous thing: it can show, at rare moments, everything which propels it. That these men had once been murderers meant that they could also be something else; at least, that was what the new wavering in this young man's voice suggested. I watched him slowly negotiate the incline of possibility, his voice swelling into a trill of astonishment, at first slow, gravelly, and then steady. Certainly this wasn't a wave of spontaneous announcement: he had seen far too much for that. More, it was the hard, pruned, strained depth-taking of someone who sensed, albeit bitterly, that the world might return nothing. But still he, with no reason that I could fathom, kept speaking, his own narrative building, gathering. Suddenly, words suggested words, listening suggested listeners, confession suggested healing; and he said, both to himself and to me, "Man, you ain't bad." And that was enough.

At ten o'clock the bell rang, and the prisoners began to file back to their cells. Of the forty I spoke with, twenty or so came up to me, shook my hand, and asked if I might come back. None of these congratulations came from the three white prisoners, something which I can only presume to understand. My poems are not overly racial: I didn't read a large number of racial poems. Possibly I had neglected them; possibly they did not like my reading. I just do not know.

The journey out of the prison seemed more efficacious. When we entered the yard this time, it was filled with inmates pumping iron, smoking, and chatting. Again we were escorted by four guards. Now the towers, with their no-nonsense sentries, were well lighted, although the lights were not dancing over the grounds as in the movies. For the first time I looked at the one-hundred-year-old granite. These walls had been made to last: hell, as Gersham Powers had so wanted, would remain interminable.

Near the first checkpoint, I saw one of the inmates who had been at my seminar. He smiled — a long, good smile — a smile that seemed almost hungry, a smile much like my brother's. I wished him well.

Then we began the elaborate countings until we reached the

last checkpoint, where they asked us to put our right hands under an ultraviolet light. The light illuminated the invisible stamp that had been placed on our wrists when we first entered the prison. It seemed such a fitting way to leave this place: the once invisible stamp, now glowing luminously green, as yet again another mystery.

KIMBERLY WOZENCRAFT

Notes from the Country Club

FROM WITNESS

THEY HAD THE Haitians up the hill, in the "camp" section where
they used to keep the minimum security cases. The authorities
were concerned that some of the Haitians might be diseased, so
they kept them isolated from the main coed prison population
by lodging them in the big square brick building surrounded by
eight-foot chain-link with concertina wire on top. We were not
yet familiar with the acronym AIDS.

One or two of the Haitians had drums, and in the evenings
when the rest of us were in the Big Yard, the drum rhythms
carried over the bluegrass to where we were playing gin or
tennis or softball or just hanging out waiting for dark. When
they really got going some of them would dance and sing. Their
music was rhythmic and beautiful, and it made me think of
freedom.

There were Cubans loose in the population, spattering their
guttural Spanish in streams around the rectangular courtyard,
called Central Park, at the center of the prison compound.
These were Castro's Boat People, guilty of no crime in this
country, but requiring sponsors before they could walk the
streets as free people.

Walking around the perimeter of Central Park was like taking
a trip in microcosm across the United States. Moving leftward
from the main entrance, strolling along under the archway that
covers the wide sidewalk, you passed the doorway to the Wom-
en's Unit, where I lived, and it was how I imagined Harlem to
be. There was a white face here and there, but by far most of

them were black. Ghetto blasters thunked out rhythms in the
sticky evening air, and folks leaned against the window sills,
smoking, drinking Cokes, slinking and nodding. Every once in
a while a joint was passed around, and always there was somebody pinning, checking for hacks on patrol.

Past Women's Unit was the metal door to the Big Yard, the
main recreation area of three or four acres, two sides blocked
by the building, two sides fenced in the usual way — chain-link
and concertina wire. It was generally in the Big Yard entrance
that you would find people "jumping." Prison sex was fast and
furious; even the threat of shipment to a maximum security
joint did not entirely subjugate the criminal libido. I walked out
to breakfast one morning and saw a set of brown buttocks
pumping between a pair of upraised knees; they were halfway
hidden in the shrubbery, but the tableau leaped out at me like
a sudden closeup in a movie. The important thing was not to
stare or look startled. I could see a hack at the far side of Central
Park, strolling along in the six o'clock morning, oblivious to the
goings on directly across the courtyard from him. As I walked
past the entryway, I nodded to a young man standing at the
edge of the courtyard and smoking a cigarette. He had the hack
under surveillance. If the blue-suited guard came too close, the
fellow would warn his friends in the bushes to get out fast.

Sex in prison always involved at least three people, two to
copulate, one to pull jiggers. It was sex in the bathrooms, sex in
the bushes, sex in the closets, sex in the little out-of-the-way
coves at the end of unused hallways. I just wanted to do my time
and get out, but by the morning of the sixth month, I was
waking up aching, so when the chance presented itself, I took
it. It was the right time of the month not to get pregnant (that's
always a little risky but desperation pushed me to play the odds),
and the boss was out sick. The hack in charge of the Sewage
Plant was forced to keep an eye on Landscape as well as his own
crew. Rick, a fellow inmate who kept the Landscape tractors
running, was a genuinely decent fellow, a real friend who was
hurting as much as I was, and when he raised his eyebrows at
me in the shop that morning I nodded yes. The whole crew
paired off that day, one woman even doing double duty. Rick
and I did it in the safest place on the entire compound — in the

warden's backyard. After, he held me gently for a long time, and it was so good just to touch another human being that I felt like crying.

Past the Big Yard you entered the Blue Ridge Mountains, a sloping grassy area on the edge of Central Park, where the locals, people from Kentucky, Tennessee, and the surrounding environs, sat around playing guitars and singing, and every once in a while passing around a quart of hooch. They make it from grapefruit juice and a bit of yeast smuggled out of the kitchen. Some of the inmates who worked in Cable would bring out pieces of a black foam rubber substance and wrap it around empty Cremora jars to make thermos jugs of sorts. They would mix the grapefruit juice and yeast in the containers and stash them in some out-of-the-way spot for a few weeks until presto! you had hooch, bitter and tart and sweet all at once, only mildly alcoholic, but entirely suitable for evening cocktails in Central Park.

Next, at the corner, was the Commissary, a tiny store tucked inside the entrance to Veritas, the second women's unit. It wasn't much more than a few shelves behind a wall of Plexiglas, with a constant line of inmates spilling out of the doorway. They sold packaged chips, cookies, pens and writing paper, toiletries, some fresh fruit, and the ever-popular ice cream, sold only in pints. You had to eat the entire pint as soon as you bought it, or else watch it melt, because there weren't any refrigerators. Inmates were assigned one shopping night per week, allowed to buy no more than seventy-five dollars' worth of goods per month, and were permitted to pick up a ten-dollar roll of quarters if they had enough money in their prison account. Quarters were the basic spending unit in the prison; possession of paper money was a shippable offense. There were vending machines stocked with junk food and soda, and they were supposedly what the quarters were to be used for. But we gambled, we bought salami or fried chicken sneaked out by the food service workers, and of course people sold booze and drugs. The beggars stood just outside the Commissary door. Mostly they were Cubans, saying "Oye! Mira! Mira! Hey, Poppy, one quarter for me? One cigarette for me, Poppy?"

There was one Cuban whom I was specially fond of. His name

was Shorty. The name said it, he was only about five-two, and he looked just like Mick Jagger. I met him in Segregation, an isolated section of tiny cells where prisoners were locked up for having violated some institutional rule or another. They tossed me in there the day I arrived; again the authorities were concerned, supposedly for my safety. I was a police woman before I became a convict, and they weren't too sure that the other inmates would like that. Shorty saved me a lot of grief when I went into Seg. It didn't matter if you were male or female there, you got stripped and handed a tee shirt, a pair of boxer shorts and a set of Peter Pans — green canvas shoes with thin rubber soles designed to prevent you from running away. As if you could get past three steel doors and a couple of hacks just to start with. When I was marched down the hall between the cells the guys started whistling and hooting and they didn't shut up even after I was locked down. They kept right on screaming until finally I yelled out, "Yo no comprendo!" and then they all moaned and said, "Another fucking Cuban," and finally got quiet. Shorty was directly across from me, I could see his eyes through the rectangular slot in my cell door. He rattled off a paragraph or two of Spanish, all of which was lost on me, and I said quietly, "Yo no comprendo bien español. Yo soy de Texas, you hablo inglés?" I could tell he was smiling by the squint of his eyes, and he just said, "Bueno." When the hacks came around to take us out for our mandatory hour of recreation, which consisted of standing around in the Rec area while two guys shot a game of pool on the balcony above the gym, Shorty slipped his hand into mine and smiled up at me until the hack told him to cut it out. He knew enough English to tell the others in Seg that I was not really Spanish, but he kept quiet about it, and they left me alone.

Beyond the Commissary, near the door to the dining hall, was East St. Louis. The prison had a big portable stereo system which they rolled out a few times a week so that an inmate could play at being a disc jockey. They had a good-sized collection of albums and there was usually some decent jazz blasting out of there. Sometimes people danced, unless there were uptight hacks on duty to tell them not to.

California was next. It was a laid back kind of corner near the doors to two of the men's units. People stood around and smoked hash or grass or did whatever drugs happened to be available and there was sometimes a sort of slow-motion game of handball going on. If you wanted drugs, this was the place to come.

If you kept walking, you would arrive at the Power Station, the other southern corner where the politicos-gone-wrong congregated. It might seem odd at first to see these middle-aged government mavens standing around in their Lacoste sport shirts and Sans-a-belt slacks, smoking pipes or cigars and waving their arms to emphasize some point or other. They kept pretty much to themselves and ate together at the big round tables in the cafeteria, sipping cherry Kool-Aid and pretending it was Cabernet Sauvignon.

That's something else you had to deal with — the food. It was worse than elementary school steam table fare. By the time they finished cooking it, it was tasteless, colorless, and nutritionless. The first meal I took in the dining room was lunch. As I walked toward the entry, a tubby fellow was walking out, staggering really, rolling his eyes as though he were dizzy. He stopped and leaned over, and I heard someone yell, "Watch out, he's gonna puke!" I ducked inside so as to miss the spectacle. They were serving some rubbery, faint pink slabs that were supposed to be ham, but I didn't even bother to taste mine. I just slapped at it a few times to watch the fork bounce off and then ate my potatoes and went back to the unit.

Shortly after that I claimed that I was Jewish, having gotten the word from a friendly New York lawyer who was in for faking some of his clients' immigration papers. The kosher line was the only way to get a decent meal in there. In fact, for a long time they had a Jewish baker from Philadelphia locked up, and he made some truly delicious cream puffs for dessert. They sold for seventy-five cents on the black market, but once I had established myself in the Jewish community I got them as part of my regular fare. They fed us a great deal of peanut butter on the kosher line; every time the "goyim" got meat, we got peanut butter, but that was all right with me. Eventually I was asked to light the candles at the Friday evening services, since none of the real Jewish women bothered to attend. I have to

admit that most of the members of our little prison congregation were genuine *alter kokers,* but some of them were amusing.
And I enjoyed learning first hand about Judaism. The services
were usually very quiet, and the music, the ancient intoning
songs, fortified me against the screeching pop-rock vocal assaults that were a constant in the Women's Unit. I learned to
think of myself as the *shabot shiksa,* and before my time was up,
even the rabbi seemed to accept me.

I suppose it was quite natural that the Italians assembled just
"down the street" from the offending ex-senators, judges, and
power brokers. Just to the left of the main entrance. The first
night I made the tour, a guy came out of the shadows near the
building and whispered to me, "What do you need, sweetheart?
What do you want, I can get it. My friend Ahmad over there,
he's very rich, and he wants to buy you things. What'll it be, you
want some smoke, a few ludes, vodka, cigarettes, maybe some
kosher salami fresh from the kitchen? What would you like?" I
just stared at him. The only thing I wanted at that moment was
out, and even Ahmad's millions, if they existed at all, couldn't
do that. The truth is, every guy I met in there claimed to be
wealthy, to have been locked up for some major financial crime.
Had I taken all of them up on their offers of limousines to pick
me up at the front gate when I was released and take me to the
airport for a ride home in a private Lear jet, I would have
needed my own personal cop out front just to direct traffic.

Ahmad's Italian promoter eventually got popped for zinging
the cooking teacher one afternoon on the counter in the home
economics classroom, right next to the new Cuisinart. The assistant warden walked in on the young lovebirds, and before the
week was up, even the Cubans were walking around singing
about it. They had a whole song down, to the tune of "Borracho
Me Acosté a Noche."

At the end of the tour, you would find the jaded New Yorkers, sitting at a picnic table or two in the middle of the park,
playing gin or poker and bragging about their days on Madison
Avenue and Wall Street, lamenting the scarcity of good deli,
even on the kosher line, and planning where they would take
their first real meal upon release.

*

If you think federal correctional institutions are about the business of rehabilitation, drop by for an orientation session one day. There at the front of the classroom, confronting rows of mostly black faces, will be the warden, or the assistant warden, or the prison shrink, pacing back and forth in front of the blackboard and asking the class, "Why do you think you're here?" This gets a general grumble, a few short, choked laughs. Some well-meaning soul always says it — rehabilitation.

"Nonsense!" the lecturer will say. "There are several reasons for locking people up. Number one is incapacitation. If you're in here, you can't be out there doing crime. Secondly, there is deterrence. Other people who are thinking about doing crime see that we lock people up for it and maybe they think twice. But the real reason you are here is to be punished. Plain and simple. You done wrong, now you got to pay for it. Rehabilitation ain't even part of the picture. So don't be looking to us to rehabilitate you. Only person can rehabilitate you is you. If you feel like it, go for it, but leave us out. We don't want to play that game."

So that's it. You're there to do time. I have no misgivings about why I went to prison. I deserved it. I was a cop, I got strung out on cocaine, I violated the rights of a pornographer. My own drug use as an undercover narcotics agent was a significant factor in my crime. But I did it and I deserved to be punished. Most of the people I met in Lexington, though, were in for drugs, and the majority of them hadn't done anything more than sell an ounce of cocaine or a pound of pot to some apostle of the law.

It seems lately that almost every time I look at the *New York Times* op-ed page, there is something about the drug problem. I have arrested people for drugs, and I have had a drug problem myself. I have seen how at least one federal correctional institution functions. It does not appear that the practice of locking people up for possession or distribution of an insignificant quantity of a controlled substance makes any difference at all in the amount of drug use that occurs in the United States. The drug laws are merely another convenient source of political rhetoric for aspiring officeholders. Politicians know that an antidrug stance is an easy way to get votes from parents who are terrified that their children might wind up as addicts. I do not advocate drug use. Yet, having seen the criminal justice system from several angles, as a police officer, a court bailiff, a defendant, and a prisoner, I am convinced that prison is not the answer to the drug problem, or for that matter to many other white-collar crimes. If the taxpayers knew how their dollars were being spent inside some prisons, they might actually scream out loud.

There were roughly 1,800 men and women locked up in Lex, at a ratio of approximately three men to every woman, and it did get warm in the summertime. To keep us tranquil they devised some rather peculiar little amusements. One evening I heard a commotion on the steps at the edge of Central Park and looked over to see a rec specialist with three big cardboard boxes set up on the plaza, marked 1, 2, and 3. There were a couple of hundred inmates sitting at the bottom of the steps. Dennis, the rec specialist, was conducting his own version of the television game show *Let's Make a Deal!* Under one of the boxes was a case of soda, under another was a racquetball glove, and under a third was a fly swatter. The captive contestant picked door number 2, which turned out to contain the fly swatter, to my way of thinking the best prize there. Fly swatters were virtually impossible to get through approved channels, and therefore cost as much as two packs of cigarettes on the black market.

Then there was the Annual Fashion Show, where ten or twenty inmates had special packages of clothing sent in, only for the one evening, and modeled them on stage while the baddest drag queen in the compound moderated and everyone else ooohed and aahhed. They looked good up there on stage in Christian Dior and Ralph Lauren instead of the usual fatigue pants and white tee shirts. And if such activities did little to prepare inmates for a productive return to society, well, at least they contributed to the fantasyland aura that made Lexington such an unusual place.

I worked in Landscape, exiting the rear gate of the compound each weekday morning at about nine after getting a half-hearted frisk from one of the hacks on duty. I would climb on my tractor to drive to the staff apartment complex and pull weeds or mow the lawn. Landscape had its prerogatives. We raided the gardens regularly and at least got to taste fresh vegetables from time to time. I had never eaten raw corn before, but it could not have tasted better. We also brought in a goodly supply of real vodka, and a bit of hash now and then, for parties in our rooms after lights out. One guy strapped a six-pack of Budweiser to his arms with masking tape and then put on his prison-issue Army field jacket. When he got to the rear gate, he raised his arms straight out at shoulder level, per instructions, and the hack patted down his torso and legs, never bothering to check his arms. The inmate had been counting on that. He smiled at the hack and walked back to his room, a six-pack richer.

I was fortunate to be working Landscape at the same time as Horace, a fellow who had actually lived in the city of Lexington before he was locked up. His friends made regular deliveries of assorted contraband, which they would stash near a huge elm tree near the outer stone fence of the reservation. Horace would drive his tractor over, make the pickup, and the rest of us would carry it, concealed, through the back gate when we went back inside for lunch or at the end of the day. "Contraband" included everything from drugs to blue eye shadow. The assistant warden believed that female inmates should wear no cosmetics other than what she herself used—a bit of mascara and a light shade of lipstick. I have never been a plaything of Fashion, but I did what I could to help the other women prisoners in their never-ending quest for that Cover Girl look.

You could depend on the fact that most of the hacks would rather have been somewhere else, and most of them really didn't care *what* the inmates did, as long as it didn't cause any commotion. Of course, there were a few you had to look out for. The captain in charge of security was one of them. We tried a little experiment once, after having observed that any time he saw someone laughing, he took immediate steps to make the inmate and everyone around him acutely miserable. Whenever we saw him in the area, we immediately assumed expressions of intense unhappiness, even of despair. Seeing no chance to make anyone more miserable than they already appeared to be, the captain left us alone.

Almost all of the female hacks, and a good number of the males, had outrageously large derrières, a condition we inmates referred to as "the federal ass." This condition may have resulted from the fact that most of them appeared, as one inmate succinctly described it, simply to be "putting in their forty a week to stay on the government teat." Employment was not an easy thing to find in Kentucky.

Despite the fact that Lexington is known as a "country club" prison, I must admit that I counted days. From the first moment that I was in, I kept track of how many more times I would have to watch the sun sink behind eight feet of chain-link, of how many more days I would have to spend eating, working, playing and sleeping according to the dictates of a "higher authority." I don't think I can claim that I was rehabilitated. If anything I underwent a process of dehabilitation. What I learned was what Jessica Mitford tried to tell people many years ago in her book *Kind and Usual Punishment.* Prison is a business, no different from manufacturing tires or selling real estate. It keeps people employed and it provides cheap labor for NASA, the U.S. Postal Service, and other governmental or quasi-governmental agencies. For a short time, before I was employed in Landscape, I worked as a finisher of canvas mailbags, lacing white rope through metal eyelets around the top of the bags and attaching clamps to the ropes. I made one dollar and fourteen cents for every one hundred that I did. If I worked very hard, I could do almost two hundred a day.

It's not about justice. If you think it's about justice, look at the newspapers and notice who walks. Not the little guys, the guys doing a tiny bit of dealing, or sniggling a little on their income tax, or the woman who pulls a stunt with welfare checks because her husband has skipped out and she has no other way to feed her kids. I do not say that these things are right. But the process of selective prosecution, the "making" of cases by D.A.s and police departments, and the presence of some largely unenforceable statutes currently on the books (it is the reality of "compliance": no law can be forced on a public which chooses to ignore it, hence, selective prosecution) make for a criminal justice system which cannot realistically function in a fair and equitable manner. Criminal justice—I cannot decide if it is the ultimate oxymoron or a truly accurate description of the law enforcement process in America.

In my police undercover capacity, I have sat across the table from an armed robber who said, "My philosophy of life is slit thy neighbor's throat and pimp his kids." I believe that the human animals who maim and kill people should be dealt with, as they say, swiftly and surely. But this business of locking people up, at enormous cost, for minor, nonviolent offenses does not truly or effectively serve the interest of the people. It serves only to promote the wasteful aspects of the federal prison system, a system that gulps down tax dollars and spews up *Let's Make a Deal!*

I think about Lexington almost daily. I will be walking up Broadway to shop for groceries, or maybe riding my bike in the original Central Park and suddenly I'm wondering who's in there now, at this very moment, and for what inane violations, and what they are doing. Is it chow time, is the Big Yard open, is some inmate on stage in the auditorium singing "As Time Goes By" in a talent show? It is not a fond reminiscence, or a desire to be back in the Land of No Decisions. It is an awareness of the waste. The waste of tax dollars, yes, but taxpayers are used to that. It is the unnecessary trashing of lives that leaves me uneasy. The splitting of families, the enforced monotony, the programs which purport to prepare an inmate for re-entry into society but which actually succeed only in occupying a few more hours of the inmate's time behind the walls. The nonviolent offenders, such as small-time drug dealers and the economically deprived who were driven to crime out of desperation, could remain in society under less costly supervision, still undergoing "punishment" for their crime, but at least contributing to rather than draining the resources of society.

Horace, who was not a subtle sort of fellow, had some tee shirts made up. They were delivered by our usual supplier out in Landscape, and we wore them back in over our regular clothes. The hacks tilted their heads when they noticed, but said nothing. On the front of each shirt was an outline of the state of Kentucky, and above the northwest corner of the state were the words "Visit Beautiful Kentucky!" Inside the state boundary were:

- Free Accommodations
- Complimentary Meals
- Management Holds Calls
- Recreational Exercise

In small letters just outside the southwest corner of the state was: "Length of Stay Requirement." And in big letters across the bottom:

Take Time to Do Time

F.C.I. Lexington

I gave mine away on the day I finished my sentence. It is a time-honored tradition to leave some of your belongings to friends who have to stay behind when you are released. But you must never leave shoes. Legend has it that if you do, you will come back to wear them again.

RUSSELL FRASER

Wadi-Bashing in Arabia Deserta

FROM THE VIRGINIA QUARTERLY REVIEW

FOR SUCCESSFUL wadi-bashing, you need four-wheel drive and
a good head of steam. Land Rovers and Cherokee jeeps are
preferred. Pulling out the throttle, you race along the wadis,
making a run at the dunes. Some dunes, enormous, dwarf a
three-story house. Lying between them are the wadis, old water
courses dry most of the year. In the rainy time they flood, and
men and animals parched for water have drowned in the desert.
The bashing isn't when you hit the wadis but when you top the
dunes, a bone-jarring experience. I learned this in Dubai on the
coast of Arabia.

A wink of prosperity under the desert sun, Dubai is squeezed
between water, sand, and a high place. The water is the Persian
Gulf, or Arabian Gulf, depending on who makes the map.
Below the Strait of Hormuz, thirty miles wide, a spiny headland,
the Ru'us al-Jibal, cuts this body of water in two. The Emirates,
all but one, huddle together on the Ru'us al-Jibal. Besides
Dubai, they are Ajman, Sharjah, Umm al-Qaiwain, Ras al-Khai-
mah, and Fujairah. Abu Dhabi, the capital, lies along the mainland coast. Behind the coast are lumpy mountains, like tufts of
carded wool, says the Sura, a verse from the Koran. The Tropic
of Cancer bisects the lower reaches of this Trucial Coast. South
and west of the imaginary line is the desert. Occupying a quarter of a million square miles, it peters out in salt plains this side
of Mecca, not far from the Red Sea. Between the foothills of
Oman and the Yemeni border, nine hundred miles away, the
land is empty. Here is a dead land, said Doughty, an English

traveler in the Arabian desert. He said men returning from it brought home nothing but weariness in their bones.

On the other side of the Strait of Hormuz, the Gulf of Oman runs south and east into the Arabian Sea. Across the water is Iran, a medieval country, where the mullahs, Islamic priests, are fighting a Holy War against the present. Soldiers in this war don't give or expect quarter, death on the battlefield counting for them as a blessing. One of their *hadiths,* a collection of sayings ascribed to the Prophet, tells them that Paradise lies beneath the shadow of swords. Oil, vital to the present, supplies the sinews of the war, and is brought from the ground by modern technology. Each day, nine million barrels pass through the Strait of Hormuz.

My host, reciting this statistic, had oil on the brain. He was USIS, a fidgety Californian with a turn for metaphor. Oil was "our vital lifeline," and he said how the enemy wanted to cut it. He divided the world into enemies and friends. Russia, an enemy, was "the bear that walks like a man." Down the road he saw a shootout between them and us, but banked on the presence, close by in Oman, of our Rapid Deployment Force. Like a Roman centurion on Hadrian's Wall, the RDF kept on the lookout, alert for signs of trouble. Surveillance planes, the AWACS, were its eyes and ears. Airborne every day, they used the fields at Seeb and Thumrait, thanks to the Sultan of Oman. He tipped his hat to the Sultan, a friendly.

Stuck over with art deco, Arabian style, the hall he put me into was a pocket version of Radio City Music Hall, where I used to see the Rockettes. A chrome-scuppered pool, Olympic size but strictly for show, separates this ornate building from the new mosque, austere as the desert. The pool is lined with jacaranda trees, and four minarets rise at the corners of the mosque. In the distance are refineries, black against a cloudless sky. Before I went on stage, I got my briefing, a list of no-no's. It included Khomeini, Israel, and OPEC. This wasn't the Chautauqua circuit, and if America had shortcomings I needn't feel obliged to tell the world. A careful young man, my host took me back to old days in the Navy. Over coffee in the ward room, officers' country, they let you talk baseball, but politics and women were out.

The American flag and the colors of the Emirates stood in sockets behind the lectern. For props I had a slide projector, a pitcher of water, and a mike that didn't work. It didn't work in Jerusalem either when I gave my lecture there, but I stayed mum on this coincidence. Seeing no evil, Arabs pretend that Israel doesn't exist. They like you to go along with their fiction. An American banker I know, having been to Israel, neglected to tell them in Tel Aviv not to stamp his visa. When he came to Dubai, they looked at this visa and put him on the next plane back to London.

Fiddling with the microphone, I counted the house, thirty bodies, all male and all but one of them Arab. Splendid in their dishdashas, loose fitting robes, they looked like Semitic patriarchs from the Old Testament. Semitic is what they are, Arabs and Jews sharing the same inheritance. Both include Abraham in their family tree. Jewish Aaron is Arab Harun, as in Harun al-Rashid, and the standard bearer of the Prophet was Eyup, or Job. Courteous but impassive, the men in the audience kept their illusionless eyes on my face. What went on in their heads they kept under their hats.

My subject was the arts, American and modern, with attention to poetry. I told them how the artist sharpened our awareness but didn't take sides, having no ax to grind. Richard Wilbur, for instance. A modern poet, he has this poem, "The Giaour and the Pasha," based on the Delacroix painting. At a signal from me, my assistant, an Arab boy, popped a colored slide in the projector. A Giaour is an infidel or "uncircumcised dog," but Arabs don't have to be told. At the rear of the stage, USIS, fidgeting uneasily on his leather campstool, wondered where I was going to take this.

"As for the infidels," God says to Mohammed, "strike off their heads, maim their fingers." This infidel, however, has got the upper hand. He sits on horseback where the Pasha, at his mercy, is down. Looking at the painting, you feel how death is imminent. But the poem has a happy ending and the Pasha gets off scot-free. People who believe that poetry is amiable lies will say this ending defines it. If the Pasha is lucky, though, the Giaour is blessed. Poised to kill, he holds his hand. Doing this, he gets beyond himself, becoming a work of art. Frozen in air, he stares without purpose and lets the pistol fall beside his knee.

The head of a victim, said the Prophet, an angry man, was better than the choicest camel in Arabia. He said this after his first battle, when they gave him a head. Their eyes crinkling skeptically, these Arabs, his descendants, considered a resolution where nothing gets resolved. Not men for half measures, they think a job worth doing is worth doing well. Falconry is a favorite diversion of theirs. The falcon, having the prey in sight, doesn't balance pros and cons but falls like a plummet. However, I was *ahl al-kitab,* "People of the Book." Oddly, this works out to unknowing. Secure in what they knew, they applauded me politely. They were *ahl al-bait,* "People of the House of the Prophet."

Shouldering his way up to the platform, Nate Yelverton stuck out a hand. He has a shrewd idea that poetry is for the birds, and sitting through my lecture must have cost him. Unlike Arabs, Yelverton is willing to say what he thinks. "More truth than poetry" is one of his expressions. Journeying around the world to tell the wogs about poetry seems labor lost to him. He doesn't like wogs, "shiftless fellaheen," and lumps them all together. Also he doesn't like Jews. Islam and Judaism, brothers under the skin, are both secret conspiracies, he tells me. Where Arabs have their *Jihad,* or Holy War, though, Jews let money do the talking. Have I read the *Protocols of the Elders of Zion?*

In Dubai on loan from Bechtel Corporation, Yelverton has taken up the white man's burden. Constructing a new desalinization plant, he is helping the Arabs augment their supply of potable water. He calls this working for "IBM," *Inshallah Bukra Mumkin.* I will hear these words often in the Emirates, he says. They mean, "God Willing Tomorrow Maybe." A good engineer, Yelverton marches with the army of progress. Bechtel, his employer, is building an industrial city in the desert, on the shores of the Persian Gulf. The railroad, coming up from Dammam, will link it to the capital, once served by camel caravans. Jubail, the new city, is almost in place. When it is finished, Yelverton says, a third of a million people will live there.

The first time we met, he was bellied up to the bar at the Mena House in Cairo. Calling for Wild Turkey, he didn't bat an

eye when he got what he called for. Yelverton expects this.
Getting things done is his business, a fight against odds. Ranged
against him are bureaucrats, do-gooders, and bumblers who
come in all colors and shapes. Battling the odds, he weaves and
lurches when he walks. Mohammed, said Arab chroniclers, had
this strange lurching walk, "as if he were ascending a steep
invisible hill." In his cups, Yelverton is apt to turn maudlin,
sometimes breaking into song. Surprising in a big man, he has
a melodious tenor, reminiscent of John McCormack. He exercises this on sentimental ballads that call the Irish home to Erin
and old tunes from the Hymnal where they wrestle and fight
and pray. The business card he gave me, fished from a plastic
sleeve in his wallet, had cabalistic signs like Greek sigmas and
gammas, all Greek to me. Bold horizontal lines connected open
loops and little corkscrews like pigs' tails. Above and under the
lines, clusters of dots inflected this mysterious writing. The other
face of the card, more forthcoming, gave his name in English,
N. B. F. Yelverton, beneath this the name of his firm. The
initials, he said, stood for Nathan Bedford Forrest, a Confederate general who got there fustest with the mostest. Putting
down his drink, he penciled in a phone number with a Dubai
exchange. "If you're ever in the U.A.E."

II

Coming all at once, day dawns in the U.A.E. like noontide. The
air is thin, and the mountains, looming, stick up like Erector
Sets. Detail, qualifying what you see, gets swallowed in immen-
sity. Sun beats on the dead land, conferring the gift of clarity, a
privilege of moribund things. Not blurred by half-lights and
shadows, contours are sharp, and good and evil look like themselves. This makes life simpler. Humbled in the dust, Arabs say
how Allah, an abstract divinity, inherits the earth, letting nothing escape. Ibn Khaldun, the Arab historian, has a hundred
litanies like this one. A Berber from North Africa, he lived on
the fringes of the Sahara. This waste of scorching sands, mountains, and stony uplands is bigger than the continental United
States. Men are minerals, he makes Mohammed say, i.e., some,
Muslims, are precious like gold, others drossy and debased. Pos-

sibly banal, this saying takes on a harder meaning in the desert. Uncounted like grains of sand, undifferentiated too, men have their brief incandescence, then lapse back in matter.

Mohammed, like Yelverton a man for sharp distinctions, began his new cult of Islam in the desert. He did this when he fled from Mecca to Medina, a ten days' journey across the empty sands. In his native place, enemies waited to kill him. There was the wife of Abu Lahab, who strewed thorns in the sand where he walked. He cursed this man and wife in one of his Suras. "Cursed be the hands of Abu Lahab: he shall perish! . . . / Faggots shall be heaped on his wife." The Hejira showed Mohammed how this wish might father the deed. Coming out of the desert, he said the sword was the key of heaven and hell. Heaven, the reward of the just, was for Muslims. His soldiers sent the others to hell. "The Lord destroy the Jews and Christians," said the Prophet, all of them in Arabia who didn't worship the God of Islam. Arab soldiers weren't troubled by doubts and hesitations, and except for Cromwell's Ironsides and the Scotch Covenanters, no better fighting men ever lived. Each day of Ramadan, the month of fasting for Arabs, begins when they can distinguish a white thread from a black one. You can do this any day in the unfiltered light of the desert. Arabs call it Rub al Khali, or Empty Quarter.

Modern hotels stand tall in the desert, and businessmen around the world have made them a home away from home. Some wear Norman Hilton suits and shoes by Ferragamo, but the briefcases they carry are plastic. Air conditioning whirs faintly inside the hotels, where the climate, neither hot nor cold, never varies. Outside, the Arabs meet the climate halfway. Square wind tunnels sit on top of their houses. The burning air, passing through these tunnels, is cooled by water or dampened cloths. This gives some relief to the people in the houses. However, they still know where they are.

Muzak, soft but perky, fills the lobby of the Holiday Inn. This is in Sharjah, just up the road from Dubai. It being early December, the music suits the season, and they are playing "Rudolph the Red-Nosed Reindeer." My Avis rent-a-car, picked up at the airport, has air conditioning, a radio, and tape deck. Upholstered in velour, the interior is red with black stripes. Arabs, reticent in last things, like their surfaces bedizened. One of their caliphs, traveling, slept beneath a black satin tent. The poles were silver, the rings were gold, and the ropes made of wool or shot silk. But their first caliph left only a camel, a single slave, and a mantle. Before he died, he spurned this mantle with his foot. "I have given back all that," he said, "and I am well and happy." When I start the car, the radio, left on, plays Kris Kristofferson and "Me and Bobby McGee."

Money, a great leveler, has homogenized the Emirates. Like tourist islands in the Caribbean, emptied of culture, they have nothing personal to show. Everything you need comes in from the outside, oil being the single exception. In the *souk*, or market, not far from the brackish creek that links Dubai to the sea, you can purchase Del Monte pineapples imported from Hawaii, Earl Grey breakfast tea, artichoke hearts, plastic yo-yos, throwaway pens, and many of Heinz's 57 varieties. The vegetable man, Bagghal, offers apples that might be McIntosh apples. Sometimes he sings, "Apples, apples, rosy as a young girl's cheek." This market doesn't stun your senses like the Bab el Louk in Cairo, where the heads of butchered animals are mounted over the doors of the shops. They have live chickens in wicker arks, though, and if you want a chicken for dinner they will slaughter it for you on the spot.

Men, idle and magnificent, kill time in the *souk*, fingering the merchandise and kibitzing with friends. They wear the familiar headdress, "a napkin with a fan belt," Yelverton says. The women wear the black veil, or *burqca*, and some of these veils are trimmed with gold thread. The nose and lips of the women are covered, but their hooded eyes are visible, like a fencer's behind his mask. An Arab merchant, peripatetic and an everyday presence in the bazaar, hawks a cluster of gorgeous tropical snakes. That is what they look like until he holds them up for inspection. Steering wheel covers, they shimmer in the sun. Ibn Khaldun compared the world to a market like this one. Set out for display, the wares were sects and customs, institutions, forgotten lore. Mutable, not constant, they didn't persist in the same form, however, but changed with the passing of days. This was a sore affliction, the historian said.

Leading to the world outside, the creek, an arm of the sea,

brings the world to Dubai. Some Arabs, strong for the old ways, say that this is how the rot gets in. The truth they honor is absolute, not compromised by the world. Platonists in their bones, they despise the world and the flesh. This goes with their notorious carnality, the principle being that what's up front doesn't count. In his *Book of Laws,* Plato put the good state far inland. Merchants and such never came there, and this provincial place kept its virtue intact. Provincialism, said Ibn Khaldun, was the key to Arab greatness. He thought that Arabs in the desert, savage, not sociable, were more disposed to courage than sedentary people, also closer to being good. They didn't obey the law, being ignorant of laws, and didn't go to school, but stood to the rest of men like beasts of prey to dumb animals. Jealous of the stranger, Arabs cocked an ear for every faint barking and noise. This xenophobic thing preserved their *casabiyah*. Rosenthal, translating Ibn Khaldun, renders the Arabic word as "group-feeling."

But the tale, baffling the teller, has an unexpected ending. Leaving the desert, Arabs bent on conquest took to the sea. This sullied their lineage. They meddled with strangers, and the closely knit group was a thing of the past. After the conquest, said Ibn Khaldun, Arabs acquired "the stigma of meekness." Our English language still remembers their sea terms. "What is our 'admiral' but the *Al-mir-al-bahr* of the Arabian Sea," Holdich asks in his *Gates of India,* "or our 'barge' but a *bārija* or warship?" Careened in the mud by the bankside, trading vessels, caulked and painted, await the next voyage. The thrusting stems of these *dhows* are like giant toggle switches for opening or closing an electric circuit.

Bouncing off the water, the sun explodes in fragments, hard on the eyes. In the street outside the *souk,* this same sun, unrefracted, creates a movie set, life imitating art. The movie is a western, *High Noon* or *Duel in the Sun,* and the hero and villain, outlined against the sky, are stalking each other. The people in the street stand up like gnomons, uncompromisingly themselves. Poor or pretentious, the buildings can't evade what they are. Nuance, Arabs think, is for effeminate people, and their art, like their politics, is mostly innocent of chiaroscuro.

My American banker friend, he who never got out of the

airport, spent two weeks in Palestine before coming to Dubai. Forewarned is forearmed, and he should have known better. Palestinian Jews, sun-spattered like Arabs, share their yen for broad strokes and primary colors. Hallucinating in the sun, I go back in mind to Palestine. In Tel Aviv, the capital, an old movie is playing, white settlers vs. redskins. The hero of the piece, clean shaven, rides a white horse. You can tell the villain by the pricking of your thumbs. Always on the alert, Israelis keep the villain in their gun sights. Out in the country, still biblical country where shepherds tend their flocks, military checkpoints, bisecting the roads, are manned by soldiers toting automatic rifles. Dressed in combat fatigues, the soldiers, men and women, are sexless. In Israel, everybody goes to war.

Barbed wire, running with the roads, separates the beleaguered state from the Jordan River. The wire, a secondary line of defense, also functions as metaphor, dividing sheep from goats. Stockades topped with wire surround the kibbutzim, lonely outposts in the desert. Outside are the hostiles. Arab merchants in the city, paying out treasure, keep these guerrilla fighters in pocket. Self-appointed vigilantes keep tabs on the merchants. "Buy Blue and White, Not Arab," read wall placards in Jerusalem, posted by the Jewish Defense League. Blue and white are the colors of the Israeli flag.

A free port on the gulf, Dubai has its own dry dock, a modern harbor nearby at Port Rashid, also a trade center, austerely modern. Along the curving drive that sweeps up to the entrance, fan palms, pomegranates, and dusty pink oleanders do what they can to mollify the hard scene. Little flame-colored blossoms surround the fruit of the pomegranate. Wood and wire screens protect these growing things; otherwise the desert, always on the prowl, would destroy them. Arabs understand this, a hard lesson learned. Centuries ago, when they conquered North Africa, they found an enormous thicket covering the wide littoral between Tangier and Tripoli. Under the shade were hamlets where men and women fostered life in society. They cultivated the land, sunk wells, and had their arts and crafts. Artificial, not natural, these little enclaves on the edge of the desert needed tending. Today the land is treeless and nine

tenths of the people who lived there are gone. The ruins of
Roman oil mills break the surface of the plain.

Admonished by the desert, Arabs in Dubai don't take their
land for granted. Outside the Hilton, my home away from
home, Rose of Sharon in concrete tubs splashes bright color
against the façade, new as tomorrow. Water from the local desalinization plant, courtesy of Yelverton, cascades in a rococo
fountain. More precious than oil in these parts, it isn't hoarded
on the Trucial Coast, Arabs having found money to burn. Getting rid of indigenous things, the Emirates have got rid of pov-
erty too. Before the gushers came in, Arab poor lived on crumbs
from the tables of the rich. For the Feast of Sacrifice, Eid Al
Adha, well-to-do Arabs, honoring their prophet Ibrahim, sacrificed a sheep and gave the meat to the poor. Now the dole, a
state subsidy, feeds both rich and poor. In Dubai, unlike the
Caribbean, nobody goes hungry.

Nobody frets about paying the doctor. If you get sick, the up-
to-date hospital, free to all, is good for what ails you. Dark-
skinned nurses in this Rashid Hospital are all starch and no
nonsense, and their voices, peremptory, sound like Mary Pop-
pins. Most of the doctors are Indian or Pakistani, but some have
degrees from London or Trinity College, Dublin. When they
come on the phone, their accents are Harley Street, plummy or
clipped. Even on the hottest days, the chief resident wears a
business suit, his pouter-pigeon belly covered by a decent waist-
coat. A gold fob with a seal, attached to a pocket watch, hangs
over his belly. Like a Harley Street doctor, he doesn't answer to
"Doctor" but "Mister."

The colonial governor has long departed from Dubai, but
their Arab ruler is still dreaming a form on the world. He is
H.H. the Sheikh, a compulsive builder, and his unreal creation
is substantially there. "As in Shake 'n Bake," Yelverton says,
correcting my pronunciation. His voice, high-pitched and fem-
inine, almost a giggle, tells of the Delta country south of Memphis, Tennessee. A homogenous country, this is where
Yelverton lives in his mind. When he was a boy growing up in
the Delta, people still honored the old ways and truths. They
knew who they were and where they were going. Living was

easy. The fat soil, well watered, produced bumper crops. Rice
and cotton were the staples, but if you put a dry stick in the
ground it put out suckers.

Living in the East for a long time, this expatriate wants to go
home. To my surprise, he has a patriotic poem, committed to
memory, that says this. "So it's home again, and home again,
America for me! My heart is turning home again, and there I
long to be." But he won't go home and knows it. The home his
heart is turning to no longer exists, and all I have to do is read
the papers.

III

Arabs in Riyadh, the capital city of the Saudis, have Yelverton
and friends to thank for their new international airport. Named
for King Khaled, this sprawl of glass and concrete is anchored
to the plateau on the edge of the city. Where Riyadh in the old
days was a sleepy oasis on the pilgrim road to Mecca, the march
of progress, says Yelverton, has changed this. Modern office
buildings are replacing the mud-brick houses, and they have an
oil refinery, a cement-making plant, also a university, the first
in Arabia. The fortress wall that surrounded the city is gone,
and Riyadh, no longer itself, is a hodgepodge where East jostles
West. Foreign workers, crowding in, give trouble to the Najdi
population. These Najders, says Yelverton, would like to keep
themselves to themselves but can't do this.

A traveled man who knows Arabia like his own back yard,
Yelverton had to see it before he knew it. I knew it before I saw
it, thanks to C. M. Doughty and his *Travels in Arabia Deserta*. The
unabridged edition of 1888, it shared the bookcase in our living
room with Palgrave's *Golden Treasury*, Creasy's *Fifteen Decisive
Battles*, and a broken set of Charles Dickens, bound in green
cloth and lettered in gold on the spine. TV was for the future,
and movies, expensive, were rationed to one a week. Grateful, I
read these volumes cover to cover. In those Depression years,
we made our own entertainment. Doughty has his longueurs,
and maybe Garnett's one-volume abridgment does a service.
But this writer is most himself when taken in large doses. An
uncommon Victorian, he harks back to stately writers of an

earlier time. The sleep of the desert refreshes his prose, or you could put this the other way round. Like Aaron with his rod, redeeming the dead land, he drew life from wasted sand rock, spires, needles, and battled mountains. It took me years to get over this gorgeous prose that reads like poetry.

"How couldst thou take such journeys into the fanatic Arabia?" they asked him. But the desert is where you find it, and Doughty knew the heart's desert better than most. More than wild beasts, he dreaded "unknown mankind." Turks in Constantinople, barbarians who couldn't be taught, would murder you, he said, but let a hound live. Abyssinian blacks, settled in the desert, saw an enemy behind every bush. Arabs, unused to the sight of a stranger, hated what they didn't know. Irately they asked each other, "Dost thou take me for a Nasrâny! that I should do such iniquitous things." A Nasrâny is a Nazarene or Christian.

But the Bedouin bade the stranger sit and eat. Doughty said he was "full of the godly humanity of the wilderness." Though he never said where the godly thing came from, you feel that it wasn't handed to this Bedu on a platter. Versed in "the desert comity," he offered a lesson in the school of mere humanity. This courtesy to the stranger set him apart. "Were the enemies upon you, would you foresake me who am your wayfellow?" Doughty asks him. "I would," he said, "take thee up back-rider on my thelûl (riding camel), and we will run one fortune together."

A cable from Washington, handed in at the Hilton, gives me new marching orders. They have scratched Beirut, where Druse, Maronites, and Shiites are killing each other, and my next speech, three days from now, is set for Chulalongkorn. This modern university, situated in Bangkok, is halfway across the world but only an overnight hop on KLM. I have time on my hands, and Yelverton proposes that we make the most of this. Next door in Sharjah, the Tourist Centre runs safaris into the Empty Quarter. "Wadi-bashing, the Brits call it." Domesticating the desert, he makes this sound like Sunday at the beach.

At first light, when the Land Rover collects us at the hotel, the sky, still empty of sun, is only a smudge, and the desert along the highway rolls like pale water. But there isn't sky or

desert, and the highway is a fiction spun by civil engineers.
Contours, blurring, melt into each other. In Arabia and elsewhere this is unsettling, and until the sun comes up we don't
know where we are. Sufi mystics in Arabia, making little of
distinctions, lived in this half-light. "I am become the wine-
drinker, the wine and the cup-bearer," one of them said. He
was Bayazid, who lived a thousand years ago.

But the sun is only biding its time. Particles of mica, embedded in the highway, gather the fierce light and hurl it back at
our windshield. We sit in front with the driver, a local tribesman
from Ra's al Khaymah up the coast. The Queen of Sheba had
her palace there, Yelverton says. The driver wears the dishdasha complete with burnoose, but rubbing elbows with Western-
ers has sloughed the old ways. A new kind of man, only just
veneered with modernity and a smattering of English, this
Abeyd-al-Malik is eager to please. "Welcome!" he says. "You
American? Is good. I like Americans. No like Russians."

The door of the Land Rover, painted red, has yellow letters
in English: "Sharjah Safari Co." Behind the enclosed cab, the
flat bed, open to the air, is fenced with wooden slats. When
Abeyd-al-Malik goes on safari into the hidden villages of the
Hajer Mountains, he carries pots and pans lashed to the chassis,
also cheap cotton goods, the rough cloaks they call *jubbah*, canvas tents and tent poles, and panniers of charcoal. In exchange
he brings back goat's hair dyed red with *kirmiz*, ropes made of
palm fiber, oil of citron, fresh dates, and date baskets. The
baskets are *zanabīl*, on sale in the market. Arab men, fastidious,
use the oil of citron, a lemony perfume. Mohammed, not all
sturm and drang, says in one of his Suras how he had loved
three things in the world, perfumes, women, and refreshment
in prayer. At any rate, says Yelverton, he had his heart's desire
of the first two.

Billboards streak past us, one advertising Pepsi in Arabic and
English. On either side of the road, the desert is littered with
the offscouring of modern life, polystyrene packing blocks,
rusted hubcaps, exploded tires, plastic junk that lives forever.
Fifty yards farther in, though, the desert is empty. Materializing
out of the sands, a market complex, spanking new, rises like a
mirage. Mixing different styles, Moorish, Turkish, and Beverly

Hills, it isn't accommodating, only eclectic, a different kettle of
fish. Some buildings, Turkish, look like nomad tents in stone,
others like Brighton Pavilion. Lapping this market, the desert,
impatient, waits to take it back again.

Outside Dubai, the road turns east, then south, following the
old Buraimi Trail. Camel caravans, crossing into Abu Dhabi,
took this trail through the Empty Quarter to the Kingdom of
Arabia. They carried their provisions with them, skins of water
and messes of barley and rice. Nothing lives in the desert, only
yellow lizards and hyenas that feed on decay. Pinnacled rocks
and broken *kellas,* old redoubts, define the horizon. The *kellas*
guarded cisterns, dry ages ago. Camel droppings in the sand
are a welcome sign of life.

IV

The oasis at Al Buraimi, a *locus amoenus* on the edge of the
sands, blossoms behind its mud walls. This pleasant place,
carved out by men, is the product of thought and painstaking.
Ghosb is their Arab word, meaning created "by effort." The
walls, layers of earth stiffened with bricks laid in athwartships,
make a palisade against the sand. Taller than the walls, the
castor-oil trees have large star-shaped leaves and fuzzy red flowers, and their skinny boles, reddish brown, are girdled like
shoots of bamboo. From the branches of the frywood trees,
yellow pods hang like tongues depressed for inspection. Woman's tongue, Arabs call the frywood. Date gardens, lush green,
glorify the oasis. A gala in the desert, the gardens are flecked
with colored lights. The orange lights are mangoes, also bou-
gainvillea. Like charity, it covers the walls of the houses,
bleached out or scabrous. Chinese shoe flowers, rosy red, grow
in plots before the houses. The ovate green leaves, edged with
teeth, are sharp enough to draw blood. Yellow flowers like puff
balls hide the dark brown bark of the gum trees, our common
acacia. Camels, not choosy, eat the leaves of this tree, prickly
with spines, and their drovers use the wood for cooking fires.

But the desert, a state of mind, has left its mark on Al Buraimi. It comes up to the walls like Moors coming up from Spain,
hell-bent for Tours. Then, without warning, it stops. This is

where Charles Martel, a great hero, has raised his baton. In 732, Moors got their comeuppance at Tours, Creasy said. So far and no farther. Startled, I can see where a line has been drawn, first the white sand, drained of color by the sun, then the alfalfa, a lushness of dark flowers. Forage for goats and camels, it unrolls beneath the date palms as if Arabs had rolled out a carpet. This is a mystery, the stuff melodrama is made of.

Black and white, in my experience never quite themselves, shade into each other, and nothing I know is black or white altogether. Day, gaining on night, and night, becoming itself, do this little by little. Some fictions, melodramatic, argue to the contrary, old Scrooge in *A Christmas Carol,* for instance. First we have the monster and a monster is all he is, then presto, the nice old man. The oasis at Al Buraimi resembles this improbable fiction. A green thought, it confronts the desert like the difference between either/or.

Cursing fluently in Arabic, Abeyd-al-Malik brakes to a stop. A drove of camels, in no hurry, lurches across the road. Their hairy feet, unshod, are squishy blobs like jellyfish, and as they move they envelop the ground. The lead camel, evil looking, has a mind of its own, narrow but determined. Coming to a halt, it collapses slowly like a jackknife being folded. The front legs go down first, then the hindquarters. When a camel sits, unless you are used to this it is hard to avoid pitching over its withers. Indignant but perfunctory, the drover jabs at the camel with his pointed crop, a piece of almond wood. He does this until it struggles back to its feet. British on the Trucial Coast complain that Arabs, hardhearted, mistreat their beasts of burden. The plight of dumb animals distresses these British, and letters to the London *Times* reflect their concern. A hundred years ago, they founded the SPCA. But camels, like the old Adam, aren't tractable by nature. If you want them to obey you, whipping doesn't come amiss.

Getting down to stretch our legs, we head for lunch and a cup of coffee. Abeyd-al-Malik, fearing for the Land Rover, chooses to stay where he is. He says that Al Buraimi people will steal the coins from a dead man's eyes. From the *shurfa'* of the mosque comes the summons to prayer, violating the desert silence, sympathizing with it too. Both blessing and malediction, this is the

Sura of Praise. Arabs, say Yelverton, recite it five times a day.
"Guide us in the right path, not in the path of those Thou art
angered with."

An uninflected crying, the muezzin's chant is tuneless, and
Yelverton, grimacing, puts his fingers in his ears. "The old-time
hymns had a tune you could carry." Surprising the locals, he
illustrates from Charles Wesley's "Soldiers of Christ, Arise."
What would the world have been, he asks me, if Mohammed,
"that fatal Ishmaelite," had never wagged his tongue.

Blocking our path, mangy yellow dogs sun themselves in the
street in front of the restaurant. Not bred or nurtured, these
dogs are all dog. Growling, they want to bite us but haven't spirit
to do this. Above the door, the signboard, scalloped with neon
tubing, is lettered in Arabic. Yelverton, cackling, makes this out
as "Al Hambra's Place." A common room like a living room with
the kitchen in back, the restaurant has a divan, taking one wall,
also a TV set. The divan, says Yelverton, is for their nightly
gatherings, *diwaniyas*. Late into the night, Arab men sit on this
divan, drinking bitter coffee and canvassing the state of the
world. The women, having their chores, stay home with the
children.

Seated at deal tables veneered with Formica, old men pick at
their food. Some, like Yasir Arafat, wear the red-checked *ghetra*
wound with *agal*, a length of black rope. Wrinkling his nose,
Yelverton advises the mutton, home grown. The fish, oily mack-
erel, is trucked in, he says, from Umm al-Qaiwain on the Gulf.
A sharp tang on the air, oil of citron cuts the smell. Their eyes
glued to a soap opera, the old men ignore us. On the flickering
screen, the black-and-white figures are tearing a passion to tatters. They speak their unfamiliar tongue, but their antics are
familiar and subtitles aren't needed to tell the good guys from
the bad. According to Yelverton, this Arab version of *As the
World Turns* is beamed to Dubai from Kuwait.

Beyond Al Buraimi, a rickrack of metal girders signals the
end of the highway. Where there was concrete, now there is
sand. The map, dispensing with lines, is all stipples and bears
the legend "No defined boundary." Stopping the Land Rover,
Abeyd-al-Malik unscrews the caps from the tires, letting out air,
then turns the car into the desert. Shy of the intruder, a flock

of camels retreats before us, but the black goats, cropping the tribulus plants, stand their ground. "Bedu country," our driver says. Rimming the desert, eroded humps that used to stand taller are crumpled like sodden asbestos. "Hajer Mountains." From the crest of a dune, a solitary camel watches our approach. Evidently what he sees from his distance alarms him, and turning tail he heads down the other side.

White from a distance, the sand, seen close up, is grainy brown, textured with pebbles. Later this changes, and the sand turns golden amber, the color of sterility. Doughty had a keen eye. Even the waste soil of the desert is full of variety, he tells us. Old rainfall, a damp memory in pockets underground, still supports a little life. The fissured bark of the ghaf tree, evergreen, is covered with gray hairs and needle-sharp twiglets. A Scots poet, Hugh MacDiarmid, says his songs are like this, tenacious shrubs that grow in the wasteland. Fending off erosion, they put "a withy round sand." Like heads of cabbage, pale green fruit hug the branches of the ghaf tree. "Food-for-camel," says Abeyd-al Malik.

A little noise in a vacuum, the Land Rover moves through silence, pervasive except for the soughing of wind. Teasing the sand, the wind plays tricks. It makes ridges and artistic patterns, as if some cunning artificer had happened this way. In a history of the dervishes, I find this about an Arab nomad who wandered in the Empty Quarter. He said he knew there was a God "by the same by which I know from the traces in the sand that a man or an animal has crossed it." In midwinter and early summer, Yelverton says, the *shamāl*, blowing from the north, drives the sand before it. Then the desert turns into a dust bowl.

Color of amber, massifs of sand float in the afternoon haze. "*Qaid*, the Bedu call them." Scoured by wind and water, the gravel flats between the dunes are dotted with outcrops of ashy white gypsum. Salt bushes, vivid green or gray-green, grow on the perimeter. Piling on speed, Abeyd-al-Malik hurls the car at the dunes, downshifting when he hits them. The front wheels, chewing sand, want to go through, not up. However, our momentum, gained on the wadis, brings us up and over. Force, accumulating, has to go somewhere. Running the obstacle course in the Navy, you hit the wall full tilt, grabbing for the top

with your fingers. If you did this in one motion, without breaking stride, simple physics did the rest. Only it wasn't much fun.

A boat in rough water, we labor up the dunes to the crest. For
a moment we hang suspended, then, holding our breath, go
down. On the other side, the sand, scooped out by wind, is a
trough in the wave. Treacherous, it gives no hint of this until
we meet it head on. The Land Rover, shuddering, threatens to
capsize. It rights itself, however, and the up and down begins
again.

Abeyd-al-Malik means to keep going as long as there are
wadis and dunes. We want him to stop but "this bugger," says
Yelverton, doesn't understand English. Understanding well
enough, Abeyd-al-Malik has a mind of his own. Sound and fury
is the element he lives in. Under the hood, however, the radiator begins to bubble, a kettle on the hob. The temperature needle swings over to the right where the gauge is colored red. It
stays there. Climbing out of the car, Abeyd-al-Malik wads up a
corner of his dishdasha, making a pot holder. Gingerly, he unscrews the radiator cap. The last of the water, vaporized, jets
into the air like breath on a frosty morning. Yelverton, furious,
yanks down the water can, attaching a length of flex cable to the
spout. He upends the can, taking care not to splash any water
on the block. In the heat we drive slowly, and the needle on the
gauge turns back to the left. Yelverton, making the worst of a
bad business, clicks his tongue against the roof of his mouth,
cursing Abeyd-al-Malik. This driver, deaf and dumb, doesn't
understand English.

Deep in the desert, the massifs make a ring like old dolmens
at Stonehenge. Inside the ring, Bedu shacks, protected from the
shamāl, hunker down on the sand. The shacks, a single building,
are stitched together with burlap, scraps of weathered wood,
and corrugated metal like the rusting doors of old box cars. A
stove pipe pokes up from the roof, and the entrance, a dark pit,
is partly hidden by a swag of canvas, looped to one side of the
frame. "Water!" says Abeyd-al-Malik, wanting to make amends.
He gives the wheel of the car a half-turn, and we head for the
Bedu encampment.

In front of the building, a racing camel grazes the salt bush.
Do I know why the camel is called the ship of the desert, Yelver-

ton asks me. "Because it's full of Arab semen." The camel, wary, lifts its head, assessing the stranger. Moist and swollen, a wad of bubble gum balloons from its mouth. Cooling itself, the camel holds this pink sac to the air, then sucks it back again. The bubble, collapsing, makes a noise like bath water rushing down the drain.

A man, a woman, and a boy emerge from the tumbledown building. Impudent, not abashed, this nomad boy has his hand out. He is dressed in rags like Robinson Crusoe on his desert island, and his avid eyes, exploring us, glitter with opportunity perceived. What he sees is *baksheesh,* dollar bills and pounds sterling mounted on three pairs of legs. Spread the wealth, he is saying, and won't take no for an answer. *Malesh!* says our driver. "Thanks just the same!" The boy persisting, Abeyd-al-Malik gives an edge to his tongue. *Malesh!* he says again. This time he means, "Forget it!"

Most Arabs, dark-skinned, are burned by the sun, but the Bedu is dark in the grain. He has kinky hair, walleyes like a pike's, and isn't bidding the stranger sit and eat. "One of the children of Ham." Arabs will tell you, Yelverton says, that Noah cursed this errant child with blackness. Unlovely to them, black is the color of evil. Ibn Khaldun says this. He thought the damned were black, like the devil in old Christian paintings. Kinky hair, a badge of servitude, goes with being black. "Great God!" Doughty has them saying. "Can those woolly polls be of the children of Adam?"

The Bedu wears the long robe, but hurrying out to defend the wagon train has left off his burnoose. His hair, mostly gray, is patchy with yellow like an adolescent girl's bleached with hydrogen peroxide. Around his waist, the rough cincture, knotted palm fibers, holds a dirk and a seamless girby. This homemade canteen, goatskin or sheepskin, glistens with droplets of water. Bedu men, says Yelverton, pulling a face, wash their hair in camel urine.

City Arabs don't like Bedu, and Abeyd-al-Malik, citified, keeps downwind of this one. Bedu flaunt their apartness, a reproach to men in cities. Indifferent to creature comforts, they live on camel milk and dates from the oases. Some tint the whites of their eyes with blue dye. Bedu don't make good neighbors. The tribe gets their allegiance, but their hand is raised against the outsider. Skirmishing like kites and crows, they have their blood feuds, passed on from father to son. Inured to shedding blood, they don't wear the stigma of meekness.

"Hey you! Ali-ben-Shifty!" Yelverton says, seeing a dark face and a bedsheet. Cupping his hands, he holds them up to his mouth.

Reluctant, the Bedu, one man to our three, hands over the girby. Tilting it, Yelverton squeezes out water. As he drinks, he takes stock of the woman. She wears the black *bukhnag*, a calico scarf edged with bright thread, also a loose-fitting gown. Her skin, unlike the man's, isn't swarthy but pale. Splotches of henna paste, rosy red like an apple, keep the sun from her forehead. The black hair, parted severely, makes a widow's peak in the middle of her forehead and falls in loose braids to her shoulders. Work and childbearing take their toll of Arab women, most being shapeless at thirty. This Bedu wife still has her young woman's body, apparent to Yelverton beneath the cheap cotton *kandura*. Deliberately, he strips off this gown with his eyes.

The Bedu doesn't need telling to understand that a line has been drawn in the sand. Not getting outside himself, Yelverton misses the anger. Arabs are Arabs, and how this nomad Arab might differ from others is a question that doesn't detain him. Eyes rolling, the Bedu thinks about crossing the line. His fingers feel for the dirk at his belt. Chattel, like goats and camels, this woman belongs to him. Pushing the boy before her, she unhooks the canvas flap and disappears into the hovel. Abeyd-al-Malik, smelling a fracas, heads back for the car.

Two cocks on a dunghill, Yelverton and the Bedu circle each other. I am their witness, impartial, and getting it down. To close the circle, all that lacks is the violence there is no going back from. A little late in the day, Yelverton thinks twice. Sweat, beading his forehead, makes dark blotches under his arms. Irresolute, he holds up his hands, a placatory gesture. The Bedu ignores this. One of the people of King Ibn-Saud, a cattle lifter and cutthroat, he likes a resolution where something gets resolved.

But the duel in the sun, a true-life scenario, breaks off unfinished. At the sticking point, the Bedu backs down. His heart, crowded with blood, is empty only of pity, and compunction is the last thing on his mind. But even in the desert, witnesses tell tales. Knowing this, he has his second thoughts, not the same as Yelverton's. Having raised his arm in anger, the Bedu lets it fall and turns away.

Fictions, in this respect, have it all over the truth. "More truth than poetry," Yelverton likes to say but misses the point. True-to-life shows a muddle, the poet showing the truth as it might be. This is what all honest writing comes down to, not imagination but the estimating eye. The writer, privileged, fills in the blanks, seeing how the ending is only the tip of the iceberg. His privilege doesn't extend to sleight of hand, though, where they want you to think that what ought to be might be.

Yelverton thinks that all fictions are like this. Hard-hearted, they take the wish for the deed. Not born yesterday, he knows that under the warm skin of the world is great cold, "more truth than poetry." I agree he has a point. This duel in the sun, sound and fury, still needs its conclusion.

Being a writer, I undertake to supply it. First, though, I have to deal with things past. I need a beginning, also a middle where important things get done. Where my scenario begins, the Bedu, not made up yet, is like the nomad boy he has sired, but different. An unwilling scholar, he needs time for study. This Bedu is lucky, and time is what they have given him. From early days they let him see how the world he lives in, various like the waste soil of the desert, isn't made in his image and likeness. On *Eid* days, celebrations that mark the end of Ramadan, the abstinent time, or the sacrifice of Ibrahim the Prophet, they dressed him in the black *bisht* edged with gold braid. They marched him off, complaining, from house to house in his neighborhood, where he bid *"Eid Mubarak"* to the neighbors. "Blessed be your celebration." Later in his sitting room — never mind that this *majlis* is the floor of a hovel — he practiced fuming the incense. He polished the *mabkhar,* fragrant with perfume, until the brass nails were gleaming and he could see his face in the mirrors. From the *marashsh* chased with arabesques, he spilled the rose-water over the cupped hands of his guest. Entertaining this guest, a stranger, he was all ears. His tongue, impertinent, he kept in his heart.

Doing this for a long time, the Bedu, schooled, becomes the hero, "full of the godly humanity of the wilderness." He has acquired the stigma of meekness. Something given, it falls like a bolt from the blue. But he doesn't take to it naturally, the way a duck takes to water. This stigma that makes the difference, separating sheep from goats, is also something he has earned.

Where my scenario ends, the Bedu gets beyond himself. Astride his victim, he swings an arm, preparing to kill. But the blow is intermitted, a broken parabola. Letting his arm fall, he doesn't do this from fear or prudence, and his gesture, not spastic, is a meditated thing.

When we regain the highway, Abeyd-al-Malik lays on the whip. He wants us home again before the desert settles down for the night. Yelverton, dejected, hugs himself against the door of the cab. Gnawed by the worm of conscience, this ill-tempered Giaour doesn't like the sorry figure he has cut. But that is only what I think, taking the wish for the deed. Earnestly, he says, "I'd rather sleep with her naked than him with all his clothes on."

Coming up on Al Buraimi, we slacken speed but don't stop. The sun, a glowing clinker, is low in the sky, and the yellow dogs that look like jackals have disappeared from the street in front of "Al Hambra's Place." But a group of Arab men, rehearsing their *diwaniya,* are chewing the fat as they wait for the restaurant to open. As we drive by them, the neon lights, winking on, illuminate the signboard. Visible for a long time in the rear-view mirror, these lights jig into the gathering dusk.

E. J. KAHN, JR.

The Honorable Member
for Houghton

FROM THE NEW YORKER

HELEN SUZMAN's principal domicile is a comfortable house in an
affluent suburb of a highly Westernized metropolis. She is married to a respected physician with a lucrative practice. She plays
a fair game of golf, and is partial to bridge on weekends. She
does not live in Scarsdale. The suburb is Hyde Park, the metropolis is Johannesburg, and since 1953 Mrs. Suzman has been
a member of the all-white House of Assembly, the main lawmaking body of the Republic of South Africa. She has never
ceased to be a dogged adversary of her country's ruling clique.
With all deference to Archbishop Desmond Tutu, who is fourteen years Mrs. Suzman's junior and likes to address her,
fondly, as "my dear child," more than a few longtime observers
of the international scene contend that when it came to bestow-
ing the Nobel Peace Prize on a South African anti-apartheid
activist His Grace would have made a splendid second choice.

The House of Assembly meets, usually for about half of each
year, in Cape Town (Pretoria is the executive branch's home
base), and Mrs. Suzman, whose constituency is called Houghton,
is now its senior front-bencher. She attained that distinction —
there appears to be no reason to believe that she will not retain
it when she runs for re-election early next month — in 1984,
when her only rival for length of service, the now universally
known Pieter Willem Botha, decided to do away with his prime
ministership and to assume the no less authoritative mantle of

president. Over the years, the two have had many exchanges, none cordial. Once, Mrs. Suzman reminded the House that when one of her colleagues in the Progressive Federal Party, Colin Eglin (its leader), was a sixteen-year-old schoolboy he volunteered for military service on the side of the Allies in the Second World War, while "the hon. the prime minister"— who, like many other descendants of the Boers, was perhaps less pro-Nazi than anti-British —"was leading gangs of destructive breakers-up of meetings all round the country and insulting men wearing the South African uniform in time of war." Another time, Mrs. Suzman was thrown out of Parliament — "asked to leave the chamber" is the polite circumlocution — for calling Mr. Botha a coward. A not untypical dialogue between them in the house, a year ago, went:

> H.S.: Stupid!
> P.W.B.: Woman!

Five years previously, after Mrs. Suzman had taken pains to watch some police wantonly dismantle shacks in a black settlement and haul some of the occupants off to jail, and after she had also been a conspicuous onlooker during a peaceful anti-apartheid demonstration in a Cape Town cathedral, Mr. Botha, then still prime minister, suggested in Parliament that her being engaged in such activities bordered on the illegal, and added, "I am telling you that if you try to break the law you will see what happens."

Mrs. Suzman responded, addressing no one in particular, "The hon. the prime minister has been trying to bully me for twenty-eight years, and he has not succeeded yet." And then, addressing him squarely across the ten yards that separated their benches, she said, "I am not frightened of you. I never have been and I never will be. I think nothing of you." Following another altercation, way back in 1966, when Botha, at the time merely minister of defence, reluctantly apologized to her in a manner she deemed unacceptable for a remark she deemed unforgivable (he had accused her of somehow being responsible for the assassination, moments earlier, of Prime Minister Hendrik Verwoerd), Mrs. Suzman resolved never to speak to him again, and she maintains that in the ensuing twenty years she hasn't. She does not count telling him off in Parliament —"I find you funnier than ever," for one comparatively mild instance — as personal communication.

During thirteen of her thirty-four years of unrelenting and singularly unrewarding efforts to save the land of her birth from its governors, Mrs. Suzman was the only member of her party in Parliament. She was often a solo voice of protest, and by now has become so celebrated at home that to millions of compatriots, of all colors and political persuasions, she is known simply as Helen. Abroad, she has probably been more frequently honored than any other South African political personage since the late Jan Christiaan Smuts, whose defeat at the polls by the Nationalist Party in 1948 launched the country on the dismal course it has followed to this day. No Nobel has yet come her way from Scandinavia (though she has been nominated three times), but not long ago a Swedish newspaper and a Danish newspaper did jointly give a human rights award to Mrs. Suzman and her friend Winnie Mandela, the wife of the imprisoned head of the African National Congress, Nelson Mandela. Last fall, Mrs. Suzman also received a key to the city of Washington, D.C. Over the years, she has accumulated two honorary fellowships (from St. Hugh's College, Oxford, and the London School of Economics) and eleven honorary degrees (again from Oxford, also from her alma mater, the University of Witwatersrand — where she has taught economic history, and which in 1979 gave her its first Alumni Award — and, in the United States, from Smith, Brandeis, and Harvard, among other institutions). The Nats, as the majority members of the House of Assembly are generally called, sometimes seem both resentful and envious of her éclat abroad. When she explained to Parliament last June that she'd had to miss the previous day's session because she was out of the country, the incumbent minister of law and order, the Hon. Louis Le Grange, with whom she has frequently tangled, asked, "Was that another doctorate?" It wasn't, actually — it was the commencement address and another award at Hebrew Union College in New York — but she did pick up two more doctorates that month.

In 1966, when a knowledgeable South African journalist was asked for proofs that his nation should not be called a police state he replied, "The English-language press and Mrs. Suzman." The journalist has left South Africa; the *Rand Daily Mail*, the bellwether of the English-language press, is gone; and much of the rest of the press, in any language, is severely circumscribed. Mrs. Suzman, who is sixty-nine but has no intention of abandoning her quixotic mission, hangs on. She still dresses in the bright colors with which in her fledgling parliamentary days she sometimes sought to focus attention on herself, but it is the wit and moral courage of her words that brighten an often monumentally drab congregation. Once, learning that three Nat M.P.s had been on a tour in the United States, she said in the House, "I am jolly sure that the hon. members exploited my existence when they were overseas. My experience is that I am held up as the No. 1 example that democracy still flourishes in South Africa." And when, as has often happened, a cabinet minister accused her of injuring their country Mrs. Suzman, who started off with a sharp tongue and has honed it to a bayonet as the years have passed, retorted, "I don't think I have really done this country much harm." After a pause for the rude interjections that nearly any such utterance of hers triggers, she continued, "If the hon. member broadened his mind and did a bit of travel abroad, he might find that my very existence in this House does this country a lot of good."

That particular hon. member, Dr. Piet G. J. Koornhof, a Nat from Primrose, has begun to do some extensive traveling; he was recently posted to Washington as South Africa's ambassador. Back in the sixties, he once informed the House, "They say that a woman's vocabulary consists of approximately five hundred words, but that the turnover is tremendous. We had a very striking example of that this afternoon. If I should come home one evening and my wife should rant and rave the way the hon. member for Houghton did this afternoon, there would by only one of two things that one could do to her. And I am a very mild-natured man. The one would be to give her a jolly good hiding, and the other would be simply to ignore her. That is really what one should do to her this afternoon, because it was an example, coming from a lady, of a really uncivilized speech."

The presiding officer said he couldn't allow the epithet "uncivilized," so Koornhof obligingly switched to "shameless." The future ambassador went on to say that Mrs. Suzman had "one purpose only, and that is to stir up unrest in the Republic of South Africa," and he added, in what may pass in his circle for displomatic parlance, "Finally I want to tell her — and I know this will hurt a little — that I think she deserves a good hiding."

Mrs. Suzman can give as good as she gets. On another occasion, after a speech by the member for Primrose, she asserted that he was "either a consummate actor or he actually believes the nonsense that he has been trying to put across," adding, "I cannot understand how a man of any intelligence could believe the things the hon. [member] has just told us." And when another member wondered one day whether she thought National Party M.P.s were uncivilized — the word got by this time unchallenged — she responded, after a moment's reflection, "No. Perhaps eighteenth-century, but not quite uncivilized." At that, he fared better than did the member whose arguments on a pending bill Mrs. Suzman felt constrained to say "really belong way back in the Middle Ages."

For more years than she sometimes cares to think about, Mrs. Suzman has occupied a precarious position that she once described to another not altogether gentlemanly member of Parliament as "amusing," explaining, "Here I am considered what the hon. member calls a sickly liberalist, a sickly humanist, and I find that in the outside world I am considered to be a very moderate, a very conservative person." A minute earlier, that M.P. had said to her, meaning just the opposite, "You are always the only one who is right," and she had snapped back, "On many occasions, sir, I think there is very little doubt that I am the only one who is right. I have no doubt about that. When I say 'I,' I should say 'I — and the rest of the world.' That is not too bad, not too bad a majority to have."

To be at once a white South African legislator and an ardent, outspoken foe of apartheid is a role hard for some people to fathom, and often it lands Mrs. Suzman in an uncomfortable spot. In 1962, visiting the United States for two months on a foreign-leadership grant from the State Department, she went south for the first time and, on reaching New Orleans, was introduced to a ringleader of the local White Citizens' Council. On learning whence she hailed and what office she held, he was briefly enchanted to meet somebody he took to be an ideological bird of a feather. While abroad more recently, Mrs. Suzman has found herself, as she put it not long ago, "in the awkward and very unpleasant position of having to correct statements about South Africa and seeming to defend the system I've spent my whole career opposing." In New York, for instance, she sat in on a forum where a speaker stated that Soweto, the huge black township outside Johannesburg, required the many workers who are forced to live in it to commute thirty-four miles to the city. Mrs. Suzman wanted to interject that a more accurate figure would have been twelve, but she let that pass. When, however, the speaker went on to say that Soweto was entirely surrounded by barbed wire, with watchtowers at the entrance gates, Mrs. Suzman, who drives herself in and out of unbarbed Soweto, using a variety of unguarded entrances, two or three times a month, demurred. "Time and again, in circumstances like that, I find myself sounding like an apologist for South Africa," she says. "And when I have to do it it infuriates me."

For some time, Mrs. Suzman, whose academic background is in economics, has been cautioning — along with Alan Paton, among other notable South Africans — against divestment and against sanctions. An anti-sanctions article she wrote for the Sunday *New York Times Magazine* last August was assessed by William Safire in the daily *Times* as "stunning and seminal." She has taken a good deal of flak for espousing that view. "I guess Alan and I are considered unfashionable," she told an American friend not long ago. "I've been against sanctions all along, because I don't think they're going to work. They're not going to bring the intransigent South African government closer to fundamental reform. They may push it, rather, into a siege economy. People outside South Africa tend to forget, if they ever knew it, that my country has no social-security safety net — no welfare, no food stamps. Sanctions will inevitably lead to widespread unemployment in export industries, and there will inevitably be even more violence than we've had lately, and more reaction to that from the government, of a more and more

oppressive kind. And once any economy has broken down it's
difficult to re-establish it."

Within the last year, Mrs. Suzman has twice participated,
while visiting England (where a lot of native South Africans,
including the older of her two daughters, now live), in spirited
debates about sanctions. Her side was judged victorious, somewhat to her surprise, at Cambridge, but she got thumbs-down
at Oxford. "Of course we lost," she said afterward. "Disraeli
couldn't have won." She has never entertained any illusions
about the outside world's impatience with South Africa, and the
widespread feeling that sanctions can accelerate necessary
changes. Back in 1979, she warned her fellow-legislators that
the demand for sanctions would "spread like wildfire if there is
any further unrest in South Africa." Last April, after nearly ten
years of far more tumultuous unrest than she had ever fore-
seen, she said in Parliament, "I can tell the hon. members that
it is a totally lost cause these days to campaign overseas against
sanctions and disinvestment, and I speak from personal experience. Unless really positive steps are forthcoming from the
government . . . I for one am going to stop banging my head
against a stone wall. . . . I am not going to go on pleading for a
lost cause unless the government, as I have said, gets off its
butt."

She relented, however; the commencement address she delivered two months later was an impassioned plea against divestment, and she followed it up with her seminal stunner in the
Times. In the fall, she lent a touch of diversity to the college
football season by giving a "Will South Africa Survive?" lecture
(her answer was, in effect, "It depends") on a number of American campuses, from Fort Worth, Texas, to the Massachusetts
Cambridge. Derek Bok, in sixteen years as president of Harvard, has had to spend a great deal of time on South Africa, and
when Mrs. Suzman arrived on the campus he asked her over
for breakfast. Bok, who keeps fit by playing topnotch tennis,
and is almost as much younger than she as Archbishop Tutu is,
said afterward, "University presidents have to hop to it if they
want to keep pace with her." He also said his guest disclosed
that before meeting him she had looked in a mirror and asked
herself, "Why have I been doing this all these years?"

From time to time, Mrs. Suzman has tried to answer her own question. Once, the answer went like this: "I've met a lot of people I'd never have got to meet as a Johannesburg housewife playing golf and bridge. I've learned a great deal about lawmaking, too. The work's been bloody tiring and bloody frustrating, but it's enabled me to take action, because of my status as an M.P. and, especially, as a serious M.P. — helping people get passports and visas, intervening for detainees, seeing that prison conditions are improved, and so forth. I've been through five prime ministers by now, and God knows how many other M.P.s have come and gone and sunk without a trace during my time."

During her American-campus tour, Mrs. Suzman, in light of her unpopular views on sanctions and disinvestment, expected to be coolly received, if not picketed or heckled. She was treated politely everywhere she went, even at unruly Harvard, and she inspired about the same number of standing ovations as hostile questions. "I guess I'm still living on my old reputation," she said at the end of the tour. "I do my best to explain to my audiences what I perceive to be the economic effects of sanctions. My emotional urge to say 'Punish this terrible government of ours,' to say 'Send in the Marines, do *anything* to bring it down,' is tempered by more practical considerations — by the reflection that one has to be rational and to wonder what would take place afterward. I'm afraid, though, that some radical blacks think of me nowadays as a scab. They think that if they keep the townships ungovernable and keep their kids out of school the government will collapse tomorrow. I disagree. All they'll do is wreck the economy. They feel that anybody who's against sanctions is letting the side down. I'm still well enough received among the older blacks. But the younger ones weren't even born during my heyday. I'm a sort of mixed-economy type — I believe in free enterprise with restraints — and that doesn't go down well with the younger generation of blacks. When one holds opinions like mine about sanctions, one finds oneself, unfortunately, with very unpleasant bedfellows — abominable ones, for instance, like Jesse Helms. It's very irritating."

South Africa has various higher-education categories: a set of universities for nonwhites, a set largely for white Afrikaners, and a set largely for English-speaking whites. When one of the last, the University of Cape Town, invited Mrs. Suzman to deliver the commencement address (and receive an honorary degree) this past June, she took the occasion to elaborate on a proposal she'd made in the House two months earlier. After remarking that most of the country's "white citizens have never set foot in the world of the blacks," she added a few comments about the majority of her fellow-M.P.s. "They have never been in a township, know nothing about the miserable conditions endured by people compelled to live in those areas," she said. "But, most of all, they know nothing of the seething anger that has built up over the years, so clearly demonstrated at [black] funerals." She proposed that every Nat M.P. be required to go to a black funeral — "heavily disguised as a human being" — so as to "get some idea of the intensity of feeling, of the heavy tide of resistance sweeping through the townships, instead of sitting on their green benches in Parliament, insulated like fish in an aquarium." If any of them ever did actually go to a black funeral, she had told them in the House — flicking her "heavily disguised as a human being" jab — "thereafter the delusion that the present unrest is but a passing phase, readily controlled by tough police action, will be dispelled once and for all."

Mrs. Suzman goes to funerals. Under one of the South Africa's recent bizarre emergency regulations, no outdoor gathering may be held without permission, sporting events and funerals excepted. At many political funerals, no more than fifty mourners are allowed. Black funerals, these days, may draw a crowd of fifty thousand, and not even the efficient South African police are quite up to collaring forty-nine thousand nine hundred and fifty at a clip. There are usually militant speeches, renditions of freedom songs, and the flourishing of the black-green-and-gold of the outlawed African National Congress. Mass arrests there may not be, but not infrequently there is what Mrs. Suzman calls "a dreadful confrontational cycle" — tear gas from the police, retributive stone throwing at the police by mourners, even more retributive shooting at the mourners by police, more deaths, more funerals, more confrontations.

Mrs. Suzman does not show up at black funerals unless she is invited. She is always glad to accept an invitation, because she hopes that the familiar sight of her will inhibit policemen whose brutalities, they are aware, she could get exposed for all the world to know in the pages of *Hansard*, the South African equivalent of our *Congressional Record*. There are many restrictions on the South African press, but — so far, at least — the newspapers are free to print parliamentary proceedings.

In 1978, Mrs. Suzman was asked by the widow of Robert Sobukwe, the head of the also outlawed Pan-Africanist Congress, to say a few appropriate words at his funeral. But by the time she got to the football stadium where the ceremony was taking place some militant young blacks had usurped the arrangements, and they wanted no white participation of any sort. "It was all part of the rejection by young politicized blacks of so-called white liberals," Mrs. Suzman subsequently told an interviewer for the Columbia University oral-history research office. "I accepted it. I mean this was something I'd been expecting for years. It doesn't hurt my feelings, and I just said, 'O.K., that's what they want. That's fine with me.' " So, instead of going out onto a platform in the center of the field, where the V.I.P.s were assembling, she took an ordinary seat in the grandstand. Next, she relates in the oral history:

> One of the black priests who'd been on the platform came across the field to us and beckoned to me and said, "We'd like you to come onto the platform, Mrs. Suzman." I said, "Well, are you absolutely sure about that, because I'm perfectly happy to stay here." "No, no," [he] said, "we would like you to come onto the platform."

When she got there, she spotted her longtime friend Mangosuthu Gatsha Buthelezi, a hereditary chief and the elected leader of Inkatha, a political movement that claims to represent some six million Zulus, who constitute more than one-third of all South African blacks. Buthelezi, who has refused to let his South African–government-spawned KwaZulu realm become an "independent" homeland, once apostrophized Mrs. Suzman as "the one flickering flame of liberty amidst the darkness." (Because his antiapartheidism does not embrace violence, and because he, too, is opposed to sanctions, many young, activist, urban South African blacks consider him antediluvian, and his having been warmly welcomed by President Reagan to the Oval Office last year, just before Thanksgiving, did little to alter that image.) The oral history continues:

> We sat there waiting, and suddenly there was the sound of chanting, and a procession came along the back of the field — a large number of blacks bearing the coffin of Robert Sobukwe and singing as they came. . . . They brought the coffin and put it at Mrs. Sobukwe's feet on the platform. Then they caught sight of Gatsha Buthelezi, and almost immediately there was an uproar. They started yelling, "Gatsha out! Gatsha out! Gatsha out!" It became very nasty, because they started advancing on the platform singing this. . . . They took not the slightest notice of [me]. . . . They say the American Ambassador [then a white] was hustled off the stage by his aides, who didn't want him to be involved in any fracas. They ended up with a very ugly scene, with Gatsha leaving in haste with his aide, who fired one shot into the air. There were no police in sight. They kept a very low profile there. It was a really humiliating thing.
>   Anyway, I think it took Gatsha a long time to forget that, if he has ever forgotten it.

Mrs. Suzman also attended the funeral of Steve Biko, who was murdered by the police in 1977 while he was in detention. Earlier, she contributed to a fund for Biko's defense. She wished her contribution to be made anonymously. The now expatriate journalist Donald Woods, who conveyed her gift, abided by her wish, but only in a manner of speaking. When Biko, whose biographer Woods later became, inquired about his supporter, Woods replied, "An M.P. She wishes to remain anonymous." Woods knew that Biko knew that there was then no other woman member of Parliament.

Mrs. Suzman describes the funeral in the oral history:

> I went down together with two of my [Progressive Party] colleagues, Alex Boraine and Zach de Beer. . . . We arrived — again, it was at a football stadium outside the town — and we were escorted across to a stand where a number of diplomats were also sitting. As we sat down on this sort of lowest rung of the stand, the grounds gradually filled up with people who were arriving by buses right through the morning. They were standing on the football field, because it had

obviously rained the night before, and the ground was sodden and wet, and nobody could sit. In the end, we couldn't see a thing. . . . So I said to Zach . . ."Look here. This is ridiculous. We haven't come all this way just to look at the backs of people. Let's work our way up to the front, so that we can see what's going on."

So we started snaking our way through this huge crowd of blacks. . . . Then, when we got right near the front, it was much more tightly packed with people, and I said, "Excuse me, may we get through?" And a young black standing nearby said, in a very hostile voice, "No, you may not. We don't want you whites here." . . . And he said a few words in Xhosa. I don't know what they were, but they were obviously "Don't let them through," because the crowd just tightened in. We could hardly move. And I got very angry then, and I turned and said, "Look here, I didn't come all this way to fight with you. I'm Helen Suzman, and I've come here to pay my respects to Steve Biko." And he said, "Who did you say you are?" I said, "I'm Helen Suzman." He said, "You prove that." So I opened my bag — I might tell you, with great difficulty, because my elbows were pinned at my sides by then, but I managed to open my bag — and I extracted a credit card which had my name on it. . . . He looked at it and said, "Mrs. Suzman, I beg your pardon. You may certainly go through." He said another few words in Xhosa, and the crowd parted like the Red Sea, and Zach and I walked through to the platform. Zach said, "Well, now I've seen everything."

It might be different today. As Mrs. Suzman has recently, and somewhat sorrowfully, put it, "The liberal road is ultimately to get squashed."

In 1960, Mrs. Suzman became increasingly disturbed about reports of maltreatment of prisoners — especially political ones — and resolved to inquire into that situation. Members of Parliament were not much better off than the general public when it came to visiting prisoners; they had to obtain permission for every visit from the Ministry of Justice. Back then, moreover, no one could talk to a prisoner unless a guard was standing by, and prisoners were not supposed to discuss the conditions of their internment with outsiders. But that, of course, was precisely what Mrs. Suzman wanted to know about. One canny political detainee at Pretoria Central Prison, when the comman-

dant was explaining the ground rules to a group of inmates in
Mrs. Suzman's presence, asked, deadpan, "You mean I can't tell
Mrs. Suzman about the time we went on a hunger strike?" No.
"And I can't tell her how we're denied food packages from
home?" No, *no!* And so it went on, until she had quite a number
of revelations to share with Parliament. One of her more important calls was paid on Bram Fischer, white, Communist, serving
a life term for treason. (In South Africa, "life" generally means
just that.) She visited him for many years, and in 1975, when
Fischer had terminal cancer, she managed to persuade the minister of justice to allow him to die at his brother's home. Not
long afterward, Fischer had a remission, and the minister, who
thought he'd been tricked, yelled at Mrs. Suzman the next time
he saw her, "You and your Communist friends!" She has been
visiting one prison or another for the last twenty-seven years.
Sometimes, after the sentimental fashion of a schoolmarm, she
refers to longtime prisoner acquaintances, out of jail or still
inside, as her "old boys."

Mrs. Suzman's first visit to Robben Island, a maximum-secu-
rity installation, where Nelson Mandela was locked up for nineteen years, was in 1967. (Mandela has since been moved to
Pollsmoor Prison, on the mainland.) Robert Sobukwe was on
the island, too, as was Hermanyo Toivo ja Toivo, the founder
of the South-West Africa People's Organization. When she first
approached Toivo ja Toivo, in an exercise courtyard, he would
have nothing to do with her. Eventually, he changed his mind,
and they spoke privately in the presence of the prison's commanding officer. Before she left that day, Toivo ja Toivo shook
her hand — the only white person's hand, the commandant
wonderingly told her, that he had ever seen the swapo man
deign to touch. By then, Balthazar Johannes Vorster had become prime minister, and Piet C. Pelser had taken over Vorster's Justice portfolio. Mrs. Suzman and Vorster — with whom
she shared a parliamentary début in 1953 and, at one time, a
golf handicap of thirteen — had now and then taken tea together when she went around to see him about a case, or for
authorization to visit a prison, but they were never friends. (One
day, touring a rock quarry, she was shown a block of granite.
"Ah," she said. "The prime minister.") She recalls that Vorster

once told her, "You allow yourself to be used too much." ("Maybe he was right," she said a few months ago. "Maybe I'm what Lenin called 'a useful idiot.' ") During one parliamentary debate, about some ameliorating changes that Vorster was thinking of instituting, she said she felt, "as one golfer to another, though his golf is infinitely superior to mine, that having started his backswing he had better see to it that he follows through."

They never played a round together. "Vorster had a certain sneaking regard for me, I think," she says today. "But that didn't keep him from nearly always being nasty. There was no geniality on his part in his relations with me. But there was one thing about me he learned early on — that, whatever job he held, I wasn't frightened of him at all." With Pelser as minister of justice, her parliamentary life became, as she saw it, somewhat less contentious and more boring. "The sort of things I said that would have made Vorster raging mad brought no more than a benign snarl from Pelser," she says, almost with disappointment. It did please her once to get Pelser to disclose publicly that when, under an Immorality Act in force at the time, seven white men and seven black women were arrested for crossing the color line in bed, all the women were convicted and all the men acquitted.

Pelser was in charge of prisons when she was first allowed to go to Robben Island, which is seven miles offshore and — separated from Cape Town by waters both frigid and shark-infested — does not lend itself to attempted escapes. "I'm very familiar with Robben Island," she says. "I could give you a conducted tour." On her maiden voyage, she went to an area housing single-cell inmates, and presently found herself in the company of Nelson Mandela, whose participation in any non-catastrophic solution to the South African problem is, she has believed ever since (as, of course, have many others), crucial and indispensable. "When he's gone," she asks today, "who knows what will happen?" During their first conversation — he in his cell, she in a corridor outside — they discovered that they were almost exactly the same age. (Of their sixty-nine years, thirty-four of hers have been spent in Parliament, twenty-four of his in prison.) More to the point, he was not prevented from relating what his life was like: no newspapers, limited study facilities, one letter and one visitor every six months, and incessant hard labor — breaking up rocks, for instance, while a guard dog nipped at the heels of inmates whom his master deemed dilatory. Another of the guards had a swastika tattooed on the back of one hand, and would stick it under political prisoners' noses and growl, "This is *my* politics." Mrs. Suzman wasted no time in informing Minister Pelser that if he didn't get rid of that guard Parliament and the press and the whole world would shortly know about South African Nazis' maltreatment of prisoners. The man was soon relieved of his duties, and general conditions did begin to improve: access to newspapers, a film once monthly, beds instead of bedrolls, opportunities for study, and, most notably, no more hard labor. "I can't say that I did it alone," Mrs. Suzman says, "but I was responsible for a considerable amount of nagging."

Though she has applied for permission every year since 1967, Mrs. Suzman has visited Mandela only five times — an average of once about every four years. Except for his family, it's doubtful whether anyone besides prison officials has called on him even that often. The two contemporaries have what she calls a "relaxed and genial friendship." During their most recent get-together, last May, she was allowed to spend two hours with him in the prison commandant's office. Mandela told her then — this commandant, too, sat in — what he had told her before: that he was an African nationalist and not a Communist, but that he would not break with the African National Congress, which he had helped to found, by asking it to purge itself of its Communist members. He would be prepared, though, to ask A.N.C. to observe a truce while he and others — and he included Buthelezi among them — negotiated with the government about South Africa's future. ("If moderate leaders are silenced," Mrs. Suzman had warned Parliament in 1963, shortly after Mandela was arrested, "they will be replaced by extremist ones.") A while before the 1986 colloquy, two British politicians had looked in on Mandela, and had reported afterward that his jailers had broken his spirit. That, Mrs. Suzman was quick to rejoin, was absurd. "Let me tell you," she said to the press. "It would take a great deal to break the spirit of a man like Nelson Mandela." There she was again — in the uneasy position of seeming to defend the operation of a system she abhorred.

Winnie Mandela has been jailed several times, for a total of about twenty months. For years, she was banned (forbidden, that is, to lead any sort of public life) and, for much of that time, exiled to a bleak spot in the Orange Free State, far from her family and friends in Soweto. Mrs. Suzman called on her three times out there. Whenever this particular M.P. went on such a mission, members of the Special Branch — the security police — would tag along. On one occasion, Mrs. Suzman's shadows, actually preceding her into Mrs. Mandela's retreat, seized and confiscated a quilt, because it had been made, not accidentally, in the black-green-and-gold of the A.N.C. — as subversive an item of bedding as ever the keen-eyed Special Branch had spotted. Mrs. Suzman saw to it that that confiscation was well publicized. She says, "I told the minister of justice afterward, 'You're the best press agent Winnie could have had.' "

Mrs. Mandela has since defied the order and returned to her home in Soweto. Mrs. Suzman has spent time with her there, too. After one chat, the two of them (with a group of reporters in tow) dropped in on a nearby high school to see what kind of education it could be offering, considering that there were armed troops posted in its yard. The principal, a black man, was understandably nervous, and his only reply to the visitors' questions ("Are things all right?" "Are you having any trouble?") was "No comment." No policemen had pursued the two women this time, but when they decided to leave they were informed by the soldiers that they couldn't until the Special Branch turned up to check them out. When it finally did, a half hour or so later, Mrs. Mandela and Mrs. Suzman were not further detained. But the fact that their movements had been blocked at all was soon circulated by the hovering press, and by the time Mrs. Suzman returned home that evening, after making a few other investigative stops, she learned that people on at least three continents were wondering if she was all right. Reflecting on that experience later, and employing one of the milder adjectives in her quiver, Mrs. Suzman said, "It must be extremely distressing for black students to be confronted at every turn by a man with his finger on the trigger."

Two Gavronsky brothers and two David sisters, at different times, emigrated to South Africa from Lithuania in the early part of the century. The brothers eventually married the sisters. The families settled in the Transvaal region, and the husbands went into the butchering business (meat, hides, tallow, bone-meal: everything the local cattle would yield) and, in due course, prospered, and branched into real estate, and prospered even more. Samuel and Frieda Gavronsky had two daughters, Gertrude and Helen. At Helen's birth, on November 7, 1917, in Germiston, then a small mining town ten miles southeast of Johannesburg, Gertrude was four and a half. When the infant was two weeks old, her mother, who was twenty-eight, died, apparently from postnatal complications. Ten years later, Samuel remarried. Meanwhile, he and his daughters had moved in with his brother Oscar and sister-in-law Hansa, who were childless.

Samuel Gavronsky, who died in 1965, was, according to his younger daughter, a sociable fellow, fond of dogs and cats, of horses, and of card games, and only passingly religious. Wherever he was lodged, candles were ceremonially lit on Friday evenings, and no on-premises consumption of pork was condoned; still, he never seemed unduly concerned about the origin of sausages grilled at somebody else's *braaivleis* (barbecue). Nor was Helen aware that her father ever gave much thought to the status of any blacks other than his domestic servants; after she went into Parliament, she once or twice attempted to remind him that, as she puts it, "blacks in South Africa were subject to many of the restrictions that he as a Jew had been subjected to in his early life"; but by then he had substantial property holdings, including a couple of hotels, and he did not appear to be moved. She herself, when it came to that, had had no contact at all with blacks—servants aside—when she was growing up.

Helen's schooling — like that of many another Jewish girl of her time and place — was at a Catholic convent. (A Nationalist M.P. may or may not have been aware of this when, during an acerbic exchange, he referred to her scathingly as "Mother Superior.") "We learned to memorize, because that's the way in which the nuns taught," Mrs. Suzman said years later, in the oral history. "We also learned to be bad losers, because we had to win at games. Otherwise, we would get whacked by the senior nun. And that was probably very good for me in politics. You're not supposed to lose in politics."

Early in 1934, barely sixteen, Helen enrolled at the University of Witwatersrand, traditionally one of South Africa's more enlightened academic institutions. (Today, with the government pretending not to notice that its rules are being skirted, some 15 percent of the students at Wits are nonwhite.) She was working for a Bachelor of Commerce degree, studying economics, accounting, and, later on, economic history. At the end of her second year, she went on a students' tour to London, where her sister, by then married to a doctor, was living. Helen had visited there the year before, and now she hoped to enroll in the London School of Economics. But her father insisted she come home, and that was that. She returned to Wits, but quit in her third year. (Later, she concluded that she'd been too immature to matriculate when she did.) Not long afterward, while on horseback at a riding academy, she found herself trotting beside a bestirruped doctor fourteen years her senior, Moses Meyer Suzman, one of eight children of a well-to-do wholesale tobacconist. The two were already acquainted, but now their friendship blossomed, and in 1937 they were married. (At eighty-three, Dr. Suzman, an internist specializing in heart, blood, and nervous diseases, is still practicing in Johannesburg. When Parliament is sitting, his wife comes up from Cape Town every second weekend, and they also manage to spend a fair amount of time together the rest of the year.) The Suzmans have two daughters, both of whom were sufficiently avant-garde as teenagers to attend interracial parties. (Now many Johannesburg discothèques are fully integrated.) The younger, Patricia, is a nephrologist, and lives and works in Boston. The older, Frances, is an art historian, and is married to a law professor, Jeffrey Jowell; they have two children and live in London. The Jowells both have graduate degrees from Harvard, and Joanna, the first of their children, was born in Massachusetts. They also lived for a while in Canada, where their second child, Daniel, was born.

Mrs. Suzman had gone back to Wits soon after Frances's birth, and she got her degree in 1942. By then, the Second World War was well under way. Vorster and others of his ideological stripe — they had never forgiven their British overlords the indignities of the Boer War — had joined the anti-Allied Ossewa-Brandwag, or Ox-Wagon Guard; and before the war was over Vorster would be interned as pro-Nazi. Moses Suzman, for his part, had got a South African Medical Corps commission, and, while his wife was pregnant with their second child, went off, as a lieutenant colonel, to serve at an army hospital in Egypt. He spent almost two years at distant posts. Helen, with what time she had to spare from her daughters, worked for the Governor-General's War Fund and then as a statistician for the War Supplies Board, where she was assigned to seeking out war profiteers. In 1945, Wits offered her a part-time job as a tutor, and not long after that she was appointed a lecturer in economic history. She stayed at Wits for eight years. Along the way, she became increasingly interested in politics, and got involved with the interracially oriented South African Institute of Race Relations.

Toward the end of 1945, Prime Minister Smuts set up a Commission of Inquiry into Laws Applying to Urban Blacks, headed by an appeals-court judge, Henry Fagan. The Institute asked Mrs. Suzman—who had quickly ascended to its executive board —to help prepare evidence to submit to the Fagan Commission. "I was a late starter in this field," she said, forty years afterward. "But once I got going I became absolutely obsessed with it." She disclosed to Parliament last June, during a debate on an Abolition of Influx Control Bill, that "it was the study of the migrant-labor system that first brought me into politics—Heaven preserve me—in the mid-forties." The Fagan Commission ultimately reported that "migration of blacks into the urban areas was a natural economic phenomenon which could be regulated and guided, but not reversed." Smuts accepted the commission's recommendation that the permanency of blacks in the urban areas be recognized and made legal, but in 1948 he and his

United Party were ousted from power. The Nationalists took control and reverted to the old idea that blacks were only temporary sojourners in the "white" urban areas.

Teaching was Mrs. Suzman's top priority away from home, but in 1949 she was deeply enough immersed in politics to organize a United Party branch among Wits teachers and students. Then the Nats began to pile on top of the existing restrictive laws and customs that divided the peoples of South Africa a whole slew of new ones, including a Group Areas Act, a Separate Amenities Act, a Job Reservation Act, a Bantu Education Act, a Prohibition of Mixed Marriages Act, a Sabotage Act, a Suppression of Communism Act (this one was eventually amended at least eighty-four times, each time getting tougher), an Immorality Act, a Ninety-Day-Detention Act, a Terrorism Act, and, perhaps most significant, a Race Classification Act. Mrs. Suzman has not once in all her parliamentary years managed to get even a private member's motion accepted, but she has had the satisfaction of witnessing the repeal of many of the laws against which she persistently campaigned—notably the Pass Laws and the Influx Control Bill. The nuns who sought to instill in her an aversion to losing would doubtless have been pleased.

Toward the end of 1952, the United Party leaders of the upper-middle-class voting district called Houghton, a few miles north of downtown Johannesburg, decided that a change in their parliamentary representation would be welcome. Houghton, which Mrs. Suzman now and then refers to as a silk-stocking area (most of its homes have a tennis court, a swimming pool, and a burglar-alarm system), was, and is, by South African standards, a fairly liberal enclave. Whoever was designated the United Party's candidate was all but guaranteed election. Mrs. Suzman, then thirty-five, and another woman were invited to compete with the sitting M.P. for the United Party's nomination. When her husband urged her to run (their daughters were thirteen and ten), she agreed, in part because she estimated that her chances of winning were slim. There was also another reason. As she later put it to a friend, "The most soul-destroying thing one can do in South Africa today is to live here and do nothing about the situation, to enjoy the fleshpots that are here

for all of *us*"—by whom she meant white people, of course—
"and do absolutely nothing about the basic injustice around us."

Mrs. Suzman got the nomination in November and was unopposed in the election the following April. "I was a member of
Parliament before I even looked around," she says. She made
her legislative début in Cape Town in July. (During that first
session, she put up at a hotel; she has since acquired a three-
room flat with a nice view of Table Mountain.) The Hon. Member for Houghton, as she has been known ever since, was then
one of fifty-seven United Party representatives. Among her
U.P. colleagues was a mining scion who would become a lifelong
friend and supporter—Harry F. Oppenheimer, who remained
in Parliament until 1957, when his magnate father died, and he
left to reign over the family's economic empire.

During Mrs. Suzman's first eight years in Parliament—in
1958, she was re-elected, again unopposed, for a second five-
year term—she continued to have U.P. members around her.
These were years notable for, among other developments, the
promulgation, in 1955, of a Freedom Charter by the African
National Congress and others ("South Africa belongs to all who
live in it, black and white"); for the rise of the political star of
Hendrik Verwoerd, who was the inspiration for many of the
restrictions that have become collectively known as apartheid,
and, Mrs. Suzman says, "the only man in the world I've ever
actually been scared of"; and for the banning of the Pan-Africanist Congress and the African National Congress after the
P.A.C. mounted a campaign of defiance toward Verwoerd's Pass
Laws, which led to the 1960 Sharpeville massacre. The United
Party, meanwhile, was having troubles of its own. Some of these
problems were personal and almost petty, as when another U.P.
woman member of Parliament said, at a caucus meeting, "Well,
I don't know about Mrs. Suzman, but when I go to a museum I
don't like it if some strange black man rubs himself up against
me," and Mrs. Suzman retorted, "Don't you mind it if some
strange *white* man rubs himself up against you?" In any event,
by 1961 the U.P. had split into rival factions, and its more liberal
members, Mrs. Suzman by now prominent among them, had
left its ranks and reconstituted themselves as the Progressive
Party. (Today, having absorbed another breakaway section of

the U.P., it is the Progressive Federal Party.) In that year, Prime Minister Verwoerd converted the Union of South Africa into a Republic, took his country out of the British Commonwealth, and called for a general election at home. When the returns came in, Mrs. Suzman proved to be the only member of her new party to hold a seat. Verwoerd announced triumphantly in Parliament that he had never for a moment believed that the Progs, as they became known, might be a threat to his Nats, but now—he turned toward Mrs. Suzman and glared at her—"I have written you off."

Scared though she usually was of him, this time she was not too frightened to reply, "And the whole world has written *you* off."

For the next thirteen years, the entire Progressive Party in the House of Assembly was embodied in the five-foot-three-inch Helen Suzman. And, for the six years following that, she was the only woman in the hundred-and-sixty-five-member House.

Those thirteen years Mrs. Suzman has referred to, in retrospect, both as "my heyday" and as "my period of trial." The *Rand Daily Mail,* then in *its* heyday, saw fit to run a poem about her titled "The Pluck to Stand Alone" and containing the lines "Give thanks for her; she raised the cry: 'This thing is evil; let it die.'" The legislators habitually ate and drank exclusively with members of their own parties. During all those years, Mrs. Suzman, having no Prog peers to consort with, never entered the members' bar, and she lunched in solitude, not infrequently off a sandwich at her desk. She had a researcher to help her keep abreast of current events and contemplated involvements, but she had no speech writers to fall back on, and if there was any Prog protest to be made against any proffered statute the oratory had to be entirely of her own composition. She says that she learned, out of necessity, to listen to somebody else's speech while simultaneously writing one of her own. Most of her fellow-legislators spoke in Afrikaans; she could understand it perfectly, but she delivered almost all her own remarks in English. She had an ally of sorts in the Speaker of the House, Henning J. Klopper, who would inform her at the outset of every annual session that although he expected to disagree with every word she uttered, he believed in certain minority rights. "I am going to see to it that you get time to speak whenever you want to," he told her. The press—the English-language press, at least—sometimes seemed to hang on her every word. After she'd been voted down in one debate, a Nat M.P. muttered crossly, "The object of the operation of the hon. member for Houghton will nevertheless be achieved. She will still be the headline tomorrow as she was today, namely: 'Lone woman opposes the measure.' " When she called for a division—a stand-up-and-be-counted procedure—the upshot would sometimes find her alone at one side of the chamber and everybody else jammed together at the other. Once, she remarked that she thought she'd seen a wistful expression on the face of a cabinet minister, whereupon another member said, "So you are a student of physiognomy!"

"I am practically everything," she replied. "I have to be, in this House."

Other exchanges have been ruder, and cruder. Some observers of the South African parliamentary scene have professed to detect "overtones" of anti-Semitism. *Over*tones? "We don't like your screeching Jewish voice" went a good deal beyond implication. In pro-government newspaper cartoons, Helen's nose was often ludicrously large. From time to time, a member who disagreed with her would shout, "Go back to Israel!" After the Six-Day War, in 1967, when South Africans began to admire Israel as a small pariah state that had thwarted big bullies, demands that Mrs. Suzman emigrate reverted to a previously suggested destination: "Go back to Moscow!" (She has also been branded a capitalist.) Even more often, she would be interrupted, as she tried to speak, by cries of "Nonsense!" and "Rubbish!" and "Sit down!" and "Shut up!"—all these, it should be made plain, terms of non-endearment to which she herself frequently and early had recourse. One of the few times on record when she was accorded a "Hear! Hear!" came after she said, teasingly, "Supposing I was to resign tomorrow; everybody would say 'Hurrah!' and 'Hear! Hear!' "

At home, during parliamentary recesses, she got accustomed to receiving hate mail and unnerving phone calls, with messages like "You bitch—which kaffir are you sleeping with tonight?"

After a while, she took to keeping a shrill whistle beside her telephone, hoping that when she blew it full blast she might give somebody's eardrums something to remember her by. (She may even have zapped a few government eavesdroppers manning illegal bugs.) Women in New York tend to list merely their initials in phone books, in order to discourage purveyors of random obscenities. Mrs. Suzman felt obliged to have "Helen" spelled out, in order to spare another female H. Suzman—a sister-in-law—unsettling affronts. In Parliament, where just about anything goes and slander is unknown, various Nats have assessed Mrs. Suzman at various times as blind, unbalanced, subversive, senile, and as an incessantly chirping cricket. She has been termed "holier than thou," a "mouthpiece for political prisoners," a "Salvation Army lassie," a "self-confessed simpleton," an "agent for revolution," and, when narcotics were on the agenda, a "dagga [hemp] fancier." (Her response to this last was that she had never tried marijuana or dagga, because she feared that if she did she might be tempted to resume smoking ordinary cigarettes.) Some of her Nat colleagues, the majority of whom are or profess to be pillars of the Dutch Reformed Church, seem to drool over innuendo. When Mrs. Suzman once spoke of some industries as being in "the hot little hands" of the minister of planning, he couldn't wait to interject, "Do not pretend that you know something about the warmth of my hands." And when she declared that she wished she "could share the dream world" of another minister, it was almost a sure thing that he would come up with "You will never be able to share *my* dream world." A member aspiring to cast slurs on her relationship with a man under discussion alluded to her six times in a single declamation as his "bosom friend." On another occasion, the same member, discussing Mrs. Suzman and a male M.P with whom the holder of the floor was also out of sorts, said, "The hon. members to whom I referred . . . revealed that rare characteristic that one finds in only one animal—the cat. They have the ability to fight and woo at the same time."

"Ever so long ago," Mrs. Suzman recently said, off duty, "I gave up worrying what these honourable members say about me." She demonstrated early that she could hold her own.

"Dense" and "dumb" were two of her milder adjudications. She is fond of expressive adjectives. A random perusal of the *Hansard*s that have chronicled her parliamentary history reveals her as having applied to other M.P.s or their articulated views, among many other pejoratives, "appalling," "desperate," "disastrous," "disgraceful," "disgusting," "distressing," "ham-handed," "horrendous," "idiotic," "malicious," "miserable," and "ridiculous." She seems to have reserved "dastardly" for P. W. Botha. Of a cabinet minister who was also a physician, and who had accused her of inciting violence, she declared, "I would not take a sick cat to that man." In the case of another M.P. who was also an M.D., and minister of health to boot, she was moved to wonder aloud (1) whether he had forgotten the Hippocratic oath and (2) whether it might not improve his health if he consulted a psychiatrist. "I do not know," she once purred in Parliament, "why we equate—and with the examples before us—a white skin with civilization." One attribute for which her Houghton constituents admire her is her cheekiness. Soon after still another minister charged that she was nothing more than a political propagandist, she applied her tongue to her ever-ready whetstone and retorted that if this particular Afrikaner politician were a tribal African woman "he would be the sort of leader of the ululators before the warriors go in to throw their assegais around." As for bona-fide tribal Africans, she favored her sometimes ululating fellow-M.P.s, in the course of a debate on the Bantu Education Act, with, "In regard to the government's concentration on trying to re-establish tribal customs and developing pride in the African people, the Africans in South Africa live in a modern industrial country and they do not want to return to their tribal structure. The Africans want only one thing, and that is to share in the benefits of the development of Western civilization, and they are not interested in wearing tribal clothing and sitting around a pot in the tribal areas."

As far back as 1963, Mrs. Suzman was telling her fellow-lawmakers, "The government . . . refuses to understand that if nonviolent protests are not allowed then [they] will be replaced by violent protests." That same year, she was the only M.P. to

vote against a statute authorizing the government to detain anybody for ninety days without trial for any reason or, when it
came to that, for no discernible reason at all. "Laws must be just
if order is to be maintained," she observed. By 1966, she had
become a front-bencher, with only ten M.P.s enjoying greater
seniority. The retired headmaster of Eton, Dr. Robert Birley,
was lecturing in South Africa that year, and he elected to extoll
Mrs. Suzman as the "foremost woman parliamentarian of the
Western world." A regional news magazine named her its Supreme Optimist of the Year 1966. Something Mrs. Suzman told
a friend that same year illustrates how much conditions in South
Africa have changed in two decades: "Few blacks seem to want
to become martyrs. Revolt seems alien to their nature. They are
quite capable of violence, but they waste it on trivia. They don't
try to overwhelm cops or garrote informers." But, having said
that, she continued, far more presciently, "Things will never get
better for the blacks before they get worse. You cannot shake
off shackles without a loud clatter."

On September 6, 1966, as the daily session of the House was
about to begin, Mrs. Suzman was on her front bench, reading a
letter that a messenger had just handed to her, when another
messenger, apparently deranged, fatally stabbed Prime Minister
Verwoerd. She was aware of a fracas, but had no indication of
what had happened until, a minute or so later, some furious
M.P.s dragging the assailant out of the chamber happened to
lose their grip and dump him at her feet. Hard on their heels,
waving his arms and shouting, came P. W. Botha, who incurred
her unending wrath by pointing his finger in her face and yelling, in Afrikaans, "It's you! You liberals did this! Now we'll get
you!"

Botha is a common surname in South Africa. There have
been as many as five Bothas in the House at the same time. One
of them, who has long since departed the scene, said of Mrs.
Suzman nearly twenty years ago, "We should not take her seriously, because she will disappear from this House in due course
in the same way as her ideas will disappear from this House."
She does occasionally disappear from her bench for a few hours,
but only after being asked to leave for the remainder of that

day's session because the presiding officer has deemed her conduct unparliamentary. When she was ordered out one afternoon and yet another Botha could not refrain from a loud "Good riddance!" it was fast made manifest that some civility obtained in South Africa: he was heaved out, too.

"The South African credo is the entrenchment of race discrimination," Mrs. Suzman told Parliament in 1967, the year in which she first met Nelson Mandela, and in which the member from Odendaalsrus told their colleagues, "The hon. member for Houghton assured us in this House about a week ago that overseas she is dubbed a conservative. I think I can understand why. It is because she is so extremely conservative when it comes to restricting the activities of Communists, who undermine the social and political fabric of this country." That year, too, the ineffable M.P. Cornelius P. Mulder — whose later mischief as minister of information (he secretly used government funds to launch an ostensibly independent newspaper at home and to try to buy a paper in the United States) proved so embarrassing that it brought down the Vorster regime — showed his mettle in a curt parliamentary exchange precipitated by Mrs. Suzman's recommendation that people hauled off by the police and not charged with anything ought at least to be allowed to have their next of kin notified of their detention.

MULDER: Even a terrorist?
SUZMAN: Yes, even a saboteur or a murderer.
MULDER: Even you.

After Mulder's exposure, a fellow-member of the Nationalist Party said, in Parliament, "If we in South Africa were ever to accept a system in which a cabinet minister who was politically responsible for things that went wrong could return to politics, we would be doing a disservice to good government in South Africa." Three years ago, Mulder was elected by the far-right Conservative Party to the President's Council, a recently created South African legislative chamber that in certain circumstances can override decisions of the House of Assembly. The Council's deliberations have apparently been far too quiet for him, and he wants to return to the rough-and-tumble of the House; he, too, is running, disservice or no disservice, on the Conservative ticket, in the upcoming election.

Over the years, Mrs. Suzman has visited a number of other' African nations, among them Angola, Botswana, the Gambia, Ghana, Kenya, Lesotho, Malawi, Mozambique, Swaziland, Tanzania, Zambia, and Zimbabwe, and for the most part — white participant in the South African government though she undeniably is—she has been cordially received. Nairobi's *Standard* has editorially applauded her "lone persistent voice" (on a visit to Kenya's Parliament she got a bigger hand than she ever has had in her own), and while Julius Nyerere presided in Dar es Salaam he told her, "When all this is over, your role will be remembered."

Back home, meanwhile, she was being increasingly remembered as someone who could get injustices corrected — or, at any rate, aired. In 1970, for instance (a year in which she told the minister whose portfolio embraced forestry, tourism, sports, recreation, and Indian affairs, "The hon. the minister is frightened of non-white people; I am not"), six mothers of young white men of draft age solicited her help. The sons were Jehovah's Witnesses. "Now, I hold no brief for Jehovah's Witnesses," Mrs. Suzman said afterward, "and, indeed, I hold no brief for a lot of the people on whose behalf I intercede." P. W. Botha, on his way up, was then minister of defence. The problem was that on reaching eighteen the young men had been summoned for a year's military service, had refused on religious grounds to be inducted, had been sentenced to two years in detention barracks, and, when they had also refused to don the uniforms prescribed for wear there, had been slapped into solitary confinement for six months; on emerging and balking again, they had immediately been given six such months more. One boy had had a half dozen of these punishments in succession and, according to his mother, had all but forgotten how to talk. It seemed possible that he could remain in solitary until he got past conscription age—thirty-five. Mrs. Suzman brought up the matter during a debate on a defense-appropriation bill, and Mr. Botha, who was notorious then for a short temper (one historian has contended that his latter-day comparative calm as head of state is attributable to medication), flared up and denounced her as a mouthpiece for all that was subversive in their nation. Mrs. Suzman, whose victories in combat with him have been few, did at least get the minister to concede that the prisoners' "recalcitrant and defiant attitude" had, "regrettably," resulted in "unnecessary hard-handed treatment by members of the detention barracks staff." This last, Botha declared, would no longer be tolerated. As a further concession, men in solitary would thenceforth be granted access to Bibles.

In time, the questions with which Mrs. Suzman peppered cabinet ministers came close to becoming her trademark. If she could not influence the making of laws, she could compel the government to reveal some of the details of their application and enforcement. "Parliament is the only place where laws can be repealed and the government can be held to account and information can be extracted," she says. "I've built up a body of statistics by asking questions—numbers of people detained, for instance, those prosecuted, those hanged. The press has found this valuable, and I've found the press valuable. I've been accused by the Nats of getting more coverage than I've any right to. I say to them, 'You say something worth reporting and you'll get publicity, too.' When one Nat M.P. accused me of giving South Africa a bad image by the questions I asked in Parliament, I said to him, 'It's not my questions that give the country a bad image. It's your replies.' "

As for the sorts of questions she had kept raising—well, if the minister of the interior had, as he reported, banned forty-nine films, exactly which ones were they, please? (*Entertaining Mr. Sloane* and *Diary of a Mad Housewife,* to name two.) Would the minister of police be good enough to identify the three still anonymous individuals known to have committed suicide while in detention? Would the minister of Indian affairs pray tell how many Indian schoolteachers had recently been sacked in Natal? For the minister of law and order: How many persons died in police custody in the year 1985, and what were the causes of death? One hundred and fifty—eighty-one from injuries sustained before and during arrest, six from being assaulted by fellow-prisoners, thirty-three from suicide, thirty from natural causes. For the minister of justice: How many people had been sentenced to a whipping over a certain twelve-month stretch, and what was the total number of strokes administered? About forty thousand sentenced; as for the strokes, "statistics of this nature are not available." That did not satisfy the persistent lone voice. "My feeling," Mrs. Suzman commented, "is that they are not available because they are so horrendous that even this retributive House might quail at the number of young people whipped."

When 1974 rolled around, and, with it, yet another election, Mrs. Suzman concluded that thirteen years alone was enough. If she won again and no other Prog made it, she would quit. But when the returns were in, so were five additional Progs. (A sixth was added soon after, in a by-election.) What joy! What luxury! Not only did she have people to break bread and have a drink with but when the minister of justice called her a "squeaking dummy" she could sit back, assured that someone else would rise to refute the aspersion. When P. W. Botha said that "the Progressive Party, throughout its history" — much of that, of course, mainly her history — "has been the intercessor of subversive elements in South Africa," there were others to shout in protest. To shout loudly enough, indeed, for him to feel obliged to substitute "*an* intercessor."

With a half-dozen Progs on the barricades with her, Mrs. Suzman was able to concentrate on areas she had long wished to make her specialties: detentions without trial (for a while, the Progressive Party distributed "Charge or Release" bumper stickers), human rights, blacks' affairs, prisons and prisoners, simple justice. She had still made no legislative headway — she once said she would faint if the House ever accepted any of her numerous amendments — but, as she told one inquiring foreigner, "the fact that you're keeping an eye on things often has a salutary effect." She adduced as evidence the fact that she had once got a young woman prisoner transferred from solitary to a three-person cell. To her oral historian at Columbia, she confided:

I became then the sort of champion of people who were detained. Although, you know, my views were probably not nearly as radical as the views of these people, because many of them were, in fact, either card-carrying members of the old Communist Party or their sympathies definitely lay in that direction. Many of then, however, were not. There were black nationalists who weren't Communists. And there were white liberals who weren't Communists. All these people were in and out of trouble. I had to intervene on behalf of a number of them to get them visits from relatives, to make sure they were O.K., and so on.

I must say very often without any — not that one wasn't thanked, but one was surprised at the hostility that afterward emanated from people on whose behalf one had intervened. It was strange, almost a resentment that they would need to use somebody like me, whom they considered to be really a — you know — part of the capitalist sort of establishment. Well, that was too bad. I happened to be in a position where I had access, and that was the important thing.

By 1979, there were times when Mrs. Suzman appeared to be getting discouraged. She told the House that the only way, as she saw it, to avoid more of the unrest that was becoming ominously pervasive was "to make changes which are meaningful, which will give black people hope about their future and about the future of their children." In her end-of-session remarks that June, she added, "Increasing numbers of young blacks are going to become despairing. More and more of them will resort to change by violence, not because they want violence, but because they see no other way to change the circumstances of their lives, which are filled with frustration and lack of opportunity."

Later that year, a former agent of the South African Department of National Security defected to London. He took along a bunch of pilfered documents, which the British press was delighted to give space to when he surfaced. He had, among other communications, a couple of private letters written by Helen Suzman, in 1976, to a member of the British Parliament, young Winston Churchill. In one missive, she had said — it would seem that her government would have applauded — "I am sick and tired of these armchair revolutionaries who live thousands of miles away from South Africa and try to prescribe on our behalf." The letters had been removed from a file captioned "Wit Vrou [White Woman] 24596." Mrs. Suzman was not taken aback to learn that such a dossier existed. She had long believed that the telephone in a small office she kept in her Houghton constituency was tapped; on one occasion, a clerk there had hung up after making a call and, on picking up the instrument to make another, had heard the first one being played back. Mrs. Suzman had been cautioned by friends concerned about her outspokenness that she really ought to stop using a mailbox conveniently down the street from her Hyde Park house. She had found all this cops-and-robbers talk rather amusing. Once, accompanying her husband to a medical convention in Moscow, she had sent home a postcard with a "Dear Comrade Louis" salutation to incumbent Minister of Law and Order Le Grange. That worthy might not have been amused if it had arrived, but when she inquired he denied having received it. She speculated that perhaps his own security people were responsible. Even so, she did not like the idea of having her mail trifled with, and she was determined to raise the issue when Parliament reconvened in February 1980.

The business about the purloined letters began to seem not quite so funny when, after Mrs. Suzman demanded to know what was going on between the Department of National Security and herself, Prime Minister Botha himself chose to reply, and said, "If you want to communicate with the Devil, use his postal facilities or allow him to use your postal facilities or your letter-heads." What the devil was P. W. carrying on about? She had no idea. "The hon. member must not push me too far," Botha continued, no more enlighteningly, "or I shall tell her who writes on her letterheads and who writes her name on the back of the envelope and signs his own name to the letter — No, the hon. member is a vicious little cat when she is wronged, but I say to her, 'Choose your friends better.' "

Still perplexed, Mrs. Suzman proposed that the House appoint a select committee to look into the matter, whatever it was or might prove to be. Botha, brushing that request aside, announced, "Things were written about secret meetings on her letterheads and her name was put to wrong use — by a person who, according to our information, is a member of a foreign intelligence service," and then proceeded to warn her and her ilk that "if they continue to associate with people who wish to jeopardize the laws of the country they are then going to make trouble for themselves."

The following day, it was the turn of the deputy minister of defence and of national security, H. J. Coetsee. He identified one of the "people who purport to write in the name of the hon. member for Houghton" as a "Mr. X," who was either an operative of or a collaborator with a "foreign intelligence agency," and who had been "accused of penetrating liberation movements, of being hostile . . . of harboring manipulative intentions." Now the deputy minister mentioned a letter written in 1978 from Johannesburg to someone abroad. Mr. X's name had been omitted from the usual return-address spot, and "in its place, was written 'Mrs. H. Suzman, M.P.,' followed by her full address." Coetsee went on to quote from the letter, whose author had watched "seven hours of ITV videotapes of programs on S. Africa which have created quite a storm in Britain. . . . They were shown secretly here and are very powerful."

Mrs. Suzman suddenly began to see the light. She had attended that seven-hour ITV rerun herself, at the home of a *Rand Daily Mail* reporter, and she had taken along an American house guest: Robert Rotberg, a political-science professor at M.I.T.; a contributor to the *Christian Science Monitor* and other publications; a frequent visitor to South Africa, about which he had written extensively in several of his sixteen books; and someone who she was positive had never been connected with any intelligence service, foreign or domestic. Mrs. Suzman phoned Rotberg later that day at his home in Lexington, Massachusetts. Did he recall anything about writing a letter while he was staying with her husband and her in January 1978? He thought back. Yes, he remembered, he'd wanted to write to his wife and kids, and Helen had given him a piece of aerogram stationery from her desk — one of those lightweight single-sheet contrivances that fold over to become envelopes, and the contents of which can be read only after the things are slit open. And, yes, it had had Mrs. Suzman's name and address printed — not written — on what ended up as its back. Where had he posted it? Oh, he supposed in that letter box at the end of her street — but what on earth was this all about? She explained, and begged him to try to find the letter and, if he could, to transmit a facsimile pronto. His wife had kept it, and within a day Helen had it. It began "Darlings all" and said toward the end — after, to be sure, alluding en passant to the "hated and feared security headquarters in Jo'burg," where he'd gone to seek a permit to visit an imprisoned editor of a black newspaper — "I send nothing but tankers of love to each of you. I wish I could send the hot sun and the swimming pool, too."

Mrs. Suzman was pleased to be able to inform Parliament on February 15, 1980 — she had already informed the press — of Mr. X's anticlimactic identity. "The whole thing is one huge giggle," she told the House. "He is as much C.I.A. as the hon. the minister for tourism and statistics." Mrs. Suzman never did get Prime Minister Botha or any of his henchmen to apologize either to Rotberg or to her, conceivably because they took seriously a tortured explanation by yet another Nat M.P. — that the professor's letter could hardly be said to have been intercepted in the first place, inasmuch as once any letter was mailed it ceased to be the sender's property.

Last June, well into Parliament's 1986 proceedings, Mrs. Suzman was happily surprised when, for practically the first time in more than three decades, a representative of the Nationalist Party — it was the member for Innesdal, Albertus Erik Nothnagel — was given the floor and used it to say a few kind words about her. The House was debating the Abolition of Influx Control Bill, a cause that Mrs. Suzman had been espousing ever since her back-bench days. "As a quite ordinary South African parliamentarian — this might sound very liberal to many people and quite off the rails, too — and as one person to another," Nothnagel said, "I should like to tell the hon. member for Houghton frankly this evening that as far as these measures are concerned, measures in regard to which she, without any assistance, took up the cudgels in this House for many years, she had a better insight into the problems and could see further than many other people in South Africa."

He had to pause. There were interjections, not recorded word for word — perhaps that was just as well — in *Hansard*.

Nothnagel continued, "I want to add that although she does lash out at us at times, taking us to task in a manner which we feel is very unfair to the N.P. [Nats] — for example, in regard to security legislation — I hardly think there will ever again be anyone in the history of this country who could do as much for human rights as she has done."

No immediate interjections, possibly because the members who could normally have been relied on to utter them had been stunned into silence.

At the start of 1986, the House of Assembly consisted of nineteen members of two parties (the Conservative Party and another) that actually stand to the right of Botha's Nats; five members belonging to a remnant of the old United Party; twenty-seven Progs; and — still far and away the overriding majority — a hundred and twenty-seven Nats. The Progressive Federal Party's ranks were soon to be thinned; two of its leading members resigned — frustrated, they said, by their inability to do more than deplore the government's ever-sterner strictures. Mrs. Suzman — who remarked to a friend at about that time, "You can only do what you try to do, and if you fail you've got to accept it" — was still there. "I hope I have enough sense to know when I should pack it in," she says. But in conversation, as in Parliament, she has seemed more and more pessimistic. "Young blacks are not only prepared to be whipped," she told her fellow-M.P.s early last winter. "They are prepared to die."

That April, she said in the House that "we are involved in a low-key civil war with rebellious young blacks, convinced that victory is around the corner if only they can keep up the pressure, since the entire world appears to be on their side," and that only if the government were to dismantle "all the laws which should never have been put on our statute book in the first instance . . . shall we be able to tackle the crucial question of political participation of blacks, and only then will South Africa stand a chance of avoiding the imposition of punitive measures by the rest of the world." The country has already been grievously punished, she tells friends and lecture audiences, by the flight of many white English-speaking natives. "I scarcely know a family that hasn't lost a child to emigration," she says. "The people who are going are those who can get jobs elsewhere, and those, of course, whom we need the most — engineers, accountants, teachers, nurses, doctors. When I tell

the House that it's a great indictment of the government that
these people have been driven away, I'm answered with things
like 'Good riddance' and 'They're not good South Africans.' "

Many people who believe that only radical measures can save
South Africa from itself think that the Progs are not radical
enough. "There doesn't seem to be a wild rush to join us," Mrs.
Suzman said in New York last fall. The Progressive Federal
Party has begun to move — if in some opinions at no more than
a glacierlike pace — in directions that Mrs. Suzman hopes will
be perceived as truly progressive. "We believe in universal adult
franchise — one man, one vote," she tells audiences in and out
of South Africa. "But we want minority rights protected by
something along the lines of what the United States of America
has in the form of its Senate." The Progs favor a national convention, with all races present, for the drafting of a new constitution and bill of rights — a gathering at which, however, two
critical matters would be non-negotiable: no oppression by any
one group of any other, and no discriminatory legislation of any
sort. "One problem with all that is that many blacks don't want
a federal system — they want unqualified enfranchisement,"
Mrs. Suzman has conceded in private. "Now, we feel, in my
party, that South Africa has many thousands of educated blacks
— in fact, millions of blacks — who want a peaceful solution and
would be prepared to become partners with the whites rather
than take over and dominate. This has never been tried, of
course, so we can't tell whether we're right. If blacks did take
over altogether and there were no rule of law and no bill of
rights, I don't think I'd stay in South Africa. I'm very averse to
bureaucratic controls, and black bureaucrats are no better than
white ones. I've stayed so far under a government I don't like,
but at least there have been elections — for those who vote —
and a fairly good legal system, and, until recently, a relatively
free press. It wouldn't bother me in the slightest to live under a
black president or a black prime minister, provided he wasn't
socialist or Marxist or bureaucratic."

In October 1985, a group of Progs traveled to Lusaka, to initiate
conversations with the outlawed African National Congress.
Mrs. Suzman had been for that all along. Last August, Minister

of Law and Order Le Grange had felt moved to ask, in Parliament, "Who is the hon. member for Houghton's No. 1 man in South Africa?" and, after a pause for not unexpected interjections, to answer himself with "It is Nelson Mandela."

Mrs. Suzman's tongue was blunt.

"Let him go!" she cried.

"She admires him with everything she has," Le Grange pressed on. "He is the only man who, according to her, can counteract the present unrest situation in South Africa and negotiate on peace."

The only interjection was Mrs. Suzman's: "That's right!"

CHARLES SIMIC

Reading Philosophy at Night

FROM ANTAEUS

It is night again around me; I feel as though there had been
lightning — for a brief span of time I was *entirely* in my element
and in my light.

— Nietzsche

The mind loves the unknown. It loves images whose meaning is
unknown, since the meaning of the mind itself is unknown.

— Magritte

I WORE Buster Keaton's expression of exaggerated calm. I could
have been sitting on the edge of a cliff with my back to the abyss
trying to look normal.

Now I read philosophy in the morning. When I was younger
and lived in the city it was always at night. "That's how you
ruined your eyes," my mother keeps saying. I sat and read late
into the night. The quieter it got, the more clearheaded I became — or so it seemed to me. In the sparsely furnished room
above the Italian grocery, I would be struggling with some intricate epistemological argument which promised a magnificent
insight at its conclusion. I could smell it, so to speak. I couldn't
put the book away, and it was getting very late. I had to be at
work in the morning. Even had I tried to sleep my head would
have been full of Immanuel Kant. So, I wouldn't sleep. I remember well such moments of decision: the great city that had

suddenly turned quiet, the open book, and my face reflected dimly in the darkened windowpane.

At such hours I thought I understood everything. The first time it happened I was twenty. It was six o'clock in the morning. It was winter. It was dark and very cold. I was in Chicago riding the El to work seated between two heavily bundled-up old women. The train was overheated, but each time the door opened at one of the elevated platforms, a blast of cold air would send shivers through us. The lights, too, kept flickering. As the train changed tracks, the lights would go out and I would stop reading the history of philosophy I had borrowed the previous day from the library. "Why is there something rather than nothing?" the book asked, quoting Parmenides. It was as if my eyes were opened. I could not stop looking at my fellow passengers. How incredible, I thought, being here, existing.

I have a recurring dream about the street where I was born. It is always night. I'm walking past vaguely familiar buildings trying to find our house, but somehow it is not there. I retrace my steps on that short block of only a few buildings, all of which are there except the one I want. The effort leaves me exhausted and saddened.

In another version of this same dream, I catch a glimpse of our house. There it is, at last, but for some reason I'm unable to get any closer to it. No lights are on. I look for our window, but it is even darker there on the third floor. The whole building seems abandoned. "It's not possible," I tell myself.

Once in one of these dreams, many years ago, I saw someone at my window, hunched over, watching the street intently. That's how my grandmother would wait late into the night for us to come home, except this was a stranger. Even without being able to make out his face, I was sure of that.

Most of the time, however, there's no one in sight during the dream. The façades of buildings still retain the pockmarks and other signs of the war. The streetlights are out and there's no moon in the sky so it's not clear to me how I am able to see all that in complete darkness.

*

Whoever reads philosophy reads himself as much as he reads the philosopher. I am in a dialogue with certain decisive events in my life as much as I am with the ideas on the page. Meaning is the matter of my existence. My effort to understand is a perpetual circling around a few obsessive images.

Like everyone else, I have my hunches. All my experiences make a kind of untaught ontology which precedes all my readings. What I am trying to conceptualize with the help of the philosopher is that which I have already intuited.

That's one way of looking at it.

The Meditation of yesterday filled my mind with so many doubts that it is no longer in my power to forget them. And yet, I do not see in what manner I can resolve them; and, just as if I had all of a sudden fallen into very deep water, I am so disconcerted that I can neither make certain of setting my feet on the bottom, nor can I swim and so support myself on the surface. I shall nevertheless make an effort and follow anew the same path as that on which I yesterday entered, i.e., I shall proceed by setting aside all that in which the least doubt could be supposed to exist, just as if I had discovered that it was absolutely false; and I shall ever follow in this road until I have met with something which is certain, or at least, if I can do nothing else, until I have learned for certain that there's nothing in the world that is certain. Archimedes, in order that he might draw the terrestrial globe out of its place, and transport it elsewhere, demanded only that one point should be fixed and immovable; in the same way I shall have the right to conceive high hopes if I am happy enough to discover one thing only which is certain and indubitable.

I love this passage of Descartes; his beginning again, his not wanting to be fooled. It describes the ambition of philosophy in all its nobility and desperation. I prefer this doubting Descartes to his famous later conclusions. Here everything is still unsettled. The poetry of the moment still casts its spell. Of course, he's greedy for the absolute, but so is his reader.

There's an Eastern European folk song which tells of a girl who tossed an apple higher and higher in the air until she tossed it as high as the clouds. To her surprise the apple didn't come down. The cloud got it. She waited with arms outstretched, but the apple stayed up there. All she could do is plead with the cloud to return her apple, but that's another story. I like the first part when the impossible happens.

I remember lying in a ditch and looking at some pebbles while German bombers were flying over our heads. That was long ago. I don't remember the face of my mother nor the faces of the people who were there with us, but I still see those perfectly ordinary pebbles.

"It is not *how* things are in the world that is mystical, but that it exists," says Wittgenstein. I had a feeling of great clarity. Time had stopped. I was watching myself watching the pebbles and trembling with fear. Then time moved on.

The pebbles stayed in their otherness, stayed forever as far as I am concerned. I'm talking about the experience of heightened consciousness. Can language do it justice? Speech is always less. When it comes to consciousness, one approximates, one speaks poorly. Competing phenomenologies are impoverishments, splendid poverties.

Wittgenstein puts it this way: "What finds its reflection in language, language cannot represent. What expresses *itself* in language, we cannot express by means of language." We are not, most certainly, thinking about the same thing, nor were he and his followers subsequently very happy with this early statement of his, but this has been my experience on a number of occasions.

I knew someone who once tried to persuade me otherwise. He considered himself a logical positivist. There are people who tell you, for example, that you can speak of a pencil's dimension, location, appearance, state of motion or rest but not of its intelligence and love of music. The moment I hear that the poet in me rebels and I want to write a poem about an intelligent pencil in love with music. In other words, what they regard as nonsense, I suspect to be full of unknown imaginative possibilities.

There's a wonderful story told about Wittgenstein and his Cambridge colleague, the Italian economist Piero Sraffa. Apparently they often discussed philosophy. "One day," as Justus Hartnack has it, "when Wittgenstein was defending his view that a proposition has the same logical form as the fact it depicts,

Sraffa made a gesture used by Neapolitans to express contempt and asked Wittgenstein what the logical form of that was. According to Wittgenstein's own recollection, it was this question which made him realize that his belief that a fact could have a logical form was untenable."

As for my logical friend, we argued all night. "What cannot be said, cannot be thought." And then again, after I blurted out something about silence being the language of consciousness, "you're silent because you have nothing to say." It got to the point where we were calling each other "you dumb shit." We were drinking large quantities of red wine, misunderstanding each other liberally, and only stopped bickering when his disheveled wife came to the bedroom door and told us to shut up.

Then I told him a story.

One day in Yugoslavia, just after the war, we made a class trip to the town War Museum. At the entrance we found a battered German tank which delighted us. Inside the museum one could look at a few rifles, hand grenades and uniforms, but not much else. Most of the space was taken up by photographs. These we were urged to examine. One saw people hanged and people about to be hanged; people on tips of their toes. The executioners stood around smoking. There were piles of corpses everywhere. Some were naked. Men and women with their genitals showing. That made some kid laugh.

Then we saw a man having his throat cut. The killer sat on the man's chest with a knife in his hand. He seemed pleased to be photographed. The victim's eyes I don't remember. A few men stood around gawking. There were clouds in the sky.

There were always clouds, as well as blades of grass, tree stumps, bushes and rocks no one was paying any attention to. At times the earth was covered with snow. A miserable, teeth-chattering January morning and someone making someone's life even more miserable. Or the rain would be falling. A small hard rain that would wash the blood off the hands immediately, that would make one of the killers catch a bad cold. I imagined him sitting that same night with his feet in a bucket of hot water and sipping tea.

That occurred to me much later. Now that we had seen all

there was to see, we were made to sit on the lawn outside the museum and eat our lunch. It was poor fare. Most of us had plum jam spread on slices of bread. A few had lard sprinkled with paprika. One kid had nothing but bread and scallions. Everybody thought that was funny. Someone threw his thick slice of black bread in the air and got it caught in a tree. The poor fellow tried to get it down by throwing pebbles at it. He kept missing. Then, he wanted to climb the tree. He kept sliding back. Even our teacher who came over to look thought it was hilarious.

As for the grass, there was plenty of it, each blade distinct and carefully sharpened, as it were. There were also clouds in the sky and many large flies of the kind one encounters at slaughterhouses that kept interrupting our thoughts and our laughter.

And here's what went through my head just the other night as I lay awake in the dark:

The story had nothing to do with what you were talking about.

The story had everything to do with what we were talking about.

I can think of a hundred objections.

Only idiots want something neat, something categorical . . . and I never talk unless I know!

Aha! You're mixing poetry and philosophy. Bertrand Russell wouldn't give you the time of day . . .

"Everything looks very busy to me," says Jasper Johns, and that's the problem. I remember a strange cat, exceedingly emaciated, that scratched on my door the day I was scratching my head over Hegel's phenomenology.

Who said, "Whatever can be thought must be fictitious"?

You got me there! Error is my first love. I'm shouting her name from the rooftops.

Still and all! And nevertheless! And above all! Let's not forget "above all."

"The Only Humane Way to Catch a Metaphysical Mouse" is the name of the book I work on between three and four in the morning.

Here's what Nietzsche said to the ceiling: "The rank of the

philosopher is determined by the rank of his laughter." But he couldn't really laugh. No matter how hard he tried he couldn't laugh.

I know because I'm a connoisseur of chaos. All the good-looking oxymorons come to visit me in my bed . . .

Wallace Stevens has several beautiful poems about solitary readers. "The House Was Quiet and the World Was Calm" is one. It speaks of a "truth in a calm world." It happens! The world and the mind being so calm that truth becomes visible.

It must be late night — "where shines the light that lets be the things that are" — which might be a good description of insomnia. The solitude of the reader and the solitude of the philosopher drawing together. The impression that one is on the verge of anticipating another man's next turn of thought. My own solitude doubled, tripled, as if I were the only one awake on the earth.

Understanding depends upon the relation of what I am to what I have been. The being of the moment, in other words. Consciousness waking up conscience — waking up history. Consciousness as clarity and history as the dark night of the soul.

The pleasures of philosophy are the pleasures of reduction — the epiphanies of saying in a few words what seems to be the gist of the matter. It pleases me, for instance, to think of both philosophy and poetry as concerned with Being. What is a lyric poem, one might say, but an acknowledgment of the Being of beings. The philosopher thinks Being; the poet in the lyric poem re-creates the experience of Being.

History, on the other hand, is antireductive. Nothing tidy about it. Chaos! Bedlam! Hopeless tangle! My history and the History of this century like a child and his blind mother on the street — and the blind mother leading the way! You'd think the sole purpose of history is to stand truth happily upon its head.

Poor poetry! For some reason I can't get Buster Keaton out of my mind. Poetry as imperturbable Keaton alone with the woman he loves on an ocean liner set adrift on the stormy sea. Or, poetry as that kid throwing stones at a tree to bring down his lunch. Wise enough to play the fool, perhaps?

And always the dialectic: I have Don Quixote and his wind-mills in my head and Sancho Panza and his mule in my heart.

That's a figure of speech — one figure among many other figures of speech. Who could live without them? Do they tell the truth? Do they conceal it? I don't know. That's why I keep going back to philosophy.

It is morning. It is night. The book is open. The text is diffi-cult, the text is momentarily opaque. My mind is wandering. My mind is struggling to grasp the always elusive . . . the always hinting . . . What do you call it?

It, it, I keep calling it. An infinity of *it* without a single ante-cedent — like a hum in my ear.

Just then, about to give up, I find the following on a page of Heidegger:

> No thinker has ever entered into another
> thinker's solitude. Yet it is only from its
> solitude that all thinking, in a hidden mode,
> speaks to the thinking that comes after or
> that went before.

And it all comes together: poetry, philosophy, history. I see — in the sense of being able to picture and feel the human weight of another's solitude. So many of them. Seated with a book. Day breaking. Thought becoming image. Image becom-ing thought.

Biographical Notes
Notable Essays of 1987

Biographical Notes

ANNE CARSON is an author (of *Eros the Bittersweet: An Essay,* Princeton University Press), translator (of Sophokles' *Elektra,* Oxford University Press), professor (of classics at Emory University), and poet. She is currently at work on a scholarly edition and critical biography of Simonides of Keos, a poet of the fifth century B.C., as well as a volume of essays entitled *The Life of Towns.* She is properly Canadian.

BERNARD COOPER is a frequent contributor to *Grand Street,* and has had work in recent issues of *The Georgia Review, Shenandoah,* and *The Western Humanities Review.* Abattoir Editions, at the University of Nebraska, is producing a chapbook of his prose, *On the Air.* He is completing work on a collection of essays and currently teaches courses in literature at Otis/Parsons School of Art and Design and the Southern California Institute of Architecture.

ARTHUR C. DANTO is art critic for *The Nation* and the Johnsonian Professor of Philosophy at Columbia University. His *The Transfiguration of the Commonplace* received the Lionel Trilling Award, and the art criticism collected in *The State of the Art* won the George S. Polk Award and the Manufacturers Hanover/Art World Prize for criticism. Twice a Guggenheim fellow, twice a Fulbright scholar, he is the author of several books of philosophy, including *The Philosophical Disenfranchisement of Art* and *Narration and Knowledge.* A book on the basic concepts of philosophy, *Connection to the World,* is to appear in late 1988, and his main work in progress is a book on mental representation.

RUSSELL FRASER is most recently the author of *The Three Romes* and *A Mingled Yarn,* the life of R. P. Blackmur. His biography *Young Shakespeare* will be published in the fall of 1988. He has contributed articles and essays to many magazines. He is the Austin Warren Professor of

English at the University of Michigan and lives in Ann Arbor and Honolulu.

GEORGE GARRETT, the Henry Hoyns Professor of Creative Writing at the University of Virginia, is the author of twenty-four books, including fiction, poetry, biography, and criticism, and has been editor or co-editor of seventeen others. His forthcoming novel, *Entered from the Sun*, deals with the murder of Christopher Marlowe.

ALBERT GOLDBARTH was born in Chicago in 1948. He is the author of several volumes of poetry, including *Optics, Different Fleshes, Original Light: New and Selected Poems, 1973–1983,* and *Arts and Sciences.* "After Yitzl" is one of a series of "essay-poems" that have recently appeared in such periodicals as *The Kenyon Review* and *The New England Review.* He is the Adele V. Davis Distinguished Professor of Humanities at Wichita State University.

ELIZABETH HARDWICK is the author of three novels, the last of which is *Sleepless Nights.* Her three volumes of essays include, most recently, *Bartleby in Manhattan.* Stories and essays have appeared in all the leading magazines and especially in *The New York Review of Books,* of which she was a founder and is at present the advisory editor.

PAUL HORGAN is the author of some two score books of fiction, history, and literature. Twice awarded the Pulitzer Prize in history, he is a member of the American Academy and Institute of Arts and Letters and of the American Academy of Arts and Sciences, and is a Life Fellow of the Pierpont Morgan Library. His most recent books, both published this year, are *A Writer's Eye: Field Notes and Water Colors* and *A Certain Climate: Essays in History, Arts, and Letters.* He is emeritus professor of English and author in residence at Wesleyan University.

SAMUEL HYNES is the Woodrow Wilson Professor of Literature at Princeton University. He has written critical books, including *The Edwardian Turn of Mind, Edwardian Occasions,* and *The Auden Generation,* and has been a frequent contributor to British and American newspapers and magazines. During World War II and the Korean War he served as a pilot in the Marine Corps. He is completing a book on English culture during the First World War.

E. J. KAHN, JR., a staff writer for *The New Yorker* since 1937, has contributed hundreds of articles to that and other magazines. He is the author of some twenty-five books, the latest of which, *Year of Change: More about "The New Yorker" and Me,* will be published in the fall of 1988.

WILLIAM KITTREDGE grew up on the MC Ranch in southeastern Oregon, stayed home with the farming until he was thirty-five, studied at the Writers' Workshop of the University of Iowa, and is at present a professor of English at the University of Montana. He held a Stegner Fellowship at Stanford University, received two Creative Writing Fellowships from the National Endowment for the Arts, two Pacific Northwest Booksellers' Awards for Excellence, and the Montana Governor's Award for the Arts. Kittredge has published stories and essays in *The Atlantic, Harper's Magazine, TriQuarterly, Outside, Rolling Stone,* and *The Paris Review.* His most recent books are a collection of short fiction, *We Are Not in This Together* (Graywolf Press, 1984), and a collection of essays, *Owning It All* (Graywolf Press, 1987). He was also co-winner of the Neil Simon Award from *American Playhouse* for his work on the script of the film *Heartland.*

WILLIAM MANCHESTER is a graduate of the University of Massachusetts and holds a master's degree in English from the University of Missouri. His numerous books include four novels; a biography of H. L. Mencken; studies of the Rockefellers and the Krupps; the critically acclaimed biography of General Douglas MacArthur, *American Caesar;* and *Portrait of a President,* a biography of John F. Kennedy. He is also the author of a memoir of John F. Kennedy, *One Brief Shining Moment,* and a biography of Winston Churchill, *The Last Lion: Visions of Glory.* The second volume of the Churchill biography, *Alone,* will be published in the fall of 1988, along with a reissue of *The Death of a President. Goodbye, Darkness* is a personal memoir of the war in the Pacific. Mr. Manchester was wounded twice on Okinawa and was awarded the Navy Cross and the Silver Star.

KENNETH McCLANE teaches English at Cornell University. He is the author of seven books of poetry, including *A Tree Beyond Telling* and *Take Five: Collected Poems, 1971–1986.* His collection of personal essays, *Walls,* will be published by Wayne State University Press in 1989.

JAMES McCONKEY is the author of *The Novels of E. M. Forster,* a critical study; *Night Stand,* a collection of stories; *A Journey to Sahalin,* a novel; *The Tree House Confessions,* a novel; *To a Distant Island,* a reconstruction of Chekhov's 1890 journey across Siberia to a penal colony; *Kayo: The Authentic and Annotated Autobiographical Novel from Outer Space,* a novel; and of a continuing series of autobiographical essays, two parts of which (*Crossroads* and *A Stranger at the Crossroads*) have been published under the title *Court of Memory.* He has also edited a collection of essays, *Chekhov and Our Age.* He is the Goldwin Smith

Professor of English Literature at Cornell University, where he has taught since 1956. Currently he is writing a book-length account of a rural Kentucky doctor and her nurse and of the hill county in which they reside.

SUSAN MITCHELL has published in *The New Yorker, The Atlantic, The American Poetry Review, The Nation,* and *Ironwood,* and is the author of *The Water Inside the Water,* a collection of poems. She writes essays and reviews for *Provincetown Arts,* and is the Mary Blossom Lee Professor in Poetry at Florida Atlantic University. Currently at work on a new book of poems and a collection of essays, she lives in Boca Raton, Florida.

ELEANOR MUNRO is the author of *Originals: American Women Artists, On Glory Roads: A Pilgrim's Book about Pilgrimage,* and *Memoir of a Modernist's Daughter,* among other books. She is an art critic and writer whose essays and commentaries appear in the *New York Times, Art in America, The New Republic,* and other national journals. She lives with her husband in New York and on Cape Cod.

RICHARD SELZER is a surgeon living in New Haven, Connecticut. He is the author of *Rituals of Surgery, Mortal Lessons, Confessions of a Knife, Letters to a Young Doctor,* and *Taking the World in for Repairs.* He is currently preparing a new collection of essays, stories, and memoirs.

MARY LEE SETTLE was born in 1918 in Charleston, West Virginia. During the Second World War she went to England, where she served as a radio operator in the Women's Auxiliary Air Force and later as a writer with the Office of War Information. Her first novel, *The Love Eaters,* was published in 1954 and was followed the next year by *The Kiss of Kin.* In 1956 she began *The Beulah Quintet,* a series of novels that came to include *Prisons, O Beulah Land, Know Nothing, The Scapegoat,* and *The Killing Ground.* Ms. Settle is also the author of three other novels, *The Clam Shell, Celebration,* and *Blood Tie,* which won the National Book Award in 1978. Her works of nonfiction include an account of her experiences in the WAAF, *All the Brave Promises.* "London — 1944" will be part of a forthcoming continuation of her memoirs.

CHARLES SIMIC has published twelve books of poems. Among them are *Selected Poems: 1963–1983, Unending Blues,* and *The World Doesn't End.* He has translated the work of many contemporary Yugoslav poets, and has published one book of essays. Simic's poems have appeared in many anthologies here and abroad. He lives in Strafford, New Hampshire, and teaches at the state university in Durham.

KIMBERLY WOZENCRAFT is a graduate of Columbia University's MFA writing program. Her work has appeared in *Quarto, Northwest Review,* and *Witness.* She has recently completed a novel. She lives in New York City.

Notable Essays of 1987

SELECTED BY ROBERT ATWAN AND ANNIE DILLARD

JERRY ADLER
Every Parent's Nightmare. *Newsweek*,
March 16.

ANONYMOUS
In Defense of Anonymity. *Virginia
Quarterly Review*, Winter.

RICHARD AVEDON
Borrowed Days. *Grand Street*,
Autumn.

JAMES BALDWIN
To Crush the Serpent. *Playboy*,
January.

RUSSELL BANKS
I Am Lost in the Flow of Time. *New
England Monthly*, March.

DOUGLAS BAUER
Broken Heartland. *Esquire*, January.

SUSAN BERGMAN
Enlargements. *North American Review*,
Summer.

WENDELL BERRY
Writer and Region. *Hudson Review*,
Spring.

SISSELA BOK
Alva Myrdal. *Yale Review*, Spring.

MARIE BORROFF
Rafting down the Grand Canyon: A
Meditation. *Virginia Quarterly
Review*, Summer.

HAROLD BRODKEY
Reflections: Family. *The New Yorker*,
November 23.

J. D. BROWN
The Peak of the Immortals. *Northwest
Review*, Vol. 25, No. 2.

ANNE CARSON
Short Talks. *Southwest Review*,
Summer.

LEO CAWLEY
Refighting the War. *Village Voice*,
September 8.

CAROL COHN
Slick 'Ems, Glick 'Ems, Christmas
Trees, and Cookie Cutters: Nuclear
Language and How We Learned to
Love the Bomb. *Bulletin of the
Atomic Scientists*, June.

HAL CROWTHER
Where the Boys Were. *Spectator Magazine*, March 14.

GALBRAITH M. CRUMP
Teaching Homer in the Shadow of Troy. *Kenyon Review*, Summer.

ARTHUR C. DANTO
The Seat of the Soul: Three Chairs. *Grand Street*, Summer.

GUY DAVENPORT
On Reading. *Antaeus*, Autumn.

ROBERT DAY
The Killing Fields. *Regardies*, May.

W. S. DI PIERO
Notes on Photography. *The New Criterion*, October.

E. L. DOCTOROW
A Citizen Reads the Constitution. *The Nation*, February 21.

STANLEY ELKIN
What's in a Name? Etc. *Denver Quarterly*, Spring.

RICHARD ELMAN
Graham Greene as I Almost Knew Him. *Boston Review*, October.

JOSEPH EPSTEIN
Sid, You Made the Prose Too Thin. *Commentary*, September.
You Probably Don't Know Me. *The American Scholar*, Autumn.

ROBERT ERWIN
The Great Language Panic. *Antioch Review*, Fall.

HENRY FAIRLIE
The Idiocy of Urban Life. *The New Republic*, January 5.

ROBERT FINCH
Bank Swallows. *Country Journal*, May.

DARWIN J. FLAKOLL
La Vida en Beya. *Virginia Quarterly Review*, Winter.

RICHARD FORD
My Mother. *Harper's Magazine*, August.

WALLACE FOWLIE
Sites. *Sewanee Review*, Winter.

PETER FREUNDLICH
The Crime of the Tooth. *Harper's Magazine*, September.

GEORGE GARRETT
The Star System: A Jeremiad. *Michigan Quarterly Review*, Fall.

WILLIAM H. GASS
Goodness Knows Nothing of Beauty. *Harper's Magazine*, April.

ROBERT A. GERBER
Bruce Weber's Pretty Pictures. *Christopher Street*, December.

TED GIOIA
Jazz: The Aesthetics of Imperfection. *Hudson Review*, Winter.

GAIL GODWIN
What's Really Going On. *Antaeus*, Autumn.

RICHARD GOLDSTEIN
AIDS and the Social Contract. *Village Voice*, December 29.

VIVIAN GORNICK
The World and Our Mothers. *The New York Times Book Review*, November 22.

STEPHEN JAY GOULD
William Jennings Bryan's Last
   Campaign. *Natural History*,
   November.

DAVID GRAHAM
Dwelling in Possibility: Reflections of
   a Homebody on the Open Road.
   Georgia Review, Winter.

FRANCINE DU PLESSIX GRAY
Charles Olson and an American
   Place. *Yale Review*, Spring.

PAUL GRUCHOW
Seeing the Elephant. *Minnesota
   Monthly*, July.
What Cranes Say. *Minnesota Monthly*,
   March.

DONALD HALL
Old Roses and Birdsong. *Harper's
   Magazine*, August.
The Way to Say *Pleasure*. *Antaeus*,
   Autumn.

LEAH HALPER
Things Lost and Found: Returning to
   Nicaragua. *Northwest Review*,
   Vol. 25, No. 1.
Managua. *Northwest Review*, Vol. 25,
   No. 2.

ELIZABETH HARDWICK
The Fictions of America. *The New
   York Review of Books*, June 25.

JIM HARRISON
Nightwalking. *Rolling Stone*, March
   26.

WILLIAM LEAST HEAT MOON
A Glass of Handmade. *The Atlantic*,
   November.

JOHN HERSEY
First Job. *Yale Review*, Winter.

EDWARD HIRSCH
Birds of Paradise: A Memoir. *MSS*,
   Vol. 5, No. 1.

EDWARD HOAGLAND
Company Men for Whatever
   Company Employs Us. *New
   England Monthly*, May.

ROBERT HOLLAND
The Duel. *Audubon*, November.

ANNE HOLLANDER
The Unacknowledged Brothel of Art.
   Grand Street, Spring.

LEWIS HYDE
The Tricks of Creation. *Boston
   Review*, February.

TAMA JANOWITZ
Adventures in Tinsel Town. *The New
   York Times Magazine*, March 22.

JUSTIN KAPLAN
In Pursuit of the Ultimate Fiction.
   The New York Times Book Review,
   April 19.

MICHAEL J. KATZ
'Tis the Gift to Be Simple. *Kenyon
   Review*, Spring.

STANLEY KAUFFMANN
Album of the Knopfs. *American
   Scholar*, Summer.

ALFRED KAZIN
Mencken and the Great American
   Boob. *The New York Review of Books*,
   February 26.
The Great American Space. *American
   Heritage*, April.

DANIEL KELLY
Love, Bill. *Minnesota Monthly*,
   December.

PETER STEINHART
The Joy of Walking. *Audubon,*
  September.

FLOYD C. STUART
The Salt Marsh. *The Atlantic,* October.

MARK SUFRIN
Losing Power. *New England Quarterly/*
  Bread Loaf, Spring.

SARA SULERI
Excellent Things in Women. *Raritan,*
  Winter.

PATRICK SUSKIND
Amnesia in Litteris. *Harper's*
  Magazine, March.

GAY TALESE
Chronicles of a Brownstone.
  Architectural Digest, November-
  December.

JOHN TAYLOR
Experience. *Georgia Review,* Fall.

SALLIE TISDALE
We Do Abortions Here: A Nurse's
  Story. *Harper's Magazine,* October.

SUSAN ALLEN TOTH
The Importance of Being
  Remembered. *The New York Times*
  Book Review, June 28.

JOHN UPDIKE
Radio Romance. *Esquire,* June.

JIM DALE VICKERY
The Land Is Alive with Wolves.
  Audubon, January.

NICHOLAS VON HOFFMANN
The Constitution — Our Ponderous
  Ark. *Grand Street,* Autumn.

KURT VONNEGUT
Skyscraper National Park.
  Architectural Digest, November.

GEOFFREY C. WARD
Jim Corbett: The Reluctant
  Executioner. *Audubon,* July.

ROBERT PENN WARREN
Portrait of a Father. *Southern Review,*
  Winter.

DENNIS WATLINGTON
Between the Cracks. *Vanity Fair,*
  December.

AMY WILENTZ
Voodoo in Haiti Today. *Grand Street,*
  Winter.

JONATHAN WILSON
Celebrity Stories. *Boston Review,*
  December.

WILLIAM S. WILSON
loving/reading. *Antaeus,* Autumn.

GEOFFREY WOLFF
A Day at the Beach. *Esquire,*
  December.

HELEN YGLESIAS
Invoking America: A Gitche Gumee
  Memoir. *The New York Times Book*
  Review, July 5.

LEE ZACHARIAS
In the Garden of the Word. *Antaeus,*
  Autumn.

ERIC ZENCEY
On Hunting. *North American Review,*
  Summer.

Interested readers will also find many essays in the following special magazine issues that appeared in 1987:

Antaeus, "Literature as Pleasure," edited by Daniel Halpern (Autumn); *Georgia Review,* "Focus on Autobiographical Essays," edited by Stanley W. Lindberg and Stephen Corey (Summer); *Sewanee Review,* "Autobiography," edited by George Core (Winter); *Witness,* "Writings from Prison," edited by Fielding Dawson (Fall); *Yale Review,* "Encounters I" and "Encounters II," edited by Kai Erikson (Spring and Winter).

The Best American
essays, 1988

$17.45   rq/

DATE